The Presence of Thought
Introspective Accounts
of Reading and Writing

Marilyn S. Sternglass

**The City College
of City University of New York**

Volume XXXIV in the Series
ADVANCES IN DISCOURSE PROCESSES
Roy O. Freedle, editor

Ablex Publishing Corporation
Norwood, New Jersey 07648

Library of Congress Cataloging-in Publication Data

Sternglass, Marilyn J.
  The presence of thought.

  (Advances in discourse processes ; 34)
  Bibliography: p.
  Includes index.
  1. English language--Rhetoric--Study and teaching. 2. Reading (Higher educa-
tion) 3. Critical thinking--Study and teaching. 4. Introspection. I. Title. II.
Series.
PE1404.S82   1988   808'.042'07   88-16636
ISBN 0-89391-568-8 (ppk)

Ablex Publishing Corporation
355 Chestnut St.
Norwood, NJ 07648

*For Ernest
and our children
Susan and Daniel*

Contents

Preface to the Series

Roy O. Freedle

Series Editor

This series of volumes provides a forum for the cross-fertilization of ideas from a diverse number of disciplines, all of which share a common interest in discourse—be it prose comprehension and recall, dialogue analysis, text grammar construction, computer simulation of natural language, cross-cultural comparisons of communicative competence or other related topics. The problems posed by multisentence contexts and the methods required to investigate them, while not always unique to discourse, are still sufficiently distinct as to benefit from the organized mode of scientific interaction made possible by this series.

Scholars working in the discourse area from the perspective of sociolinguistics, psycholinguistics, ethnomethodology and the sociology of language, educational psychology (e.g., teacher-student interaction), the philosophy of language, computational linguistics, and related subareas are invited to submit manuscripts of monograph or book length to the series editor. Edited collections of original papers resulting from conferences will also be considered.

Volumes in the Series

Author's Note

In the spring of 1983, I read an article that a colleague of mine, Sharon Lynn Pugh, had written in the *Journal of Reading* (under the name Sharon Smith). The article described a reading activity that she had designed for graduate students in the Language Education Department, asking them to describe and analyze their processes in making sense of an article for which they had virtually no background information. After reading Sharon's article, I proposed to her that we collaboratively develop a course for graduate students in English and Language Education in which we would design a varied sequence of tasks and ask the students to examine their reading and writing strategies. She was enthusiastic about this plan, and we then developed the course, "Introspection in Reading and Writing Processes," which was offered in the spring of 1984 at Indiana University. We collected copies of the papers the students produced and the introspective journals they wrote throughout the semester, tape-recorded all the class sessions, video-taped six class sessions, and recorded the final small group conferences we had with the students at the end of the semester.

During the 1984–85 academic year, Sharon and I presented two papers together (at the New Hampshire Conference on Reading/Writing Relationships and at the Conference on College Composition and Communication), and we wrote one paper together, "Retrospective Accounts of Language and Learning Processes," published in *Written Communication* in 1986. In the spring of 1985, Sharon agreed to direct the Learning Skills Center at a technical college in Malaysia associated with Indiana University, for two years beginning in the fall of 1985, and I accepted a position at The City College of the City University of New York. We then decided that it would be best to pursue separately our analyses of the information we had collected, especially since we agreed that there were numerous perspectives that could be taken on this rich source.

Thus, although I may be listed as the sole author of this particular work, it is impossible to describe fully how important the collaborative process of planning, collecting, talking, and thinking about this material has been. I look forward to the publication of Sharon's perspectives on the research and wish to thank her for her insight, intelligence, and good humor, especially when things didn't turn out exactly as we had "planned."

In the spring of 1986, after I had completed a draft of the first four chapters of this book, I sought responses and reactions to the descriptions and analyses of the seminar activities from the perspective of the participants in the seminar. Ten of the participants agreed to read the draft and provide comments. I have incorporated their responses into the manuscript. I wish to thank them for being willing to take the time to respond to the draft and for their many helpful insights.

Marilyn S. Sternglass

CHAPTER 1

The Nature of Introspective Accounts in A Classroom Setting

This book is about an extended conversation, a conversation between instructor and instructor, between instructors and students, between students and students, between students and others, and between students and themselves. This conversation took place in the spring semester of 1984 at Indiana University, in a graduate course titled "Introspection in Reading and Writing Processes" that Sharon Lynn Pugh and I team-taught. Seventeen graduate students from the English and Language Education Departments enrolled in the course. We asked them to undertake a series of reading and writing tasks and to keep introspective journals describing their processes throughout the semester. With their consent, we audiotaped all of the class meetings and the final small group meetings we had with the students, and video-taped six classes. We duplicated all of the papers written for the course and the journal entries.

The purpose of collecting all of this material was to document and explore the range of strategies that a competent group of language users would employ to respond to a range of reading and writing tasks over a semester's time in a more naturalistic instructional setting than has been used in prior studies. The descriptions provided in these ongoing multifaceted conversations suggest new insights into the language processes involved with literacy events. Shirley Brice Heath has defined a literacy event as "any occasion in which a piece of writing is integral to the nature of the participants' interactions and their interpretive process" (93). Scribner and Cole point out that asking people how they have gone about a task, and explaining their reasons for responding in a certain way, has a long history in literacy research: "This distinction between doing and talking about doing is as old as the developmental tasks themselves and is explicitly included in a number of theories as a crucial marker of level of intellectual development"(115).

1

The roles of reading and writing in classroom settings have undergone significant changes in the past fifteen years as there have been increasing efforts to bring these language events together. But, even as the "process" movement has swept into new instructional materials, there is still a sense that there are specific ways to approach classroom tasks, whether, for example, heuristics have replaced outlines in writing, or macrostructures have replaced main points in reading. The material collected in this study allows for the first time close examination of the actual range of strategies employed by sophisticated language users in response to a range of reading and writing tasks over a semester's time, thus also documenting the development of learning when classroom materials are selected to foster knowledge-building over significant periods of time. The material also reveals, perhaps ironically since the participants in the study were simultaneously graduate students and instructors of undergraduates, that there is still a large gap between what is taught as practice in the classroom and what is actually practiced. Furthermore, it reveals that there is no single monolithic "best" way to approach even a specific task in a specific setting. Each language user sets goals, discerns audience, interprets and responds to the task in a way that will best facilitate learning for himself or herself.

Currently, models of the composing process attempt to account for how readers and writers make sense of existing texts and create meaning in their own developing texts. These models state or imply that individuals call on prior knowledge to build new knowledge, altering existing schemas as necessary in doing so. The implication is strong that there may be variations in sequence or emphasis, but essentially the processes are the same. Although I do not wish to argue that the processes are idiosyncratic, I will present evidence here that interpretations of reading and writing tasks are so influenced by a range of contextual, intellectual, and personal factors that individuals cannot help but interpret tasks based on complex *sets of factors* that are unique for each individual. Admittedly, the graduate students in this study shared many intellectual views and practices, the most dominant being their professional commitment to intellectual activities centering on the use of language. They, therefore, naturally constituted a highly verbal community. But this study will demonstrate that, even within such a community, highly original and diversified responses to tasks are produced because of significant individual interpretations.

The sets of complex factors influencing interpretations cannot be captured by computer-simulated models or studies undertaken in sterile, laboratory-like settings. To understand what affects interpretations of tasks in classroom settings, it is necessary to fully account for the factors in a real setting over real time. The varieties of strategies used by the students will be shown to differ between tasks and between individuals on the same task. Students use their preferred strategies as long as they prove functional;

teachers must help them build on their strengths and learn to recognize those approaches that are dysfunctional. In this way, the sets of complex factors that influence interpretations of literacy tasks and selection of strategies to carry them out can take into account essential individual differences.

Before these language events can be described, it is essential to consider the nature of the introspective journal reports which described these processes and the context within which they were produced. In Chapter 1 I will discuss the nature of these reports and in Chapter 2 describe the specific classroom setting within which the language activities were carried out and the effect of that context on the types of responses that emerged. Chapters 3 and 4 will describe the range of reading and writing strategies employed to respond to the tasks within the specific setting. Chapter 5 traces the origins of the actual textual responses that were produced in the first sequence of teacher-designed tasks. Chapter 6 will present implications for instruction and research.

A brief description of the class requirements will facilitate interpretation of the initial journal and class comments as they emerged from the classroom context. The semester was divided roughly in half, with the first seven weeks consisting of teacher-designed reading and writing tasks and the last eight weeks consisting of work on a self-designed research task and reports to each other on their review of their reading and writing strategies over the semester. During the first seven weeks, the students were asked to read articles on the topic of introspection itself and to write summaries, reaction statements, synthesis essays, and position papers. The readings included: Elizabeth Valentine, "Perchings and Flights: Introspection" (1978); Daniel C. Dennett, "Where Am I?" (a science-fiction story that served as the last chapter in a book of philosophical essays exploring the mind's relation to the body and an individual's sense of purpose titled *Brainstorms* (1978)); D.O. Hebb, "Self-Knowledge and the Self" from *Essay on Mind* (1980); Graham Quinton and Brian J. Fellows, "Perceptual Strategies in the Solving of Three-Term Series Problems" (1975); J. St. B.T. Evans, "A Critical Note on Quinton and Fellows' Observation of Reasoning Strategies" (1976); Peter E. Morris, "Why Evans is Wrong in Criticizing Introspective Reports of Subject Strategies" (1981); and J. St. B.T. Evans, "A Reply to Morris" (1981). The latter four articles all appeared in issues of the *British Journal of Psychology*. In the second half of the semester, the students individually selected an area for research and wrote a report on their research. We asked them to keep ongoing journals of their progress on the paper, reporting each week what they had done, even if they had done nothing specific on the project for that week.

I have given the students in the class pseudonyms. The English students are referred to as Crystal, Robin, Rose, Violet, and Lila (literature majors minoring in composition), and Amber, Chip, and Heather (students enrolled in an English Language Program concentrating in composition). The Language Education students concentrating in the area of reading are Pearl, Opal, Ruby, Jade, Topaz, Garnet, Daisy, and Jay (the only foreign student). Lionel is an English Education student.

INTROSPECTION OR RETROSPECTION

In considering the nature of the journal and classroom accounts produced in the course, a natural question arises about whether they should be characterized as introspective or retrospective. In both cases, the individual is providing a verbal report of mental processes. Fodor has argued that there must be a language of thought. Gardner, discussing Fodor's work, notes, "If cognitive systems involve representations, if cognitive operations involve the manipulation of symbol-like representations, then these representations must exist somewhere" (83). For Fodor, this language of thought is very much like natural language. In the case of introspection, the implication is that the account of the mental process is instantaneous with the experience. But accounts that are instantaneous with experience, if such accounts are even possible, are always thought of as oral reports, or speech. Culler, for example, has noted that speech "seems to be the one point or instant in which form and meaning are simultaneously present" (169–70 quoted in Eakin 224). Husserl, similarly, has argued that consciousness can be fully *authentic* only when its workings express the present activity of a human subject (cited in Norris 45). Husserl set up a distinction between *retention* (immediate sensory traces, what today is identified with perception) and *representation* (experiences recalled over a greater distance of time). This distinction seems very close to the one often made between introspection and retrospection.

If information is verbalized just at the time the individual is heeding it, Ericsson and Simon label the report as *concurrent verbalization* (what I have been calling *introspection*). If an individual reports on a cognitive process that occurred earlier in time, Ericsson and Simon label the procedure a *retrospective verbalization* ("Verbal Reports" 218). As Ericsson and Simon point out, talk-alouds and think-alouds (usually called *protocol analysis*) attempt to report what is being heeded in short-term memory, while retrospective reports are more often based on information from long-term memory. They are thus more vulnerable to error and incompleteness (*Protocol Analysis* 16). However, these retrospective reports fall within Ericsson and Simon's cognitive model because they assume that the cognitive processes leave in long-term memory a "subset of the originally heeded information in the form of a retrievable trace of connected episodic memory. Retrospective reporting involves retrieval of these episodic memories and verbalization of their content" (*Protocol Analysis* 149). The information becomes accessible from long-term memory through information and cues in short-term memory. There is, however, the problem that the individual could confuse other retrievable information with information actually heeded during the processes being recalled (149). For our students, this could mean the possibility of generalizing about literacy tasks rather than attending to the particular task at hand. We tried to anticipate this difficulty by varying the tasks so that each had specific characteristics, thus increasing the likelihood that the report would speak to the specific experience at hand rather than to generalized processes. Ericsson and Simon believe that, by acknowledging that the accounts can only reflect heeded information, it becomes possible to avoid the long-standing argument over whether all mental content is verbal or at least verbalizable. The information that is heeded has been heeded in a form retrievable through verbalization and thus becomes reportable as information for analysis.

> Saussure argued the priority of speech over writing: In speaking one is able to experience . . . an intimate link between sound and sense, an inward and immediate realization of meaning which yields itself up without reserve to perfect, transparent understanding. Writing, on the contrary, destroys this ideal of pure presence. It obtrudes an alien, depersonalized medium, a deceiving shadow which falls between intent and meaning, between utterance and understanding. . . . Writing, in short, is a threat to the deeply traditional view that associates truth with self-presence and the 'natural' language wherein it finds expression (quoted in Norris 28).

Against this, Derrida argues that writing is the precondition of language and must be conceived as prior to speech. "Writing, for Derrida, is the 'free play' or element of undecidability within every system of communication. Its operations are precisely those which escape the self-consciousness of speech and its deluded sense of the mastery of concept over language" (Norris 28–29). But, for Derrida, neither writing nor speech permits the "desire for presence" and both are already "at one remove from the reality of being" (Eakin 224).

Since a major part of our accounts, the weekly journals that accompanied the carrying out of the tasks, were in written form, they would seem to come closer to Husserl's category of representation. The class meetings, of course, were in spoken form, but they often served as elaborations of what had previously been discussed in the journals, since one of the conditions under which the class operated for the teacher-designed tasks was to carry out the tasks without consultation or discussion with any other class members. At the time that Sharon Pugh and I constructed such a limitation, it was to ensure that each student would have the experience of producing a "pure" response to each task. We soon came to realize that we were jeopardizing important components of the learning experience, the natural collaboration that goes on among graduate students and the social nature of learning. We decided, nevertheless, to continue this restriction until the period of teacher-imposed tasks was completed. We would then be able to contrast the composing experiences on another dimension in addition to teacher-designed and self-designed tasks, the dimension of "solitary author" (Cooper 367) versus the social-collaborative experience. Langer's ("Children") socio-cognitive view of reading and writing emphasizes the importance of language learning as socially based and interactive, and points out "that cognitive factors are influenced by context, and that they, in turn, affect the meanings that are produced" (7). In this study, both conditions constituted part of the context, and their effects are described and evaluated.

Discussions in class corroborated the distinction between introspection and retrospection. At the second class meeting, Garnet wrote in her journal: "I also found the discussion about introspection as retrospection [in the Valentine article] interesting in terms of what I was engaged in doing. Retrospection seemed to be what was occurring for me, but the thoughts run so close together that it is difficult to know whether to include those in this account or to try and only strictly record what I remember thinking about as I read." She is raising the issue here that thinking about a subject is an ongoing activity, and it is difficult, if not impossible, to segment the thinking that takes place at one specific moment. Her comment thus exemplifies Derrida's notion that each moment is made up of the present moment in combination with all previous moments (Norris 47). But since that is the case, any "moment" that is reported will reflect the writer's thoughts and perceptions at that point in the process, even though it must be a moment cumulative of all previous experiences. Those perceptions, then, across students and across time, could give us freeze-frame looks that would eventually fuse into longer, more coherent, narratively structured films depicting this range of students on this range of activities. That was what we were seeking.

Language and Thought

While the label introspection appears to suggest instantaneous reports on thoughts while they are occurring, it is clear that it is impossible to capture the complete stream of consciousness while it is occurring or at any later point in time. From a constructivist perspective, Reid argues:

> . . . language and thought exist in separate domains: thought falls within the domain of the personal and individual, whereas the semantic categories of language are part of a public social structure. It is to be expected then that moving from one domain to the other would involve a transformation. This

disengagement of thought from language also allows for the possibility that certain thoughts exist in a non-linguistic state as complex as conceptual gestalts (9).

Thus, even speech falls short of the ideal of capturing all thought, and so surely must writing. Attempts at verbal records of this stream of though t are as close as we can come to capturing them so there is no priority of spe ech over writing in recording them. In reading this manuscript, Garnet, who is interested in semiotics, pointed out that it would be possible to have ' 'people introspect using sign systems other than language" (such as movement or art). Although this is certainly true, I can only focus on verbal rep orts in this study, since these were the only sign systems we invited.

At the seventh class meeting, Rose objected to the use of the term int rospection, defending the term retrospection on the basis of her analysis of the relationship between her thoughts and her language. She said, "I don't think that anyone can introspect. It's all retrospection, a matter of time." Whether one talked about "a couple of seconds or a couple of minutes," she fel t there was still a time lapse and then a translation into language. For her, there was "always some kind of gap between them." But when one sees th is gap as simply the normal lapse between direct experience and the individ ual's conscious awareness of it, it is easy to see that this is the close st we can ever come to instantaneous recording of experience. Instead of bemoaning what is inevitably lost, we should revel in the degree to which experien ce can be represented through language. Even protocol-analysis, which purports to record instantaneous experience, must be seen as reconstruction of experience. The translation of thought into language is always a process of selection from the stream of consciousness which occurs too rapidly for verbatim recording. Since consciousness itself is selective, the selections may not be wholly voluntary or conscious acts, but they may be rooted in the entire make-up of the individual. Rosen makes a similar point about the construction of narratives. He says:

> The unremitting flow of events must first be selectively attended to, interpreted as holding relationships, causes, motives, feelings, consequences—in a word, *meanings*. To give an order to this unmanageable flux we must take another step and invent, yes invent, beginnings and ends . . . [N]arrative is the outcome of a mental process which enables us to excise from our experience, a meaningful sequence, to place it within boundaries, to set around it the frontiers of the story, to make it resonate in the contrived silences with which we may precede it and end it. But to perceive it and invent a story is not enough, it must be verbalized, it must be told. There must be a telling which delivers it as narrative (13–14).

The construction of a narrative from selections from the stream-of-consciousness also bears on the completeness of the accounts, which is discussed later in this chapter. And the items selected to be reported become significant, as do the reasons why the individual decided to select just those items for reporting.

It is likely that this discussion about whether these accounts should be called introspective or retrospective would be irrelevant to the deconstructionists. The issue is raised because I want to characterize the nature of these accounts and argue for their usefulness. To characterize these accounts as retrospections seems more appropriate, because such reports must always be reconstructions, whether they are prepared after the experience that is described in them or recorded at least in part while the tasks are being carried out. The journals and the classroom discussions constituted the ongoing conversation of the course, written and oral, yet both reconstructive and retrospective. Regardless of the closeness of time when the accounts were recorded, as Derrida has argued, there is no moment of pure reflection or perception; everything is experienced over time. And these accounts were not only influenced by what was happening to our students in their immediate context, but they were also being affected by all their prior experiences, as is true for all types of experiences. Thus, each moment constitutes itself and all moments that preceded it and contributed to it.

No matter what they are called or how they are characterized, these types of self-reports have been questioned in regard to their usefulness in efforts to understand human thought processes. As Sharon Pugh and I pointed out in a preliminary article (Sternglass and Pugh 1986), there have been four major objections to the use of this type of report: the validity of such accounts, the completeness of accounts, the depth of the accounts, and the effect of introspecting on the processes being examined. I would like to explore each objection and cite some examples from the students' journals and classroom comments that illuminate both the limitations and values of such accounts.

THE VALIDITY OF SUCH ACCOUNTS

The validity of such accounts is always called into question because the suspicion lurks that the reporter of the account will consciously desire to please the listener or reader. Thus, it is appropriate to have a healthy skepticism about such data. From a psychoanalytic perspective, Spence has pointed out that, when a patient has the greatest need to please, the account may have the maximum distorting effect (86). It is not too far-fetched to consider the classroom setting as similar to the psychoanalytic one in the sense that there is a similar feeling of the need to please instructors on the part of students. Therefore, the potential to tell us "what we want to hear" must always be seen as a possible distorting factor.

The question of access to thought has been raised as an issue in the validity of introspective accounts. Ryle questioned whether there were actually happenings in the mind to which an individual might have privileged access. He believed that the same things could be learned from the individual through observation and direct questioning. He took a behaviorist stance indicating that people are predisposed to act in certain ways under certain conditions (cited in Gardner 67).

Hebb has argued that introspection is always inferential and never the result of direct observation. For him, the implication is that the subject will be compelled to make things up because the knowledge gained from such self-reporting is only very indirectly related to actual internal processes (30). But, as has already been suggested, that part of experience which rises to the surface and can be expressed verbally is crucial because it represents the choices of the individual doing the reporting. (It developed that the items selected for reporting were frequently those that represented problems in responding to the tasks and thus were the experiences that were heeded.)

Ericsson and Simon contend that

> thinking-aloud protocols and retrospective reports can reveal in remarkable detail what information [subjects] are attending to while performing their tasks, and by revealing this information, can provide an orderly picture of the exact ways in which the tasks are being performed, the strategies employed, the inferences drawn from information, the accessing of memory by recognition (*Protocol Analysis* 220).

Although the reports we received could not be characterized as "the exact ways the tasks were being performed," they nevertheless reveal strategies, inferences, and accessing of memory, just as Ericsson and Simon contend can be done.

The issue of validity of the journal accounts was raised by the students in the second class meeting. Pearl suggested that, because "there's so much happening that you cannot write it all down," perhaps if the instructors had given them a guide they might have selectively chosen something else to report. But Amber noted that, although such guidelines on methodology might have increased reliability, that would have been at the expense of validity, because, as Sharon Pugh pointed out, they would then in effect have been answering our questions instead of their own. In other words, we would have been directing the selections from their stream of consciousness rather than requiring them to make their own selections.

In her journal for the fifth class meeting, Ruby introduced an analysis of her work using the terminology of her discipline, reading and language theory. She refers to *schema*, which Kucer has defined as the "complex structures of information that represent the individual's past encounters with the world. They contain the language user's knowledge of objects, situations and events, as well as knowledge of procedures for interpreting, retrieving and organizing information" (321). Ruby said,

> The process of writing this paper helped me come to grips with one of the aspects that had been bothering me—the effect of schema in reporting an experience. I finally realized that, as a person who accepts mental activity as schema-driven, I could accept even schema-biased reports as valid reflections of a subject's mental processes. If our mental processes are schema-derived, then even a report of an experience which has been affected by the subsumption of the experience into the larger schema will reflect people's general approach and strategies in problem-solving and decision-making.

But two months later, at the fifteenth class meeting, Ruby became suspicious of the educational jargon that she and others had been using to describe their processes. She brought up the issue of the need for naive introspectors. She felt that our class discussions had been "rampant with theoretical jargon as we imposed our theoretical background on our interpretations of what we observed about ourselves. This may result in data more reflective of our theoretical bents than the sort of unvarnished human experience you may want to observe through introspection." For example, she noted, "I don't think people in the general public run around talking about top-down, bottom-up, schema." Ruby went on to point out the danger of having little compartments that could fit the information that could be too easily labeled, so that we lacked accounts that were "simply on the raw side." Amber supported that point by commenting that when the labels were too easily accessible, it obviated the necessity of "checking out more closely to see if that was indeed what was going on."

Although there is certainly a danger in this too easy recourse to metalanguage and educational jargon, there is an advantage to have sophisticated language users be the first group to describe their strategies and processes over an extended period of time. (It is a decision similar to Emig's selection of Lynn (*Composing Processes*), an especially articulate twelfth-grader, as the primary focus of her seminal study of composing processes.) These language graduate students are prepared to be sensitive to the changes that may occur in their reading and writing processes, and equipped to describe nuances that could easily go unnoticed and unarticulated by less linguistically aware individuals.

Rationalization

From the notion of inference raised by Hebb, it is only a short step to the argument that these kinds of accounts constitute rationalizations. Jones has defined *rationalization* as an unconscious activity:

Everyone feels that, as a rational creature, he must be able to give a connected, logical, and continuous account of himself, his conduct and opinions,
and all his mental processes are unconsciously manipulated and revised to
that end. No one will admit that he ever deliberately performed an irrational
act, and any act that might appear so is immediately justified by distorting the
mental processes concerned and providing a false explanation that has a plausible ring of rationality" (6 quoted in Sherwood 175).

Sherwood considers the issue of rationalization from a causal perspective.
He argues that rationalizations may have logical form as reasons, but that,
if, in a given situation, they are not causally relevant factors, then they have
become rationalizations. He says that "a reason is a 'real reason' precisely
when it is a causally relevant factor, and it is only a 'rationalization' when it
is not in fact a causally relevant factor even though the agent may assert that
it was a consideration causing him to act in the way that he did" (176).

Introspective accounts as rationalizations came up for discussion in the
fifth class meeting. Amber brought up what she labelled a "self-justification,
a self-hypothesis" (using terminology she had picked up in reading Morris's
article). She had decided that she needed to account for why an idea that
she had felt important while she was reading Evans' article had not appeared
as one of the major positions described in the paper she had written for that
day. "And then I marked, I just decided it was subsidiary. It didn't get in
there but I thought is was important so I was figuring out why it didn't get in
there. That was not the reason it didn't get in there and I was figuring out
why, after the fact, a good logical reason why it wasn't there." When Ruby
characterized that explanation as a rationalization, Topaz disagreed, saying
that "it may not necessarily be a rationalization." Amber concurred, "That's
what I decided. It may be a real reason." And then, as occurred frequently
during the class discussions, Topaz brought up the issue of the way in which
introspection was viewed within different research paradigms. She commented, "It's almost as though any time an empirical scientist cannot measure something very neatly, it's a rationalization. Or it's not worth studying." For example, in one of the earlier readings, Valentine had presented
introspection as a kind of probing tool to assist research methods that are
more rigorous in the traditional sense (19). When I commented that Amber
had had an idea floating around which didn't appear in the writing, and that
she was trying to account for that, Amber defended her use of the term rationalization to describe her activity by defining it as "some behavior that
had already occurred and after the fact of its occurrence trying to figure out
what happened." In other words, as Chip pointed out, she was constructing
an explanation after the fact. And Amber's concern remained about whether
the explanation she provided was the real reason.

Honesty of the Accounts

For the seventh class meeting, when the students were just beginning to work on their self-selected projects, Amber brought up in her journal the issue of the dilemma of the journal writer deciding just how honest the account could or would be with the recognition that the journals were "public documents," even though individual writers would never be identified by name. She wrote an account in her journal of previous family problems, and then went on:

> Twice I've torn out journal entries and re-written them, because they got too deep into personal things. My impulse was to do so with this one too. But it gets to be too much extra work, and really if you want to know 'why' I select a topic, then this kind of account is more 'valid' than one centered on intellectual or academic reasons (though those are involved too). I'm afraid of being thought immature or dumb—crazy is an attractive option among those choices (save face, see?).

Opal later commented that she had had similar feelings which she attributed to her lack of confidence which had its genesis in her status as a first-year doctoral student, intimidated by other more advanced students in her program in Language Education. Thus the issue of presenting an acceptable persona to the instructors and any others who might eventually have access to these journals, either directly or through published accounts, has to be acknowledged as a factor in the presentations of self reflected in the journal accounts.

In a critique of Erwin Steinberg's (1986) defense of protocol-analysis, David Dobrin notes the difficulty of describing the constraints exerted by an audience. He says that providing an exhaustive list of the constraints and some description of meeting those constraints would be required before such a description could be viewed as an actual mechanism showing how problem-solving works (721–22). Although I want to argue that writing processes do not follow neat problem-solving strategies, I do wish to provide a description of the constraints of complex writing environments (both internal and external) that affect composing processes. Although Dobrin says that he is "completely unable to imagine what [an exhaustive explanation] would be like" (722), I would like to submit the descriptions of this book as an additional argument that the complexities of the composing environment mitigate against a "model of the writing process [that] would be so complete that one could plausibly try to program a computer to perform the same analyses"(722).

On reading a draft of this manuscript, though, Crystal commented:

> If this study had been carried out over a shorter period of time, then this factor

[of presenting a favorable persona] might have been very important. But because we were all able to become compatible with each other over an extended period, the 'masks' were soon dropped. My opinion is that, except initially, this need for self protection prejudiced your data very little, if at all.

Rather than seeing these protective features, though, to the extent that they existed in the accounts, as prejudicing the information, I believe that they reflect the varying ways in which individual students negotiated their relationships with their instructors.

THE COMPLETENESS OF THE ACCOUNTS

It would appear on the surface that the more complete the report would be, the more credible it would be. But as Spence points out, the most impressionistic journals may require the most reconstruction on our part, but they may be the truest to the writer's experience; the more neatly laid-out journals may "flourish only at the cost of unfaithful reporting" (86). The reason Spence offers for this is that, if the individual is truly free in his or her reporting, the account may not be understood; on the other hand, if the report is too easily understood, the individual may not be freely reporting. Similarly, Rosen points out that as individuals construct narratives, they embed evaluations of the events into their narratives (cited in Short 394).

> For successful interchanges to occur, a shared language must develop over time for the participants. Words which we initially hear in their common meaning without fully understanding their sentences gradually acquire, as we hear them in different contexts with varying degrees of understanding, the sense intended by the patient. But for this to happen, both parties in the conversation must make an active effort to achieve a negotiated understanding (Spence 86).

Our classroom setting had obvious advantages for achieving that "shared language" over time. We all started with a fairly common vocabulary of language concepts that we could use in discussing the reading and writing processes we were interested in (although we did consciously spend part of the second class meeting going over some terminology that seemed related to our concerns. We wanted to know in particular if the students from the reading and composition fields were using these terms in the same way). We had the class meeting times as opportunities to expand on or, to use Spence's term, "unpack" the journal entries. Thus, when the accounts were not self-explanatory, not only the instructors, but also the students, were sensitive to the need to try to fill in the gaps and the class meeting times provided opportunities to do this. Central to Spence's notion of "unpacking" accounts is the idea that the context within which they appear must be fully available to readers of those accounts. So, just as we attempted to unpack the journal accounts at the class sessions, so will I attempt in Chapter 2 to unpack the entire conversation of the semester by providing the full context of the class and its effects on the accounts.

Sources of Incompleteness

Ericsson and Simon have pointed out that incompleteness in the reports may result from 1) the information not having been heeded initially and thus never having been stored in short-term memory, making it inaccessible for verbal reporting; 2) not all the information available in short-term memory at the time of the report actually being reported; and 3) not all the information previously available in short-term memory having been retained in long-term memory, or retrievable from long-term memory ("Verbal Reports" 236). These limitations surely affected the completeness of the reports we received, but they did not invalidate the reports that were given. Furthermore, by gathering reports from a sizable group of individuals, we were able to discern patterns in their responses as well as individual variations. Instead of dwelling on the potential incompleteness of reports, Ericsson and Simon believe it more fruitful to rephrase the question thus: "Is the verbal report a complete or sufficient description of the information the subject actually has and uses?" ("Verbal Reports" 239). They conclude that the report that is received is not invalidated by its incompleteness (243).

In considering how the relationship of language to thought affects completeness, the reports in the introspective accounts are selected and simplified, often influenced by time pressures and the human wish to present oneself favorably. Questions arise such as how the writer decided what to include, or for what ulterior purpose. In reading this chapter, for example, Chip noted: "The really tricky thing is that we want to make ourselves look good to *ourselves*, never mind the outside audience." In regard to such issues, Evans is afraid that admitting introspective accounts into the approach of experimental psychology would represent a regression to the "methods of nineteenth century introspectionists" ("Critical Note" 518). In response to Evans, Morris distinguishes between "self-hypotheses," attempts to describe causes of one's behaviors, and strategy statements, reports on consciously chosen strategies for tackling problems (465). These strategy statements generally focus on relatively narrow issues and are therefore not as likely to be susceptible to interpretation, selection and omission.

Many of the journal accounts describing what the students actually did in responding to the tasks can be characterized as strategy statements. Attempts to describe the causes of behavior, so called self-hypotheses, also appeared in the journal accounts. Both types of responses are described later in this chapter.

At the second class meeting, I asked the students to comment on how much they felt the journal accounts reflected what they really did, and how much they felt was lost in the process of communicating what they had done. Chip said that he felt that a lot had been lost. Amber said that, if she tried to write about the whole writing process, all of it that she could remember, she would be writing for days. Lila noted that she was very conscious that her journal would be handed in. This had led her to adopt a tone in her journal that she characterized as very different from her personal journal, an academic tone. Amber also noted that, although she had tried to include discussions of where the most important ideas had come from, "one of the things that is not in there is very much about what didn't fit in." Along with this difficulty of not having any record of the multiple options that may have occurred to the individuals who were in the process of making decisions, Chip noted another dilemma we would have to take into account in interpreting their journal accounts:

> I tried to explain some decisions that I had made in my writing but if you explain every decision you've made—you don't remember why you made every decision because you were busy making the decision. But certainly some of them stood out for me because there were things on the surface. You might think I made this decision because I'm so well-structured, but actually it was a matter of one word which reminded me of something else.

Thus, unless the connections to prior knowledge or immediate insight were explicitly stated in the journals, we could not be aware of every potential relationship that individual students would have to any of the readings or tasks.

For a few students, the issue of cooperation in the study was a major factor. Trying to be compliant, even when she had to report some lack of success in her introspecting activities, Jade reported in her journal for the fourth class:

> I would like to give more specific information as to what took place in the process of synthesizing, but I don't know. I spent a lot of time in the car this week and did a lot of thinking then. I don't recall that anything specific resulted from that thinking, but I'm sure it was important. I do it all the time before writing a paper, but I don't know exactly what I do. It ultimately results in a plan. That plan is often changed during writing, but I have always thought about it first.

For her, as for all the others, the incubation period was essential, and although Jade did not record any of the specific insights gained from this mulling period, she recognized its significance. (She later reported to me that writing was always difficult for her and that she relied on her memory as preparation for writing.) Although the importance of the time element for undertaking these tasks will be discussed at some length in a subsequent chapter, it is sufficient to say here that we felt that one of the most important advantages our material has over protocol analysis reports is that they reflect the more natural element of time (a minimum of one week) that our students had to complete the reading and writing tasks. And, as will also be seen in later discussions, the time period of the complete semester allows for the description of the incremental growth of knowledge that develops in a particular field over periods of sustained learning. The students had two major topics: introspection during the first half of the semester and their self-designed research projects in the second half. Chapter 5 deals extensively with the building of knowledge on the topic of introspection.

Where Attention is Focused

Tomlinson makes a distinction between cognitive process and composing processes. She argues that individuals have great difficulty describing their cognitive processes because they have limited access to them (431). She believes, though, that it is possible to study retrospective accounts of composing processes for what they do reveal: "As writers construct representations of their writing processes, they reveal to us their conceptions of how one should think and talk about writing processes; about what composing is, what one can and should know about it, how one goes about doing it, what problems are inherent to it, and what the meaning of composing is or should be" (442–443).

At the fourteenth class meeting, Lionel brought up the issue of how writers construct representations of their writing processes.

> We've been talking about how we're trying to understand each other's processes and how different and unique they are. And they sound pretty unique when we describe them. But we just had a perfect example of somebody [describing physical movement while writing] and everybody said, "Oh, yeah, me too." But nobody [else] brought it up in their own personal description. Maybe it wasn't high in their own personal description, but I've been sitting here doing that the whole time. Somebody talks and I think, "Oh, I do that." And somebody else talks and says the opposite and I say, "I do that." Maybe what we're getting at as much as differences as we're seeing ways of perceiving our processes more—or at least as much as we're seeing differences in processes.

Violet offered the opinion that perhaps different things about their behavior bothered different people and so they tended to focus on the things that bothered them. It seems that, as they "heeded" the points that bothered them, they selected them from their stream-of-consciousness for reporting.

These comments are central to the notion of how complete we can regard the accounts to be. It is probably true, as Violet cautioned, that individuals often mentioned and described the elements in their language processes that were brought to the conscious level by some dissatisfaction in their activities, so that many of the automatic successful coping strategies were simply not mentioned. Ericsson and Simon point out that, if individuals are experienced in carrying out particular types of tasks, the processes may become automatic and not accessible to conscious examination and verbalization (*Protocol Analysis* 190). They also note that, while attention is necessary for learning or changing cognitive structures, "it is no longer necessary when the same cognitive process has been executed many times" (226). The reason for this is that, as a process becomes highly practiced, it becomes more and more fully automated. Thus, the intermediate steps are carried out without being interpreted, and no input or output uses short-term memory. While this automation speeds up the process, it makes verbal reports from short-term memory unavailable, since the information was never consciously heeded (225). This factor would account for the particular mention of dissonant events, since they would always be heeded. It also suggests that, if a population of less proficient readers and writers were studied, that group would likely report on some cognitive activities different from those our graduate students chose, because it is likely that complex reading and writing processes would be less-fully automated. Ericsson and Simon point out that, with "increase in experience with a task, the same process may move from cognitively controlled to automatic status, so that what is available for verbalization to the novice may be unavailable to the expert" ("Verbal Reports" 235). Thus, although some information may well be lost for our proficient language users, it is not likely to be that which the individual attended to during the carrying out of the task itself.

Yet, particularly in the beginning weeks of the semester, several of the students commented in their journals about their ordinary, everyday strategies for approaching reading and writing tasks and noted that, even if they didn't mention these activities specifically in later accounts, we should assume that they would be carrying them out. But, because there is a danger that the students might describe a "typical" response rather than a specific response to a task, thus generalizing a process that was not actually used in carrying out a specific task, I have limited my descriptions to the specific accounts related to the specific tasks. Clearly, a selection process was operating, but the selection criteria differed for individual students. As to the ultimate completeness of the reports, Ericsson and Simon conclude that "the information that is heeded during performance of a task is the information that is reportable and the information that is reported is information that is heeded" (*Protocol Analysis* 167).

That information does not always have to be information that directly translates into a response to the reading or writing task. Dobrin points out that what may appear to be "irrelevant" traces (i.e., irrelevant to the immediate carrying out of the task) may in fact be relevant, and researchers should not discourage the production of such traces nor ignore their significance when analyzing the writing process (719). So, although the journal accounts produced by the graduate students in this study may not contain every factor that influenced their responses, these accounts have not been produced in a context where some aspects of the experience have been discouraged nor labelled irrelevant by the investigators while the accounts were being produced. Except in the "practice" session of the first class, no investigator was ever present while a journal account was being produced.

DEPTH OF ACCOUNTS

Perkins believes that introspection induces the "border between the conscious and the unconscious to shift" (38–39). Even though there are limitations to the amount and kind of information that can be obtained from a subject, the information can be valuable and can be extended by conscious reflection. As Sharon Pugh and I pointed out in an earlier article, questions remain about what material is conscious, what subconscious, and what borderline. It is legitimate to ask whether we can usefully deal with conscious material not knowing what is going on beneath the surface. But this issue may be as unimportant, finally, as deciding between labels of introspection or retrospection. The journal accounts seemed to represent the level of introspection that could be captured by language, and it was perhaps fruitless to conjecture about those intuitions that could not be translated into verbal reports. In relation to Tomlinson's point, the students were always providing what they considered to be appropriate descriptions in their journal accounts for the particular demands being made on them.

Level of Accessibility

Pearl raised the issue of level of accessibility at the third class meeting, when she asked how we could know why she made the introspective decisions she did. She pointed out that we couldn't assume that she reported everything that she did. And we would also not know precisely how her decisions were guided. Sharon Pugh summarized the groups' conclusion about this: "We're getting at below the surface, but not at the bottom line or anything like that." In other words, we were receiving the items selected from the accessible stream-of-consciousness flow.

In her journal for the fourth class meeting, Crystal was having difficulty describing how she identified relationships:

> How did I "see" the general conclusion, the "synthesizing idea"? After reading each essay, I was left with an impression as to a central idea or thesis statement [using the language of the experienced instructor of composition]. . . . The only way I can describe my conceptualizing a central idea for each essay is to say that after reading something it leaves me with an "impression" as to what it generally says.

At the fifth class meeting, she was still having difficulty describing her experience, and she told the class that there always seemed to be something elusive in her experiences that seemed more perceptual—it was perceived, it was latent, and it remained indefinable.

At that same class meeting, in relation to there being "something beyond access," Robin was ready to take issue with that elusiveness. He objected to the authors of the essays on introspection that he had been reading calling

> that thing that they can't talk about, genuine, authentic. All those wonderful words are attributed to this thing that they don't know is there. And it's true, it's not biased. All this stuff. I think it's a myth. . . . I think there are things that are hard to verbalize, but I don't know whether they are true or genuine or unbiased.

His major objection was that these researchers seemed to be searching for introspections that would be beyond the reach of language and he couldn't believe that even if such accounts were accessible that they would necessarily be more valid. The inaccessibility to the origin of the insight can have two causes according to Ericsson and Simon: the absence of intermediate stages of acts of recognition from short-term memory, and failure to report transient contents of short-term memory. Thus, "sudden insights" emerge without the individual being able to account for them (*Protocol Analysis* 160). Durkin, though, maintains that, when concurrent think-aloud protocols are collected, it is possible to trace the steps leading to the emergence of the insightful idea (cited in Ericcson and Simon, *Protocol Analysis* 160).

In reporting at the thirteenth class meeting on her processes throughout the semester, Daisy reflected that she felt she had been very poor at writing in the journals:

> I was uncomfortable with it all semester. Less so the second half where I could just write what I was doing and what I planned to do. But I don't think that I ever introspected in the way that you people did. I don't know the metaphors. I don't put things on the back burner.

And, indeed, Daisy was accurately describing what had been in her journals throughout the semester, accounts of what she had been doing to carry out the tasks, what Morris had called strategy statements. When commenting on this manuscript two years later, Daisy noted that initially she had been uncomfortable and had felt the need for more direction in the class. She had wanted to discuss the assignments with others. But then she explained why her journals had taken the form of strategy reports rather than describing processes: "I was unable to put personal anxieties and feelings in writing for others to read." So her personal inhibitions had strongly shaped the form of her responses. But she went on to comment that her "frustration decreased as the class ceased being composed of individuals and became a unit, as the restrictions were lifted on collaborating, and as I began working on material in which I was interested." Her later observations must make researchers and teachers sensitive to how the effect of individual personality traits may be undetected while they are influencing the behavior of students.

The issue of the depth of the accounts appears almost to be a moot issue. The students reported on what they could capture in language of their processes and what they felt comfortable revealing to others, and their concentrated conscious reflection likely increased the amount of information that could be obtained, as Perkins had pointed out. As Tomlinson noted in relation to cognitive processes, the value of whatever could not be captured, that which might be said to be on the unconscious level, inaccessible to language, or that which was consciously suppressed, cannot be assessed.

EFFECT OF INTROSPECTING ON PROCESSES BEING EXAMINED

As Perkins mentioned, when introspection causes the border to shift between the conscious and the unconscious, the knowledge that one is being asked to introspect or retrospect will affect the processes that are being examined. For some critics like Evans, this represents a form of contamination, but for others, notably Perkins, this is not a serious problem. Ericsson and Simon reviewed a large group of studies that purported to show that verbalization changed the course or structure of thought processes, but they found that this did not occur except in studies of perceptual-motor tasks and tasks requiring visual encoding processes (*Protocol Analysis* 106), neither of which were called for in our study. They concluded that

> the processes associated with verbalization should be treated as an integral part of any model of the cognitive processes for a given task whenever the articulation takes the form of direct verbalization (i.e., vocalization of heeded information). The model should also include the processes for storing information in LTM [long-term memory] to account for the phenomena of retrospective verbalization at the end of experimental trials. The gross model we have

proposed is focused on the verbalization of ongoing cognitive processes, but the postulated close link between information attended to and information stored should make it a relatively straightforward matter to model retrospective verbalization (106–07).

Thus, while Ericsson and Simon have mainly examined studies of introspective (i.e., concurrent) reports, they feel confident that retrospective reports can also be valid.

At the first class meeting, in describing her experience in preparing to write the summary of the Valentine article assigned for that day, Garnet commented: "When I first started that article, I reread that first paragraph three times because I was trying to concentrate on what I was doing and it interfered for me." Clearly, at that early stage in trying to examine her own reading and writing processes, the knowledge that she was being called upon to introspect upset her normal unselfconscious practices. Amber noted the same difficulty in her first full journal entry for the second class: "Reading: an unnatural act. I read *in order to* lose self-consciousness: too many watchers watching too many watched."

In a report to the class on a preliminary look at the information collected in the journals, Sharon Pugh noted that, early on, one of the students had written:

> I'm finding it much more difficult to remember what processes I went through as I wrote. I was concentrating on the content of what I was writing and really do not remember much about the thought processes I went through in doing the writing. I will have to start making notes to myself and more consciously try to focus in on my processes as I write [Garnet's journal].

Garnet wanted to be more sensitive to the various "moments" in the writing process because as a reading major, she had heretofore primarily paid attention to her reading processes. As Sharon Pugh commented, there were quite a few of these types of comments early in the semester as students indicated that they saw some things on the surface, but then often felt that other things went under; however, after a period of time, these kinds of comments dropped out of the journals. The students seemed to become increasingly satisfied and less self-conscious about the act of self-reporting.

Characteristics of Journal Writing

The relationship between the individual students and their journals varied enormously. Some examples will illustrate the range. Daisy mainly confined her reports to accounts of what she had been doing to carry out the tasks. Opal, from the very beginning, shared her anxieties and insecurities as she grappled with the early tasks, and then her triumphs as she gained mastery over the readings on introspection and her organized way of dealing with her final paper. Amber came closest to writing a stream-of-consciousness journal as she described her thoughts flitting from past to present, to connections with ideas, individuals, and experiences that were sparked by her present activities. Jade and Lionel offered cooperation but openly expressed resentment about what they were being asked to do, the conditions under which they had to work, and the lack of feedback being received. Robin portrayed his reactions with a refreshing combination of directness and sincerity that made it impossible to take offense at his criticisms. The feeling always emerged that he was trying to understand and learn from his observations of his own responses.

Crystal was the only student who adopted a really personal stance toward her journal, treating it like a communication to an intimate friend, addressing it (on the computer screen) as "Dear Journal." In her journal entry for the thirteenth class, Crystal described this relationship:

> Another point came up in class yesterday regarding an awareness of "audience" for these journal entries—I think that I was very aware of audience at the beginning of the course. But that feeling has diminished considerably. In fact, I feel as though I'm "talking" to the computer screen almost entirely, and as I see the text on the screen, I "react" to it in some obscure way; it "talks back" to me. Just sitting and thinking doesn't accomplish much. But when I start "talking" to the computer, when my thoughts are up there where I can see them, then I can work them out. It's actually much easier to talk to the computer than it is to another person. To how many people can you admit your doubts, fears, insecurities? Also, how many people want to hear them even if you could get up the courage to talk about them? I used to talk to myself all the time (you know those embarrassing moments when you're just carrying on a conversation with yourself like crazy and suddenly realize that someone's looking at you? and then you try desperately to pretend that you were whistling or chewing gum?) But now, and this is due to the habit of journal writing that started in this course, I talk to the computer instead. Although I have all the journals on a computer disc, I haven't looked at any of them after I've run them off, and I've done this deliberately so that each "conversation" is new, so that what I have to say at any given time isn't influenced by what I might have said before.

For her, then, the introspective journal writing seemed to constitute, in part, a dialogue with herself as she "talked" her thoughts through with herself in the role of an intimate, non-judgmental friend, and, in part, a dialogue with us. She took both dialogues quite seriously. But, later, when reading a draft of this manuscript, Crystal offered a tempered analysis of her earlier behavior and its relationship to composing directly on a computer:

> I wonder about this—about the implications for word processors in the process of writing. Any writer knows (and apparently our class did, also) that talking

with someone about a project can help "order" his/her thoughts. The computer screen is not as satisfactory as another person in the sense that it can't offer suggestions. But the screen is a definite "presence" (for me anyway).

It may have been the case that Crystal's heavy work load during her single year at Indiana University caused her to be more isolated (and thus self-reflective) than she was when she returned to her familiar home environment.

For almost all of the students, after the first few weeks, the conscious interference of the introspecting activities appeared to diminish. There were still occasional mentions of such interference, but for the most part the students used the journals and class meetings to monitor their strategies in responding to these typical literacy tasks. This is not to say that they did not frequently analyze their own behavior, but the analysis was of the behavior, not of the process of introspection.

To this point, I have been considering the nature of introspective reports and the reasons why they should be taken seriously as useful accounts of the thought processes of the individuals reporting them. As Ericsson and Simon concluded in their 1980 article:

> [V]erbal reports, elicited with care and interpreted with the full understanding of the circumstances under which they were obtained, are a valuable and thoroughly reliable source of information about cognitive processes. It is time to abandon the careless charge of "introspection" as a means for disparaging such data. They describe human behavior that is as readily interpreted as any other human behavior ("Verbal Reports" 247).

In the balance of this chapter, I will describe the nature of the reports relating to the reading and writing strategies that emerged from the journals and the classroom discussions. The actual range of strategies will be described in Chapters 3 and 4.

REPORTS OF WHAT THEY DID

Many of the accounts in the journals were detailed descriptions of how the students carried out the reading and writing tasks over the semester. Toward the end of the semester, at the thirteenth and fourteenth class meetings, the students reviewed their individual journal entries and summarized what they had come to understand of their own reading and writing processes. Chip noted he had discovered in his introspections that he had a very hard time sorting out different kinds of processes that he used when he wrote:

> For example, a lot of times it seems to me that I'm making some sort of stylistic decision. I'll look at a sentence and it doesn't look right to me. It doesn't bal-

ance. It seems like it needs something else. I have a feeling that that's a stylistic judgment I'm making but then in trying to correct it, I come up with some more material and another idea and then that idea might end up influencing other things in that part of the text. So I feel that there is some sort of mixture of different kinds of processes, different kinds of intentions going on driven by different motives but all affecting each other very much.

Violet had been grappling throughout the semester with completing a literature seminar paper for a course in which she had taken an Incomplete grade. As she worked on this paper, she felt that the introspections she had done on her processes for our course were giving her an insight into the writing of this other paper also. In her journal for the eleventh class meeting, she reported that she had been working on this other paper. Recognizing that our instructions for the latter half of the semester had been to simply report whatever they were doing that week, she commented on her progress with her literature seminar paper:

> Now that I'm actually writing, I've become aware of how much rereading I do *while* writing—or rather, in the interludes between actual bouts of composing. I've gone back to my notes a lot, and I've looked back at some articles (though mainly I'm working from my notes). I've done a lot of rereading of sections of _____ and _____ as I come up to the point of writing about them, even though I was careful to read those sections when I was still in the "reading stage" of the project. I don't think I was aware before of how much moving back and forth between reading and writing I actually do when I'm working on a complicated project like this. I knew that I tended to reread what I'd already written, but that's all I was very conscious of doing.

This pattern, which worked so well for Violet, would not likely conform neatly to a flow-chart model of composing, no matter how many dual-directional arrows were drawn.

At the fourteenth class meeting, Heather described how the journal writing helped her to organize her material for her final paper.

> I tried to solve a lot of the big issues in the journal and it was fixed in print for me. And that resolved the issue in a lot of other ways and I could get beyond that. In the past, it wouldn't have happened until I was at the point of drafting and I would have all kinds of anxiety attacks about not being able to get at the issue. So, in that sense, the journal was wonderful.

In this instance as for some others, the journal writing reflected what the student was doing as she was doing it, her composing process for that particular task.

REACTIONS TO OWN AND OTHERS' TEXTS

Early in the semester, we began to find associations with other knowledge to the essays assigned in the course. (This topic is developed more extensively in Chapter 5 with the discussion of textual origins.) For example, in her journal for the third class meeting, Crystal noted the artificiality of being restricted to write on one essay.

> I found it difficult to consider Hebb's article in isolation. Instead, I kept thinking of Valentine's article and Dennett's. I also kept thinking of the little I know of Freud. I see in myself when I read a need to find structure of some sort, to find order or even to impose it when I don't find it. That's why Valentine's article angered me. Is this because I perceive the disorder that lurks beneath the surface of my own thoughts?

Through her critique of Valentine's article, which she had found difficult to understand partly because of its poor organization, Crystal describes how she found it hard to consider one article in isolation.

In the journals, we found many such instances of reference to other texts, individuals, and settings. Just as any moment in time is thought of as cumulative of all prior moments, so is reading and responding to any text an accumulation of the individual's prior knowledge and experience with all other texts. Associations that are triggered are naturally individualistic, but the idea that associations are triggered and that such triggering is valuable has become a commonplace. Opportunities exist in classroom settings to consciously select and sequence materials to help individuals construct knowledge through cumulative associations with a range of texts on a particular topic or thematic area, but this is seldom done in the setting where most formal instruction in language skills takes place, the freshman composition classroom. In reading the draft of this manuscript, Heather noted that her own experience of "seeing the introspection stuff come together" had changed her approach to the teaching of reading in some of her composition classes. There, if reading is included at all, it generally consists of discrete items, unrelated thematically or informationally. Students are rarely given the opportunity to simultaneously build their knowledge and their power of expression. If more sophisticated thinking leads to more sophisticated writing, it is because the power of cumulative language and concept building underlies both. The connections to other materials and experiences that our graduate students made and demanded of themselves must be nurtured in all classroom settings, but especially introduced to those who need to have it demonstrated that knowledge-building is cumulative and benefits from associations with other connections.

CONTINUATION OF PROJECTS

The journals often served as an outlet for continuing a discussion that had begun in one of the assigned short papers or raising an issue that was not directly included as part of the "official assignment." For example, Amber used the journal entry for the fourth class meeting as such an outlet:

> I'm feeling frustrated because I do have a reaction to Hebb that wants [to be] spoken and no such "task" to do, so I'm gonna sneak it in here. There is immediate experience, but not of the self. Immediate experience can be neither an act of introspection nor what is introspected. Introspection posits a self looking, but in the act of splitting the self into a seen and a seer (!) there is no longer a unitary self—which is the experience of immediacy. The act of introspection is, in a sense, a self-alienating act. Immediate experience arises only in the relation of a non-self-consciousness with non-self. The *knowledge* of immediate experience, that there is such experience or that one has experienced it in such a way cannot be simultaneous to the experience (this knowledge must be after the fact, i.e., retrospective).

Thus, the journal permitted Amber to explore and share with us her criticisms and observations about Hebb's discussion of introspection which were not demanded in the assignment asking for a synthesis between Hebb's and Dennett's writings. Her point, of course, was well taken, and brought up the issue of how any retrospective awareness of the experience has the potential to confound the report of the immediate act. But, analogous to the issue of the "moment" of reporting, experience cannot be reported until it is known nor can thought be communicated until it is realized in language.

Lionel also felt frustrated by the confines of the synthesis task and continued his discussion of the issues in his journal:

> I explained that my synthesis doesn't accurately say what I think. In fact, I'm not sure what I do think about introspection and location of the self. So far, the arguments against introspection haven't persuaded me that it doesn't exist, although I'm not sure it does. I still wonder, for instance, about human beings' intuitive sense of divine existence—God or gods. Discrimination of senses gives no help, because sensory experience gives no stimulus for constructing or conceiving an extrasensory world or force or being, does it?

As well as continuing the discussion of the ideas he raised in his paper, Lionel attempted here to use the journal as a dialoguing device with the instructors. But we never responded to this question or others that he and some other class members raised in their journals, except in class discussions. (We had decided not to respond in writing to the individual students in order to encourage them to explore their own thinking freely, and we responded orally only as participants in the class meetings.) This lack of individual response had an extremely alienating effect on Lionel, perhaps more so than for any other participant in the seminar. He seemed always to want feedback and response, and, when he failed to receive it, other than in classroom discussions where he received little personal feedback, he increasingly distanced himself from the experience. When Heather commented on the draft of this manuscript, she noted that she felt "sympathy for Lionel" and wished she had known about his feelings at the time. This comment made me reflect that perhaps Lionel, an English Education student, felt more isolated from not only his instructors but his peers than anyone else in the seminar. He was at Indiana University for a single year (as Crystal was), taking as many courses as possible, but not really connected to a doctoral program as all the other students in the seminar were. He seemed not to have real "colleagues," as all the other graduate students did. Jade also told me that, although Lionel had socialized with the reading students in the Language Education Department, he had felt intellectually separated from them while he took most of his courses under the rubric of English Education. I met Lionel, by accident, at a professional conference in late 1987 just as this book was about to go into production. He told me that, initially, in the class, he had felt that he could be a member of both the English and reading groups since he had an M.A. in English but was then a student in the School of Education. He soon came to see that he was a member of neither group, although he felt closer to the reading students because "they talked to him." He did strike up an acquaintanceship with Robin on the basis of their both having been students in Oregon, but this friendship was limited to before-class discussions. Although he didn't feel completely an outsider, neither did he achieve insider status with either of the groups.

Chip noted, when he read the manuscript, that he had not minded so much the lack of response to the journals, but, in retrospect, he felt it was strange not to have any response to the academic papers. He said, "It made them seem even more exercise-like." Since we would clearly have wanted to avoid such an assessment, we regretted any effect of this lack of feedback on the writing. Nevertheless, as the analysis of the texts in Chapter 5 reveals, the students were sufficiently intrinsically motivated to undertake serious study of the topic of introspection.

Violet, also using the journal as a conduit for information that didn't fit into a formal paper, wanted to communicate some of the thinking she was doing about her self-selected topic of understanding schema theory that didn't fit in with the assignment for the eighth class.

> I did a lot of speculation that didn't actually wind up in the paper, partly because it seemed so unfounded and partly to limit the size of the paper. (For example, I tried to imagine what a freshman non-English major's poetry reading schema might actually be like. What "slots" are they trying to fill in? What

finally convinces so many of them that poetry can mean anything at all, but that they'd better learn the teacher's interpretation of what a particular poem means?) In such a case, is more than one schema operating, like a poem schema and a classroom-course schema?

It was often the case that Violet's extended comments were statements relating research to pedagogical practices.

We had had an opportunity, we realized more fully after the semester was over and we were starting to analyze the materials, to have used the journals in the dialoguing way that some of the students clearly wanted us to. We could have written replies to the journal entries, particularly those so clearly conversational in tone, filled with questions begging not for answers but at least for responses. We had unnecessarily limited the interaction to its face-to-face dimension (in the classroom, in our offices, or in casual conversations), treating the journals like artifacts for analyses rather than thinking of them as materials dialoguing with us. We had seen the journals as opportunities for the students to explore their own thinking with themselves and had not picked up on the rich opportunities to extend the interaction to ourselves. In responding to this manuscript, Garnet registered her strong agreement about the opportunities lost when we failed to respond to the journals. She noted, "Thinking with yourself is always embedded in thinking with others rather than being something one does in isolation." (Had we commented on the journals, we would doubtlessly have muddied the research aspect of the seminar, but we would likely have improved the instructional aspect. Although these conflicts were not conscious issues for us at the time the seminar was being offered, we recognized later that this dual instructional/research design did affect the responses we received and perhaps unconsciously affected the responses we gave. This issue is dealt with more fully in Chapter 2.)

INTRUSIONS FROM THE OUTSIDE WORLD

Rarely are instructors sensitive to the factors of life outside the classroom that are affecting their students. The journals provided one way for students to share the complications in their lives that were having an impact on their performance in the classroom. When these descriptions occurred in the journals, we never felt that they were being offered as excuses, but rather they were presented with the purpose of showing us what their full lives were like. For example, in her journal account for the eleventh class meeting, Ruby shared with us a problem that she had been having:

> I am having a lot of trouble concentrating on my reading lately, because I have recently found out that I will have to go somewhere out of state to fulfill the

internship requirements for my bilingual fellowship. I am totally up in the air about where I will have to go and the people with whom I must deal on campus are rather difficult. It is also somewhat of a blow because I will not be getting the experience with the Groups program [a summer preparatory program for disadvantaged students admitted to IU] I was hoping for if the bilingual people decide on something they want me to do. Of course, not getting the money involved in Groups is also a source of worry. Anyway, wondering what on earth I am going to be doing and how I am going to arrange my summer is making concentration on reading very difficult. . . . I just sat down to get some good intensive reading for my paper done and the phone rang. It was one of the bilingual people calling to tell me something about the possible internship plans for this summer. The whole business is so complicated that it drives me berserk. I mention this situation because it makes concentration so difficult and affects my ability to concentrate on my work.

Understanding the effect of such complications could improve the attitude of instructors toward students' sometimes legitimate requests for flexibility in fulfilling their commitments.

Throughout the course, Jay, the only foreign student (a Jordanian), maintained a reserve and appeared reluctant to participate freely in the discussions. In fact, in one of the latter class meetings when the students were summarizing their descriptions of their introspective processes for their classmates, after Jay completed his report, Sharon Pugh attempted to ask him some probing questions. So marked were the responses by the other class members to Sharon Pugh's questions that she directly asked the class to explore why they were answering Jay's questions instead of waiting and giving him a chance to reply. Heather later noted in commenting on this manuscript that this "shock of recognizing what we all were doing" was something that she wanted to remember so that she could apply this insight to her teaching. In his journal entry for the twelfth week, Jay gave some indication of why, in addition to his obvious difficulty with spoken English, he had so often been reticent:

In the same time [I was working on other papers] I was still thinking of my project on schema theory [for this course] and preparing for working on it and having it finished within the limitation of time I have. I feel very confused these days because I have a lot of work to do, beside my heavy responsibility toward my family. I recognize very well that it is very anxious to be in a position like that I am. To achieve my goal perfectly and completely is not an easy task. I think writing a good paper needs besides availability of information need[ed] for completing it, the ability to go through this information and achieve something that is new and different from that which is available. It is a creative achievement and not just repeating what is found in books. It is difficult to have the opportunity to be a "creative" writer within this framework and pressuring environment. Pressure may have a positive side effect when it stimulates who has it to increase his/her effort to achieve the planned goals. In

many occasion, I was in the same spot and my feeling was that it is better for
me to have this kind of pressure to achieve the tasks I am supposed to do.

This dilemma of quoting information directly or synthesizing and interpreting it had been a difficult problem for Jay throughout the semester. The
language difficulties, the time pressures, and perhaps an educational style
which in the past had rewarded close adherence to source texts had made it
almost impossible for him to draw away from the exact language of the experts whose works he was reading and reporting on. For one of the short
papers in the course he felt that he had achieved success by giving his personal interpretations, but as his journal comments indicated, by the end of
the semester he saw that he was about to revert to his old habits, which he
did. But at least now he knew that there was a difference, and he wanted to
aim for the more "creative" interpretation when he could.

It might at first appear that the types of responsibilities these mature graduate students have would differ substantially from the more carefree life that
we normally associate with undergraduates. But my hunch would be that a
great many undergraduates have equally complex lives outside of the classroom, even if their experiences might differ markedly in the details. Heather
later noted that this would be especially true on an urban campus, where
almost all students have jobs. I certainly found that to be true when I began
teaching at City College in New York. The point is that everyone's life is
complicated in one way or another, and, though we do not want those complications to be excuses for performance in the classroom, being aware of
them can make us more responsive as instructors to the individual experiences and needs of our students.

COMMUNICATIONS AND NEGOTIATIONS WITH INSTRUCTORS

At the second class meeting, Jade, who often adopted an alienated de-
meanor in the classroom but who pictured herself in her journal as wanting
to be "cooperative" in this dual instructional–research setting, described
how from the very beginning she was tailoring her journal accounts to what
she thought would be helpful to us in our research:

> I found myself deciding—really concerned with what to enter and what not to
> enter because I was thinking, now what information do they want, what infor-
> mation do they need? Whereas when I'm reading a book or anything like that
> kind of text, I have another purpose. I'm going to use this information later for
> some reason so those decisions [about notes in a journal] are made very natu-
> rally, whereas here I was—what do they want me to write down? What do
> they want to know about my reading?

Two comments seem appropriate here: first, that the notion of an external audience for her notes seemed to divert her from what she regarded as her natural motive for reading, and it may well have had this effect. Second, she perceived the notes about her process to be useful solely for us in our research, and she had not incorporated into her personal goal-structure what we had tried to communicate to the class, that the major purpose of the course for the student participants was to gain further self-knowledge about their own processes. We believed she had exaggerated our authority as classroom instructors, but felt bound to comply with that authority as she had defined it. When reading the manuscript, Garnet commented that "it was difficult for all of us to initially incorporate into our goal-structures the purpose of coming to understand ourselves."

But not until two years later, when she read a draft of this manuscript, did Jade explain to me why she had been so concerned with the research aspect of the course. She had enrolled with the expectation that it was a course on learning to use introspection as a research technique. She had even expected to do a small research project of her own as part of the course, and she had thought of some tentative research designs to try out. She never explained this conflict between her expectations and the actual design of our course to us, so we did not understand at the time the reasons for her displeasure or her apparent fixation on her willingness to be a compliant research subject for us. She felt compelled to participate in the activities of the course and used the journal as an opportunity to comment on what was happening. She told me that she never considered dropping the course, such a possibility apparently not having been a part of her instructional history or behavior.

In almost her ultimate attempt to be cooperative in her journal, Jade accounted to us for her prospectus for her final paper being a week late:

> Well, as you probably noticed, I didn't hand in my prospectus on time. I decided that since I didn't know what one was, I wasn't going to do it. No, seriously, I felt a certain degree of uncertainty as to what was expected of me along with a sense that this was busy work since I had already discussed this with Sharon. From the time you gave us the assignment I knew what I wanted to do [examine methodologies of foreign language instruction]. I told Sharon about it and it remains unchanged. I felt absolutely no need to put it into writing—so I didn't. What changed my mind was when I started considering the consequences of my action. I didn't think I would be penalized in any way, but I was afraid I might screw up your research. I figure you may be looking at these proposals in terms of our final products and any changes in direction that may have taken place. Whether or not that is your intention, I decided that the completeness of your data collection is more important than my aversion to less than challenging activities.

This comment was characterized as Jade's "almost ultimate attempt to be cooperative" because her ultimate attempt turned out to be the writing of the final paper, which she also felt was unimportant because it required formalizing understandings for us that she felt she had already achieved for herself. She consistently characterized the "thinking" activities of her experience as the crucial ones, and, unlike others, did not feel that, in the composing (the writing), new insights developed. Thus, writing up the products of her thinking held little attraction for her. Perhaps this belief was related to her agonizing process of writing. Two years later, she commented that writing was still not a mode of exploration for her although she was attempting some free writing to increase her fluency. Her major use of writing was for articles that she wished to submit for publication, and she treated her graduate course papers as prospective publications.

As early as the second class meeting, Pearl had set up her own agenda for the course and wanted us to know that. She said, "I would guess that because each of us set up our own agenda, so what sort of introspections we would record, that every single set will have that characteristic and which will make them very different." She later explained to me that, since we had not made clear how the assignments would fit together, instead revealing them week by week, she had felt the need to create a structure for herself. She would figure out a way to make the course useful for herself. By the fourth week, Pearl was considering the value of these introspective accounts for research purposes. She wrote in her journal:

> Are we just reporting *external* images of various sorts? Does this matter for purposes of educational research? (In either case, the Subject is reporting images, etc. which the Experimenter *cannot* observe. These would seem to help provide us with more insight into how the Subject *reacts* to the environment anyway, and then the mental processes can be inferred. This sort of data seems better to me than *pure* guesses from *only* outwardly observable reactions.) I just realized that the last point above seemed right to me. Perhaps this is because I can't observe my own mental processes and they still surprise me, but I just observed a mental image that is a reaction to these stimuli??? This is getting tough—[emphasis in original].

Writing for exploration was proving fruitful for Pearl.

Thus, these types of journal accounts gave the students opportunities to let the instructors know directly what was on their minds. In addition to giving at least Jade an outlet to explain her behavior, it gave students like Pearl an opportunity to share her thinking about what we had always hoped would emerge, a notion of the collaborative research that instructors and students were doing together. Most of the students knew one of us fairly well before the class began, and some knew both of us. Most had a positive attitude toward the course and the research, although for some there was a strain between the dual roles of student/research subject (as is already clear from Jade's journal comments). Some others, like Opal and Topaz, seemed quite uninfluenced by the research component and thought of themselves only as students with assignments. Thus, it was possible for the participants to choose among several stances for their roles in the course, primarily traditional student, research subject, or collaborator with the instructors in a study of self and others. Of course, the stances taken varied even for individuals at different points in the semester.

SELF-ANALYSES AND SELF-CHARACTERIZATIONS

Throughout the semester, influenced by the readings, the tasks, and the class discussions, the students not only reported on their thinking, reading, and writing activities, but they often analyzed their own introspections. Some, like Derrida, might argue that the students could not be reporting the presence of their thoughts because "speech and the writing that records it are always at one remove from the reality of being" (Eakin 224). Eakin posits that, "psychologically speaking, reflexive consciousness—the self's sense of itself as a self—is liveliest and most immediate in the moment of speech" (225). The immediacy of speech would be lost, of course, in the journal accounts, but as the discussion of introspective and retrospective reports demonstrated, both spoken and written accounts are reconstructions that provide verbal reports of mental processes that would be inaccessible in any other way.

In considering the nature of autobiographical writing, Eakin presents the writing of autobiography as the recording of moments in time as they reflect all earlier moments. Eakin proposes a

> conception of the autobiographical act as both a re-enactment and an extension of earlier phases of identity formation. . . . That is to say that during the process of autobiographical composition the qualities of these prototypical autobiographical acts may be re-expressed by the qualities of the act of *remembering* as distinguished from or in addition to the substantive content of the *remembered* experience (226).

Eakin goes on to consider the elusiveness of self-knowledge in the autobiographical act:

> [T]ime and again the self as an object of inquiry seems to dissolve in direct proportion to the intensity with which it is pursued. From this perspective, the Deconstructionists emerge as only the most recent to remind us of the perennial gulf between life and language, person and text, which has always been one of the principal truths taught by the practice of autobiography. Yet the enduring autobiographers . . . help us to cross this gulf, introducing us into the illusion of presence even as they make us know it for the illusion it is (276).

In a sense, the participants in our seminar could be considered as mini-autobiographers. Perhaps the records they produced were only "illusions of presence," but, in their attempts at self-analysis, they create a sense that they feel the presence of their thoughts strongly and are capable of communicating these thoughts to others.

Increasing Consciousness

In his journal for the sixth week, when writing the position paper, Robin noted that

> This assignment was the easiest and most rewarding of all the projects we've done so far. As a contrast to my fears when the synthesis assignment was given, I felt relief and even a little eagerness to write this assignment. The fact that I had these feelings *to begin with*, before I even tried doing the assignment, leads me to believe that I'm doing "top-down" type thinking. I had already decided, with the synthesis assignment, that Dennett's deal (story, article, parody) didn't have a clear point of view and I had already written that in my journal. Otherwise, I have been "defending a position" all along in my journal, a position that I had come to before I took this course. One interesting aspect of this, now that I think of it, is the feeling I learned a lot in writing this last paper, or during the last few weeks culminating in writing this paper. Perhaps I've shaped my inquiry into introspection according to my belief that social relations are the determining factor in most (all?) human actions. Maybe I haven't learned at all, but I just feel pleased that my point of view still works for me. The position that "introspection" is social—or that social concerns motivate introspection—is something that people who know me would predict. Once I wrote a long history (autobiographical) about why I think like I do—and it seems clear to me that my family's values are essentially ones that necessitate seeing one's identity socially. One of the taboos of our family was to close your bedroom door!

Robin's analysis reminds him of a similar autobiographical account about the way in which he perceives all of the experiences of his life, and he feels very comfortable with these types of accounts. In addition, he sees that his analysis of introspection as social is intimately connected with his philosophy of social interaction, and he fits new knowledge comfortably into that framework. His own dissertation addresses the social nature of learning. For him, connections to his belief-system and philosophy are central to making meaning out of any new experience. He would be incapable of treating any text as an isolated entity.

The Development of Self-Understanding

The lack of feedback, audience and intrinsic incentive had been discouraging to Jade from the beginning of the semester. In her journal entry for the fifth class meeting, she revealed that this was not her only difficulty:

> Not until I was well into my writing did I realize that the kind of reporting I do in this journal is what Evans would call rationalization and what Morris called self-hypothesis. Although I agree with Morris that they have some value, I share the skepticism of Evans.
> . . . This semester I have a lot of shorter papers to write and I find that I'm not allowing myself to reflect too much about the writing because that takes a lot of time. Reflection for me leads to so much revision that I feel like I'm hammering out my text, or perhaps a better metaphor is one of slowly chipping away at it. That is the way I usually write and when I do, I feel more comfortable with the product. But it makes writing an incredibly slow process. That just won't work for me in this context. So I've become almost neurotic about putting my writing off until the deadline and then be forced to produce. (Gee, this is starting to sound like a confessional instead of a journal.)

What is happening, though, is that Jade has brought her discomfort to the surface and has begun to analyze the behavior she has adopted in response to her problems.

By the ninth class meeting, many of the students were becoming aware that they were indeed increasing their consciousness as a result of writing the introspective reflections. Heather noted in her journal:

> I learned something about myself with that last assignment before this. When I am in a foul mood about something related to or even totally unrelated to my studies, I have a tendency to constrain the limits of the assignments I have been given. I am not relating this for any other reason than I want to remember it. When I reread my own paper and journal, I realized I had set a false boundary for the writing assignment. Between the two writings, I managed to do what I ultimately thought I should have done, but I wanted to divide it up, giving authority to someone else for setting the limits. Why this is valuable is that I have done it before and will probably do it again. In this case, knowledge will be power; I can talk myself out of the boundaries in the future.

At this point, at least, Heather believes that the self-analysis will be enough to help her shift her strategies to more satisfying ones. Furthermore, unlike Jade, who had acceded authority to us as researchers, Heather has consciously decided to assert her own authority in her work.

When reading the draft of this manuscript two years after the seminar was completed, Heather reflected on how her ability to shift her strategies to her own needs had matured:

> I've discovered since that if I am truly mentally exhausted, I don't seem to be able to fight the limits and end up doing a bad job of it. The extension the other direction is that when I am totally without limits or classroom expectations, my own sense of my writing is much improved. The two papers I did for conventions this year have been my best work yet and the only limits were my interests.

So, even though Heather cannot always fight the limits, she does feel more satisfaction in contexts that she can control and she is clearly aware of the causes and implications of her behavior in each setting.

For the twelfth class meeting, Crystal began to understand what her difficulties had been in writing the research paper for our course and she had started to resolve them. She reported in her journal that, although she had planned to spend a particular day reading, she had procrastinated by writing her parents' wills (although they weren't needed until the summer), had gone to a movie in the afternoon and an opera in the evening,

> the whole time feeling guilty about slacking off? So why didn't I work on [the poet whose work she was studying in preparation for writing her dissertation]. I think I know the reason: which is, that I'm afraid my "idea" concerning her late poetry won't pan out and I'll have to start again in a new direction. Even so, if this is the case, then it makes sense to find out. Still, I'm procrastinating.

The next entry in the journal reflects an incredible change in her confidence and her attitude:

> Hello, Journal! After a productive day in the library yesterday, I'm sure that I no longer will procrastinate regarding [the paper]. In fact, I was so excited when I left the library that I practically ran home to read some more. Maybe the reading I've been doing hasn't been so desultory after all, maybe somehow it all "digested." Because I'm convinced that my idea about androgyny figuring in [her] poetry is right. Found a fantastic book . . . that puts all my reading and intuitions in perspective. And this means that not only I've got a paper, but also that I've got a dissertation.

Perhaps there is nothing so remarkable about this description over time of a student grappling with, despairing about, and finally overcoming her concerns with a major topic. In fact, two years later, Opal commented that this had been exactly her experience when studying for her qualifying exam for the Ph.D. But such instances are documented very infrequently while they are occurring. And all too rarely are they shared with novice writers who have the illusion that everyone else's path is smooth, and only their own is troubled. After reading Crystal's description of her experience, Heather felt very strongly about sharing these experiences with students. She noted that her own experience was that she couldn't write about something until she felt she knew about it, and that students should not be urged to "get busy" or "write to discover" too early in the process.

At the next class meeting, Crystal, who had produced both expository and fictional responses to the tasks over the semester, summed up her reflections on her composing processes and the effect that introspection had had on her:

In thinking about how my writing strategies might have changed, I was actually surprised with what I came up with. I mean this change is the result of introspecting, of thinking about this. . . . There is a difference [between] academic writing and creative writing. In academic writing or the research paper or whatever, I need a shell of some sort or I find that I can write reams and reams of paper that are nothing but digressions that I have to throw away. Creative writing starts with an idea and then just sort of goes from there right into the computer. It starts to take shape on the screen . . . I think that doing these journal entries, getting into the habit of thinking about writing, has affected what I do and what it's done is making me more self-conscious about writing as I'm doing it. I think I can see in myself an attempt to be more careful in phrasing sentences, in making connections between sentences and between paragraphs, instead of just writing like crazy as I used to. And so I really think that this habit of thinking about it has made me more self-conscious. I think it helps. I think I throw away less trash than I used to.

And I wondered about a week or so ago, because I had already decided that this had happened—that I could see it happening. I wondered if my self-consciousness had gotten me in trouble because I had the worse case of writer's block that I think I've had in years. I couldn't do this [final] paper. I'd sit down and not even be able to get a few words together. I threw pages away, I don't know how many pages. And I wondered if this self-consciousness had done that. Have I gotten afraid of what's up there on the screen? Have I gotten too critical of it? So that that's blocking my ability to put the words together. And I thought about that and came to the conclusion that instead I think there were two other factors at work in this case of writer's block.

One was that I attached to this project, all sorts of self-imposed anxiety. Was the idea going to work into a dissertation? It if wasn't, would I have to junk all the research I already had? . . . I have thought about it quite a bit and I think that the writer's block wasn't really an increased self-consciousness but really due to other factors.

To use Morris' terminology, Crystal's reports of her strategy statements had led her to create self-hypotheses about the sources of her behavior.

Opal had repeatedly reported her difficulties with the tasks assigned in the course until she had finally felt she had had some success with the "position paper." Toward the end of the semester, for the twelfth class meeting, she wrote a long journal entry reflecting on what she had learned about herself as a result of the introspecting activities. She noted that the lack of organization and structure in her work had been one of the causes of her almost consistently high anxiety level. She was trying to overcome this lack of organization by structuring her activities for the final paper in our course very rigorously, and she was having some success with that. She acknowledged that procrastination had been an important mode of operation for her, and as if to demonstrate that she would become master of her own behavior, she was now going to force herself to take a dreaded statistics course in the upcoming summer. But she felt that coming to understand herself had been enormously valuable:

> I'll admit that until approximately three weeks ago, I really disliked this course. I hated the tasks and felt intimidated by many of the participants. But now, perhaps because of the above mentioned realizations, I find myself viewing it as one of the courses in which I have learned the most. I say that not in the sense of the amount of content material learned but in that knowledge gained about myself—why I'm so anxious, [about my] learning style, etc. It has aided me in looking both within and outside of myself. I'm still uncertain as to what introspection is, but I know I do a lot of it.

It is interesting that Opal feels compelled to make a distinction between learning content and learning about herself. Actually, the learning about herself *was* the content of the course. This confusion about what they were supposed to learn in the course continued throughout the semester for some.

Aside from the distinction between content and "learning about oneself" that Opal made, some students persisted in the notion that what was important was that Sharon Pugh and I learn about them, rather than that they learn about themselves. When reading this section of the manuscript, Garnet commented that she had felt initially confused by the goals of the course. She said, "While [the goals] were clear in your's and Sharon's minds, we did not get a clear message. We did not feel that we were exploring with you but that you were exploring us." This distinction appeared to decline markedly for most of the students at least by the time they began working on their self-designed projects. (Perhaps, in a perverse way, our "exploring them" was a less threatening outcome than their "exploring themselves.") Violet commented, when she read this manuscript:

> It is interesting that graduate students are so concerned with being "safe," especially since we so often complain about our own undergraduate students' concern with grades and inability to take risks. The concern mentioned here and several other points raised in the study (concern about evaluation, for instance) suggest that our class was actually a good general model of student

behavior. Graduate students may seem more sophisticated, but they still seem to have a lot of the same concerns—and perhaps behavior as undergraduates do.

Few seemed to regard evaluation as a central factor in the course, but all had internalized models of what constituted appropriate graduate student behavior, the personas they would then present to their instructors.

ATTEMPTS TO DESCRIBE THE MIND AT WORK

Not surprisingly, one of the major focuses in the journal writing was the attempt to describe the mind at work. Hayden White, in *Tropics of Discourse*, considers the relation of language to thought:

> The human power to consign meaning is mysterious insofar as it is conceived to precede, logically if not ontologically, all of the efforts of the thinking, feeling, and willing subject to determine the meaning of meaning, or the status of meaning in the world. Language or speech is mysteriously invested with the power to create meanings and, at the same time, frustrate every effort to arrive at definitive meaning (276).

Yet we are inevitably left with language as the major source of access to thought and meaning, inadequate and frustrating as it may appear at times.

Heather was in a reflective mood when she wrote her journal for the twelfth class meeting. Interested in analyzing her mind at work, she wrote:

> Now for some introspection images. I have tried to give shape to how these issues are coming up and as they relate to the paper. There seems to be some middle ground between total awareness and total unawareness. That middle ground I envision as a pool. All the information touches the shoreline and acts together in the pool. I can't quite describe all of it—I still see my file drawers as the unaware information, but I have a strong sense that it is there. If I choose to deliberately process, I can feel the pool moving, the waves rolling—movement. But when I write I undergo a similar submersion as when I read. I still can't be "in" it if I'm observing it. Consciously trying to observe it is more possible at less creative points—editing, proofing, rereading. I also think that language's linearity creates infinite problems in trying to describe it, which may be why you're getting so many figures and metaphors. I can conceive of my pool holding and processing say five chunks of information, but if I try to describe it, language demands one word after another, not five interactions happening at once. By stringing out the description, I lose the sense of what actually happened. It's too thick, too difficult to get at the ease with which some of the connections happen.

But, two years later, Heather felt much less frustrated with this simultaneous aspect and just accepted the fact that it would happen. As she points out, metaphors were a favorite way to describe the mind's operations, since they could convey the multiple layers the writers were aware of. They were forced to select, from the larger stream-of-consciousness, those items they were "heeding" and could thus report.

In her journal entry for the eleventh class meeting, Opal found her perceptions of her processes growing, and she accounted for this at least partly through her introspective examinations:

> The more I read [on literacy], the more questions are formulated. It's not that the initial ones are gradually being answered but rather that extensions seem to be forming. But it's not the same process that has occurred in other paper writing tasks. In other projects I would find myself becoming angry and frustrated when I recognized that I really didn't know enough about the subject but for some reason I don't have a sense of frustration but rather one of simply being led further and further into something. Perhaps I'm not really formulating more questions than I normally do in the writing process, but rather that I simply have greater awareness of their presence. Actually I've become quite sensitive to the presence of thoughts. That is a very strange statement to make. I don't mean to imply that I'm always cogitating on great and wonderous ideas; the majority are quite mundane—but I'm now aware that I'm thinking about something and often question it (the thought not the awareness). I've also started to write a lot of these thoughts down—not a journal exactly, but various situations that need attending to. I may not come up with answers, but the process has the effect of lowering anxiety and frustration.

Two years later, she expressed very positive feelings about her experience and noted, "These realizations have changed and influenced everything." She wrote to me saying the course had been "by far the most influential of courses—perhaps so because of its effect on multiple aspects of my life, both professional and personal." When Opal, a reading student, came up with the phrase, the "presence of thought," I doubt that she realized its implications for the deconstructionists. For her, it meant simply an awareness of her thinking processes and a beginning of greater self-control over her life as a result of this awareness.

The Emergence of Insights

From the very beginning of the semester, Topaz was extremely interested in describing and analyzing her mental processes. She characterized one level of her thinking as her "back burner," a term she had apparently been using for some time. In her journal account for the fourth class meeting, she described her approach:

As I wrote, my "back burner" was busy "stewing" the concepts of creativity, claims and grounds, satire, testimony and non-theoretical discourse vs. theoretical discourse. I was also very concerned about why Dennett had chosen the creative form to deal with an academic concept—this was "back burner" level also. I concentrate on concrete aspects as I write—I am *very* conscious of this level. However, I am also conscious of my "back burner" working, even though it is not conscious thought that is going on at that level. Sometimes I think it is a computer processing data; other times I think of it as my subconscious; most of the time I just accept it as my old, familiar, dependable "back burner" which never fails me. By the time I had finished writing about the four points, I called up the data from my back burner and wrote the last two paragraphs of my paper.

These last two paragraphs were evaluative (as Rosen's concept of narrative predicts), indicating that she had delayed presenting her assessments of the arguments raised in the articles read for that week until she had summarized them. But she had been evaluating the arguments all along, simply holding those judgments in abeyance on her "back burner" until she was ready to present them. Her willingness to take this evaluative stance is examined more fully in Chapter 5, where Topaz's orientation toward argumentative structure is seen to dominate her reading and writing strategies.

Topaz's description of the simultaneous operation of her "front burner" and her "back burner" is evocative of Bleich's idea of cognitive stereoscopy. Bleich ("Cognitive Stereoscopy") maintains that

Knowledge is always a re-cognition because it is seeing through one perspective superimposed in another is such a way that the one perspective does not appear to be prior to the other. Because the perspectives are different, or heretofore unrelated in our minds, the new knowledge is sometimes described as the "aha" experience (99).

But, as can be seen through some of the students' reports, sometimes even these "aha" experiences can be traced.

Topaz continued to be interested in describing her introspective processes, and for the eleventh class meeting, she provided an elaborate discussion in her journal in which, as she wrote, she learned something more about her processes:

Introspection comes in layers. It's not a "one right answer" process. *All* my burnout explanations are valid for me—it is not *really* a choice of one *or* the other explanation. On different mental levels, I have different reasons for what I do. One reason (programming myself for thought time) may be more superficial/conscious than the next (pushing to natural capacity) or the next (termination of compulsive tendencies). It is a case of first level introspection, second level, third level, etc. (I say "etc." because there is no limit to the levels a given person might list. In fact, *my* fourth level is that I want to get through the reading so I can get to the writing process which is more important to me than the reading is.

Each level is different but each level is valid. Just because they do differ does *not* make one the "right answer" and all the others "rationalizations"—to use Evans' term.

The last paragraph was an "ah ha" perception based on the preceding four paragraphs of deductive reasoning. Therefore, perhaps "spontaneous inspiration" is not so "spontaneous" after all. Perhaps it just *appears* to be because we do not normally see/recognize all the reasoning that went on before it [emphasis in original].

As previously mentioned, Ericsson and Simon corroborate this view of "sudden insight." They believe that such reports are the result of the absence of recognizing intermediate stages from short-term memory and failing to report the transient contents of short-term memory ("Verbal Reports" 238). Topaz's experience provides an example of the claim made by Durkin that the emergence of insightful ideas can be determined through careful examination of protocol reports.

Emerging Self-Hypotheses

By the ninth class meeting, when she was preparing her prospectus for he r final paper on the topic of validity and reliability, Amber was beginnin g to feel that she was learning something about her way of working: "Thinking about what I've said thus far in the journal, I see frustration is a pre tty strong motivator for me for pushing my thinking—usually in over my head though I'm beginning to trust, more and more, that my doggie paddle will get me *somewhere*, even if only in deeper."

At the eleventh class meeting, Jade again raised the issue of the relationship between introspection and language:

> I feel a great deal of discomfort in terms of talking about the language that people are using in their journals . . . I started thinking about my use of language and often times it's very sloppy. It's simply a function of my experience. I find myself, for example, when I talk about education using a lot of sports language, because that is a function of my experience. And yet to conceive of education in those terms, make any parallels at all is so diametrically opposed to the way I think of education. It's totally inappropriate for me to use those other metaphors when I'm talking about my views on learning. And yet I do that because it's a function of my experience that's comfortable. I think often times the language that we use is simply a function of the things that are going on around us.

Or, she might have added, the things we know and care about. Lionel, too, was concerned by how literally his language would be interpreted. He noted:

> This introspection is hard enough to do and see anything very clearly, but even if it were clear, language itself may not be the appropriate way to communicate what is happening precisely because it's not necessarily a linguistic experience. But [and here, of course, he raises the paradox of all those who wish to separate thought from language], how else can you describe it? And so you start writing in your journal and just start tossing stuff up like typical figures of speech.

The selection of language must, of course, reduce to some extent the complexity that thought in linguistic or non-linguistic form takes, but the choice of language and metaphors must reflect the perspectives and prior experiences of the individual attempting to express these thoughts.

Throughout the semester, there were indications that there were difficulties with precisely defining introspection or even knowing for certain that someone was engaging in it. At the fourth class meeting, Lionel objected to our characterizing some of the behaviors we were discussing in class as introspective accounts. He said:

> I'm not sure I know what introspection really is and I'm not sure I'm doing it. You said earlier that we were introspecting and I thought, "I'm not introspecting, I'm just talking. I'm just thinking about it." I'm not sure what it is and I'm not sure when I do it and I'd kind of like to get more clear on that but so far, I haven't been convinced by any of the writers [we have read].

Three years later, when I asked Lionel whether he felt more comfortable now with the concept of introspection, he jotted down some answers to my questions:

> . . . Also incomplete at the end of the course was an idea of what introspection was, really, its nature and functions. I had to continue to think about it, to rework my notions of introspection, particularly to come to grips with the limitations—that I just can't get as deeply into my own or anybody else's thinking as I would like to—as my curiosity desires.

For Lionel, it was still not clear that thinking about one's processes and then describing those thoughts in the language that gave form to them was introspection. But what else could introspection be?

THE VALUE OF INTROSPECTIVE ACCOUNTS

Though there have been criticisms of introspective accounts, they still remain the most direct way to capture the thoughts and feelings of individuals undergoing any experience that a researcher wants to understand and describe. I have tried to convey the limitations that researchers in language and psychology have felt about such reports. I have tried to include the reservations the students themselves had, at different times, about such reports. But I hope that what has come through this account so far is that, even within such limitations, there is a richness of experience that can be conveyed from these examinations of self that can be achieved in no other way. Heather later commented that, if protocol analysis reports had tried to account for "and then" and "at the same time," etc., the task could never be completed. But the journal accounts, collected over time, permitted the picturing of such simultaneity with less distortion of the actual composing event.

Prior studies of the composing process, whether through protocol analysis or stimulated recall, have neglected to consider the issues that have been raised here about the nature of such reports: their validity, their completeness, their depth, and their effect on the process being examined. I do not want to claim that I have overcome all the limitations inherent in such reports, but with seventeen students reporting on five teacher-designed tasks and one longer self-designed task over a semester's time, there is a range and a depth to this set of materials never put together before. With this number of students and tasks, it is possible to trace and describe the complex ways in which individuals define and design their responses to reading and writing tasks. All too often, teachers think of monolithic tasks, monolithic responses to those tasks, and monolithic strategies to produce those responses. Through these introspective accounts, I now have the means to describe the range of ways in which actual students individually interpreted and responded to this range of tasks.

And some of the issues that might appear to weaken the validity of such accounts can begin to be seen as supports for their usefulness. For example, the notion that the writer wishes to present an acceptable persona *is* a factor in a classroom setting and may well influence the actions as well as the accounts of the individual. The fact that the reports may not be complete may indicate that the items selected for reporting are the ones that are causing the highest level of anxiety for the individuals reporting them, or they may tell us what students believe *should* be reported in such accounts. The depth of the reports takes us very far into the workings of the mind, as far as language can carry us, and it seems useless to speculate about what lies beyond the ability of consciousness to be reflected in language, particularly when we are looking at language events themselves. And, finally, although it is impossible to deny that every research methodology affects the processes being examined, as Perkins pointed out, shifting the border between the conscious and the unconscious, however awkward, has the possibility of improving the ratio of that which is able to be accounted for.

What I do know about these accounts is that they are extraordinarily varied and complex. When reading the manuscript, Chip commented that he thought we got beyond cognitive processes which he characterized as "rather low-level, automatic, and unconscious decision-making processes." He thought "the journals got at higher level processes which might be called 'habits,' 'attitudes,' or 'personality traits.' " The journals reflect a range of reading and writing strategies that can make us sensitive to the variety of issues that surround such literacy events in our classrooms. They also help us to see, as will be shown in Chapter 5, on textual origins, how students' preferred approaches to learning and writing can be traced through analyses of texts and journals in ways previously inaccessible to researchers. But responses to tasks never exist in a vacuum. So before taking a detailed look at the reading and writing processes and the resulting texts, I must describe more fully the context within which these events took place and the effect of that context upon the students' responses to the demands of the course.

CHAPTER 2

The Role of the Specific Classroom Setting

Far too often, literacy events have been set in sterile, "laboratory-like" environments and examined as essentially a-contextual events. But, as researchers such as Brandt have come to see writing as a social experience, there has been increasing demand for the study of literacy events in relation to the complex dimensions and demands of their settings. Harré, Clarke, and DeCarlo maintain:

> each adult human being has his or her own repertoire of beliefs and habits, the personal domain; but all human action occurs in a social context—sometimes explicit, sometimes implicit which constitutes the social domain. What any body does on a particular occasion, therefore, can be fully explained only by reference to both the personal and social domains (21).

Kantor, Kirby, and Goetz have called for "discovering and elaborating upon specific features of context" (296). Scribner and Cole have noted that "[l]iteracy is not simply knowing how to read and write a particular script but applying this knowledge for specific purposes in specific contexts of use" (236). Similarly, Mishler notes that "context should be viewed as a resource for understanding rather than an enemy of understanding" (cited in Kantor et al. 296). Myers has contrasted rationalist, positivist, and contextualist studies. He notes:

> Although positivism has been the dominant method of research in writing, an increasing number of researchers has started to criticize the positivist assumption that in the pursuit of general laws in the social sciences one must strip away context and put subjects in an experimental or laboratory setting.
> Contextualism differs from positivism in that it examines subjects in their natural settings without imposing any experimental constraints from the out-

side. . . . Contextualism differs from rationalism in that contextualism examines writing as an evolutionary process, collecting data over extended periods of time in a "natural" context, whereas rationalism examines writing as a product, collecting examples of the end result. (19–20)

Harré, Clarke, and DeCarlo point out that "one of the most important basic units in the system of behavioral analysis is precisely that which refers to long-term as opposed to short-term patterns and . . . this has largely been missed by laboratory analyses. Activities in the laboratory, however naturalistic, can represent only relatively fleeting and fine-detailed patterns of human activity" (28). In arguing for an ecological model of writing, Cooper proposes a model of writing "whose fundamental tenet is that writing is an activity through which a person is continually engaged with a variety of socially constituted systems" (367). Cooper states that an ecological model goes beyond a contextual model in that it "postulates dynamic interlocking systems which structure the social activity of writing" (368). Such a model accounts for how writers affect others and are affected themselves in the act of writing.

CHARACTERIZING CONTEXTS

In *Narrative Truth and Historical Truth*, Donald Spence makes a crucial point about the importance of understanding the full context within which any materials for investigation arise. Spence is concerned with the interpretation that the reader of any analysis may make. He argues that there is a difference between normative competence and privileged competence. With normative competence, readers of such reports base their interpretations of the data on their own theoretical assumptions and personal experiences. Only when the data is "unpacked" by supplying as many elements from the original context as possible, including the researcher's own basis for providing input at transition points, can a reader come close to the privileged competence of the researcher. Spence calls this unpacking the "naturalizing" of a text (218–236).

Tannen likens the contextualization of a conversation to the filling in of background for literary works. In the literary process, the reader creates a world according to the writer's instructions. The most dramatic use of this type of literary language is poetry "in which the goal is to evoke the most elaborate sets of associations in the reader by use of the sparest verbal representation" (156). Tannen notes that a similar process of contextualization is basic as well to conversation. Conversations that are transcribed and considered by themselves appear incoherent (156). They must be explained or elaborated to recover as much of the original context in which they appeared as possible for meaning to be derived from them.

From the same perspective as set forth by Spence and Tannen, I believe that it is crucial for readers of this book to have as complete an understanding as possible of the context within which the students in this study responded to the reading and writing tasks. But, as Robin pointed out to me when he read a draft of this chapter, it is also essential to note that there is no such thing as a monolithic context; in fact, each student in the seminar was creating a specific context for himself or herself as he or she interacted with the instructors, the tasks, and the other participants in the seminar. Chip also noted this in reading the manuscript, pointing out "particularly the context of the inter-personal relationship between student and teacher, which was quite different for various members of the course." He commented also, "Students and teachers are assumed to have only a limited relationship (one semester, one room). Maybe that is okay (i.e., a valid assumption) for research involving freshman composition, but clearly here the situation was quite different." (By this, I believe that he meant many of the students knew one of the instructors in the course from previous courses and other interactions, and some knew both of us.) In this chapter, I will be describing the tasks that were assigned to the students, the conditions that were prescribed for their being carried out, and the ongoing reactions of the students and instructors to the contextual factors as provided in the journals, the papers, and the classroom discussions.

Robin Lakoff has made the distinction between discourse being reciprocal or nonreciprocal. She defines *discourse* as *reciprocal* only when both or all participants are able to do the same things, and if similar contributions are understood similarly. Thus, in a fully reciprocal discourse, any participant can ask a question and expect an answer. If one can make a particular sort of statement or ask a particular kind of question, so can others. If one can refuse to answer, so can others ("Persuasive Discourse" 27). Lakoff recognizes that the classroom setting may present a problem because of the power relationships that customarily exist between instructors and students. Power, in this instance, means the power to motivate a discourse in a certain direction, to begin or terminate it explicitly. Although power is generally considered an evil and its appearance in discourse a sign of the corruption of the discourse, Lakoff suggests that, "as long as it is explicitly acknowledged that the imbalance exists, there is no problem" ("Persuasive Discourse" 33).

It is, of course, the case that, in the graduate seminar that Sharon Pugh and I taught, the students were enrolled in a conventional classroom setting (with the understanding that such a graduate seminar will differ markedly from secondary or undergraduate level classes). Harré, Clarke, and DeCarlo suggest that such a setting will capture what they label as the second level in a three-level hierarchy of decision and control (in psychological theory). We would thus have access in our graduate seminar to how "plans are made, verbal formulations considered, and carefully chosen tactics put into effect"

(32). Their third level of control, relating to social orders, might not ordinarily be captured in such a setting, but I believe that the students' journals do picture some affective changes that were triggered by their participation in the events pictured here.

The students had the expectation that they would be evaluated and graded as in any other course. Although we tried to defuse the evaluation aspect in ways that will be described, we could not completely eliminate the power relationship inherent in such a setting. And, as Spence pointed out in relation to noting the significance of transition points in a conversation, we often initiated and terminated specific areas of discussion during the class meetings. However, I hope that through "unpacking" the conditions of the course, I will meet Lakoff's condition of "explicit acknowledgment."

Origin of the Course

The impetus for the course was a discussion that Sharon Pugh and I had in the spring of 1983 after I read an article that she had published in *The Journal of Reading* (under the name Sharon Smith). In this article, she described a reading activity that she had designed for graduate students in the Language Education Department, asking them to describe and analyze their reading processes in making sense of an article for which they had virtually no background information. I proposed to her that we collaboratively develop a course for graduate students in English and Language Education in which we would design a varied sequence of tasks and ask the students to examine both their reading and writing strategies. The purpose of the course would be to make the students examine their own modes of operation in carrying out a range of tasks and to become aware of the modes of others. Sharon Pugh enthusiastically agreed, and we began an ongoing series of luncheon meetings to design the course.

Our initial idea was to locate a sequence of readings on the topic of introspection itself and give the students a series of short reading and writing tasks for the first half of the semester. We decided that the writing tasks should encompass the genres normally associated with the teaching of writing—summaries, reactions, syntheses, and the like—because we believed that all of the students who would enroll in our course would also be teachers of reading and writing, most as graduate student instructors in either the Learning Skills Center or the English Composition Program. They would thus be familiar with those genres both as instructors and students and would feel comfortable producing such written responses. (We did not anticipate the degree of analysis of these genre terms that took place in response to the assignments.) We felt that, by designing the course so that the first half of the semester would include teacher-designed tasks and the second half a longer self-designed task, the students would have an opportunity to explore their reading and writing strategies under two important contrasting sets of conditions. Although Hillocks' analysis of research on written composition was published after our study was undertaken, he urged studies that would examine writing under contrasting conditions: "Useful research might examine changes in writing over a period of time with no assigned topics in one condition [like our students' self-designed final tasks], randomly assigned topics in another [nothing comparable in our study], and topics selected is some sequence [like our teacher-designed tasks in the first half of the semester]" (239).

Only after the course was designed, did it occur to us that we would have access to an incredibly rich set of materials that would allow us to reflect on and analyze the experiences of an extremely linguistically sophisticated group of students. At that point, we saw no conflict in our roles as instructors and researchers, because we expected to conduct the class as a normal class and simply collect the information as the semester went on. We knew, of course, that we would have to have the permission of the students to document the proceedings of the class, but we did not expect that to present any difficulty. (We were later surprised to what extent being "subjects" in a study affected some of the participants in the class.) The Learning Resources Center of Indiana University supported all our costs of documentation.

To our delight, seventeen of the best graduate students in the Language Education Department and the English Department enrolled in the course. Although we had initially hoped to hold the enrollment down to twelve, we were inundated by requests from individual students who were interested in the course, and we found it hard to turn them away.

At the first class meeting, we explained the conditions under which the course would operate for the first half of the semester. After receiving the students' approval for us to collect the materials of the course for later research purposes, we turned on the tape recorder which would run then throughout the semester at the class meetings. I explained that we had no syllabus to distribute for the course, but the assignments would be revealed week by week.

NATURE OF THE TASKS

Each assignment was to be accompanied by a weekly journal entry in which the students were to describe their thoughts and activities as they responded to the task. Although we gave fairly explicit directions as to *what* was to be accounted for in the journal entries, we gave no directions as to *how* the students were to approach the accounting. In this way, as was pointed out in Chapter 1, we hoped to receive valid accounts from "naive" introspectors, and we valued this individuality for the freedom it would give the students in selecting what aspects of their responses to include in the accounts.

Ericsson and Simon predict, on the basis of their model, that retrospective reports can be accessed and specified even without the subject being provided with specific information about what to retrieve, particularly in the ideal situation when the individual is giving the report immediately after the task is completed (*Protocol Analysis* 19). Their model postulates that verbal behavior can be accounted for in the same way as any other behavior, by developing and testing an information-processing model of how information is accessed and verbalized in response to stimuli (61–62). But, as in our case, when the relevant time period and particular type of event to be recalled are specified, the recall increases considerably because of the availability of retrieval cues. As Ericsson and Simon point out, this type of recall is very time consuming and could hardly take place in studies allotting short time periods to fill out a questionnaire (45) or demanding recall in an environment which does not allow normal associations to prior knowledge and social encounters to take place (as in protocol analysis or stimulated recall reports).

A description of the tasks and accompanying journal assignments is presented in Table 1.

The First Class: Modeling the Process

For the balance of the first class meeting, we distributed one of the articles on introspection (by Valentine) and asked the students to read a section of it that we had designated, summarize that section, and then write a journal entry accounting for their reading and writing processes. We thus hoped to model in class, with a very brief assignment, the kinds of tasks they would be undertaking in the course. We gave them thirty minutes for the activity.

In addition to describing their responses to the task, e.g., the difficulty of reading the "middle" of an unfamiliar article, their definitions of summary, their uncertainty about the purpose of the activity, and their initial self-consciousness with introspecting, they noted their discomfort at having to do the task in class and under time pressures. Later, in their journals, some noted that they had also felt insecure in this initial setting where they knew some but not all of their fellow students and had had varying prior experience with their instructors. For some, like Chip, knowing both instructors well "was a significant factor in my general reaction to the course and what I was being asked to do." The students were sensitive to the fact that they were starting to adopt public personas for themselves.

Jade later commented to me that, although the classroom environment

Table 1

Class Meeting	Task	Journal Assignment
Teacher-Designed Tasks		
1. 1/11/84	In-class: Read and summarize a section of the Valentine article.	Account for your reading and writing processes.
2. 1/18/84	Read entire Valentine article and write a reaction statement.	Write description of process of coming to understand article and devising reaction to it.
3. 1/24/84	Read "Where Am I?" (Dennett) and "Self-Knowledge and the Self" (Hebb). Write a summary of each.	Write about how you decided what to include in the summary.
4. 2/1/84	Write a synthesizing essay drawing on the information from the Dennett and Hebb readings.	Write how you selected synthesizing idea and how you used information from source texts to produce own text.
5. 2/8/84	Read four articles from *British Journal of Psychology*. Summarize two positions being argued.	Describe how you identified the two positions and selected major arguments to support each.
6. 2/15/84	Write a paper in which you defend a position on the issues we have been discussing.	Describe how in defending this position the re-reading of the texts was affected.
Self-Designed Tasks		
7. 2/22/84	Select topic about which you would like to know something and select an aspect in which you have little specific knowledge. Read and summarize the two articles you have chosen on this topic.	Describe how you chose topic and how you chose the two articles.
8. 2/29/84	Write paper relating information from the two articles to area you already know something about.	Describe how you integrated new with existing knowledge.
9. 3/7/84	Write a prospectus for your major project paper with a selected bibliography.	Write an account of how you selected and planned this project to this point.
10–15. (3/21/84–4/25/84)	(Final paper due 4/25/84.)	Keep journal accounts of your work on the major project as you are working on it.

seemed to feel freer for most of the English students than their experiences in literature seminars, some of the reading students had found it to be more structured than their other graduate courses. In particular, this was true for reading students like Garnet, Pearl, and herself who had been working with Language Education faculty who had treated them like colleagues and serious researchers, not like academic apprentices. They also felt more comfortable arguing in classes where all the students had similar backgrounds. In our course, especially early in the semester, some of the reading students had felt uncomfortable, Jade told me, during discussions of philosophers' work, but later they felt more secure when the talk turned to naturalistic research and schema theory, concepts with which they were more familiar.

The Second Class: Reaction to the Valentine Article

For the second class meeting, the students were asked to read the entire Valentine article and write a reaction statement to it. In their journals, they were asked to write a description of their process in coming to understand the article and devising their reaction to it. When she described her reaction statement to the class, Heather noted that, in the class context, since "I know that the two of you are being experimental, . . . I too can be experimental." She had thus removed herself from concerns with evaluation and felt free to explore her own thinking. Since we had "pitched" the course from the very beginning as one in which we would try to learn as a community about the range of individual reading and writing processes through introspective accounts, we were delighted by this stance. It was reiterated frequently throughout the semester as comfort with the group increased and confidence grew that evaluation was truly not a large issue on the agenda. (Only Lionel continued to resist this perspective throughout the semester.)

The Third Class: Summaries of Dennett and Hebb

The assignment of the third class was to work with two of the readings from the packet of materials we had prepared for the class. They were to first read "Where Am I?" by Daniel Dennett, and write a summary of it. Then they were to write a journal entry in which they described how they decided what to put in the summary. Then they were to read a second piece, "Self-Knowledge and the Self" by D.O. Hebb, write a summary of that, and write in their journals how they decided what to put in that summary. In trying to define the assignment more precisely, Garnet asked whether they were to introspect on their reading only as it affected the writing of the summary. This comment was an example of what Tannen, citing Lakoff, called indirectness in conversation. Lakoff had argued that speakers prefer not to say what they mean directly for two reasons: "to save face if their opinions or wants are not favorably received, and to achieve the sense of rapport that comes from being understood without saying what one means" ("Why You Can't Say" quoted in Tannen 156). Thus, Garnet, a reading graduate student, appeared to be asking if their major focus of attention was to be on the writing process rather than the reading process. My response was that I doubted that they could be separated that neatly. That appeared to satisfy her at the moment (at least she pursued the topic no further at that point), but in her journal entries for several weeks she commented on her difficulty in describing her writing processes, stating that she felt much more familiar and comfortable with describing her reading strategies. At the end of the semester, though, when reviewing her journal entries, Garnet found that, although she was conscious initially of struggling to write about her writing processes, she had consistently been writing about both her reading and writing processes.

Sharon Pugh commented that we would be focusing on their decisions for this task. What the students could not yet know was that these two readings were quite different in their nature, the Dennett reading a science-fiction type of story dealing with the separation of the mind from the body and the Hebb reading a conventional research article analyzing introspection as a research methodology. We were interested in knowing whether the students would find their reading and writing strategies different in responding to these contrasting types of materials.

The Fourth Class: Synthesis of Dennett and Hebb

When it came time to synthesize the two readings for the fourth class meeting, Robin decided that the readings

> didn't synthesize and it was easier for me to write this than it was to try to fake one. Although in my real one that I handed in, when I was done with it it was too short so I added two paragraphs [of synthesis]. It was only a page and a little bit and it just didn't seem like it was enough to be a good student.

If Robin, who is one of the most open, sincere, and straightforward of the graduate students, felt the need to portray himself as a serious student, it seems clear that all students must be adopting personas at least to some degree that they hope will be acceptable in a classroom setting. Proponents of a "psychology of action" contend that "[l]anguage is not only a device for passing on information, setting out plans and projects and so on. It is also a medium through which people display their worth, publicly express the sort of person they wish to be taken to be . . . A certain sort of language is called

for by the conventions in use among the members of the community"
(Harré, Clarke, and DeCarlo 10–11).

On reading this manuscript, Garnet gave a very good picture of the personas that serious graduate students adopt. She said,

> Those of us who get to doctoral programs are usually pretty good at playing the
> academic game and that involves portraying ourselves as serious students. The
> research made this even more a factor because we were making ourselves
> public as learners in a way that went far beyond what we would have nor-
> mally. While comments made in class are usually public, they aren't recorded
> for others to read and our processes along the way aren't kept track of. Usually
> there's just a final product (paper) at the end, but no one knows if we put it
> together in two nights or a whole semester. This class opened a lot up to the
> public that is usually private and so I'm not surprised that you found examples
> of us trying to be "serious students."

Violet also commented on the topic of presenting oneself as a serious graduate student. She noted:

> [Robin] and I once had an interesting conversation about the written Ph.D.
> exams, when we talked about the need not to seem "too radical" in the an-
> swers to exam questions. We felt there was some pressure to respond to the
> questions more or less in the way the [exam] writers intended. I don't think
> such pressure was present in your course at all, but behavior patterns of "good
> graduate students" may be hard to break.

As all these comments suggest, instructional histories and specific contexts
both play important roles in influencing behavior. And the pressures inherent in this context doubtlessly focused the students' attention particularly on
their public personas.

In that same class meeting, Sharon Pugh made a casual comment that
had ramifications for the next several weeks. While the class was discussing
the various possible approaches to synthesizing, she asked whether they
had all followed a more or less conventional approach or whether it had
occurred to anyone to do anything different such as writing up Hebb's article with Dennett's style and approach. When Amber suggested that that
would not be synthesis, Sharon Pugh replied: "Why not? It brings two things
together. . . . In a sense that's really going far out with the assignment but
had that occurred to any of you, to try something that was kind of bizarre?"
Crystal noted that she had briefly flirted with the thought of writing two
Tarzan scripts, but abandoned the idea because it would have taken a lot
of time. (This was the first hint of her interest in creative responses. The
evolution of her creative writing is fully traced in Chapter 5.) Sharon Pugh
described a hypothetical dialogue that a student in a previous class had con-

structed between two researchers whose work the students had been read-ing. Lionel immediately wanted to know whether the class was now being directed to try something in "a non-linear fashion." We, of course, never gave them a direct answer, but, as subsequent weeks revealed, a few felt that they were now mandated to try something "bizarre," a few considered but rejected such approaches, and a few were uninfluenced by the discussion. (Lionel's immediate interest in the dialogue form must have influenced him because his final position paper emerged in that form as will be seen more fully in Chapter 5.)

The Fifth Class: Summarizing Four Researchers' Positions

In her next journal entry, Crystal, who the week earlier had resisted the temptation to write a "creative" paper, noted that she "was encouraged in the tendency to [write a parody] by last week's class discussion, which obvi-ously opened the door to creative essays." However, along with her parody, she attached part of one of her drafts in which she stated "seriously" the meaning of the essays and a memo: "Having stated these conclusions as evidence of my serious intent in reading the assigned material, I now feel free to submit an essay of my own which I just couldn't stop writing once I had begun." Regardless of her feeling encouraged to write such a response, like Robin earlier, she still felt the need to protect herself by covering all the options and behaving as she believed a "good student" should. Two years later, when reviewing this manuscript, Crystal noted that she thought often about her reaction and had "tried, because of it, I think—to put my own students more at ease. It's hard to do, though. We have been so 'pro grammed' regarding the academic experience." Clearly the prior educa-tional histories of our graduate students (and their own undergraduate stu-dents) had so socialized them to make assumptions about proper academic behavior that it was extraordinarily difficult to break away from.

Jade, on the other hand, felt that the cues in the previous class had not simply opened creative options but had mandated them. Still wanting to be helpful to our research, she went right along with these "directions" and produced a dialogue as her formal paper. In her journal entry, she explained her decision:

> All right sports fans, this week I decided to do something different. You have said that you want us to feel free to express ourselves in alternate ways so I did.
>
> Actually I would be more honest if I said that you gave cues to indicate that was what you were looking for. I know you're not thrilled with the stance I'm taking in this class, but I'm finding it extremely valuable. It's not so much a question of giving you what you want, but rather responding to the cues in the context in much the same way that my students and/or research informants

might. Trying to not cue a certain type of behavior simply does not work. The cues are always there. I'm learning a lot about what form they take, what effect they have, and possible ways of dealing with all of this.

So since you cued alternate response forms, this is what I produced. I resisted initially because of the increase in time I saw as being involved in this type of thing. I don't know what made me decide to go ahead with it after all.

As I began there was a certain amount of anxiety involved. I have never been completely comfortable writing anything that even smacks of fiction. But the fact that this will not go public allowed me to relax and write.

She expressed surprise at the next class meeting that not all of the class members had followed these "cues." And after reading a draft of this manuscript, she expressed further surprise that the others may not have even recognized the cues. (Of course, because of her interest in the course as a research enterprise, she may have been particularly attuned to what she interpreted as cues.)

When the students were discussing the four articles from the *British Journal of Psychology* that they had been assigned to read for the fifth class meeting and which they had had some difficulty with, Sharon Pugh asked if anyone had tried to find out more information. Both Daisy and Ruby acknowledged that they had considered the possibility and felt the need to do so, but neither had. Ruby said that she had rationalized that "that was not in the assignment and it was going to be cold [that night]." When I pressed her about whether that was the way she customarily treated assignments, she admitted that she usually went out and got more, but it depended on what she was going to use the information for. Heather wondered whether we had had some expectations that the students would seek outside sources, and Ruby was also curious to see whether we were waiting to see whether anyone did go out. We told them in class that we wouldn't share that information with them at that time, but in fact we had speculated in advance whether anyone would seek out additional information. It seemed clear that they had found at least minimally sufficient information with which to work and there did not seem to be sufficient motivation to pursue the issues beyond the assigned reading. When reading the manuscript, Garnet noted that our unwillingness to answer those types of questions had reinforced their notion that we had ulterior purposes related to our research goals and that the students were put into a position of having to guess what we were trying to do to them. It is true that Sharon Pugh and I had formulated questions about the students' possible range of responses to certain of the tasks, but we were not sufficiently sensitive during the class meetings that our noncommittal responses would strengthen some students' perception of the course as a research enterprise.

The Sixth Class: Writing a Position Paper

Concern with the process of decision making came up in the sixth class meeting, when the students discussed their options in responding to the task asking them to defend a position on the issues we had been considering in the course. Garnet, in particular, noted that she had had to decide whether to defend a position or *her* position. She preferred to select an issue of her own rather than choosing an issue that had been defined in the readings. Ruby, Amber, Daisy, and Lionel all quickly agreed that they had made the same choice. Jay indicated that he had felt the assigned readings were not sufficient to give him the information he needed to defend a position, so he had gone to the library and read additional articles and chapters from books.

Several other students indicated concern with having adequate information, but they reported that they had used only additional sources or materials already available to them. Amber said that she had outlined enough material to write a fourteen-page paper, but then selected from the materials to produce a three-page paper. Crystal indicated an insecurity with the concepts, so she reported that she had handled it the only way she could fairly competently, and for her that meant creatively. When Sharon Pugh pressed her as to the distinction she was making, Crystal responded:

> I guess I'm opposing creative writing and academic writing. Creative writing gives free rein, in my definition anyway. There can be connections of one kind or another, but there is no judge as far as to say your argument is not logical here or your sources aren't adequate. Whereas in academic and scholarly writing, writing does require logical development and adequate support for points made.

The genesis of this perspective can be seen more fully in the consideration of the textual origins of Crystal's work in Chapter 5.

For her "topic," Crystal had selected the argument between empirical and naturalistic research as to the validity and usefulness of introspective reports. A brief excerpt from Crystal's tale will illustrate how she approached the task. She tells of an Emperor whose subjects construct a labyrinth beneath his castle and challenge him to find the route. He dispatches "empirical" legionnaires to study the problem. When they finally fail, he admits defeat to his "subjective host":

> Finally the day of reckoning came. Aged and shaken, his empirical domain crumbling around him, the distraught sovereign conceded defeat to the subjective host. As he bade them enter the fortress in which their presence had never before been recognized, however, he stopped dead in his tracks.
>
> "My God, you're a bunch of women!"

"Sure are, Honey," said the leader as she helped herself to a handful of grapes, "and since we'll be on a first-name basis from now on, my name's Rita Mae but my friends call me David."

"David?"

"You know how many jobs there are for 'subjective' females in this world? You'd call yourself David too."

"Well since you're here, do you mind explaining the labyrinth to me? Did I underestimate its complexity?"

"No, Sweetheart, you didn't underestimate the labyrinth; you underestimated the power of what you so condescendingly refer to as the 'subjective element.' . . . Anyway, each one of us built a different section of the labyrinth according to her own plan, and thus only the builder had direct access to her own section. Your empirical guys did a good job as far as they went, but their information was just too limited . . ."

Thus, Crystal had raised an appropriate issue and deftly dealt with it by satirizing the position she wished to criticize. Furthermore, as she pointed out in her journal entry, academic sources are not required to justify points in a creative paper.

The Self-Selected Projects

At the end of the sixth class meeting, we took some pains to try to describe fully the nature of the self-selected task the students would be working on for the remainder of the semester. We stressed that we wanted the students to select a topic for purposes of their own, so that they would feel motivated and would feel that the inquiry had some intrinsic value for them. In the journals, we wanted them to keep an ongoing record so that we could "develop a sense of what the stages in this process are like for people who have to go out and do some kind of a research project. How do you identify a topic, how do you identify the appropriate sources, how do you relate them to what you already know?" We ended the restriction of not being allowed to collaborate with their classmates or others.

At the next class meeting, it was clear that the energy levels of the students had risen as they began discussing their prospective topics with each other. Robin's comment was typical: He noted that he had been trying to read a certain book for a long time and it was "really hard. And I finally thought that this was a perfect time to really understand it and so I sat down and did it." Opal later commented that by this point in the course the students "finally felt some 'ownership' of the tasks."

The Remaining Class Time

A large part of the following class meeting was spent in negotiating just what should be done with the class time for the remainder of the semester. During that time, the students would be working on their final research projects. We had planned that in the last two class meetings the students would share the substantive content of their papers with each other. In the interim class meetings, we had considered the possibility of inviting some graduate students and faculty members on campus who had been using forms of introspection in their research to come and share their experiences with the class members. We asked for reactions to these tentative proposals.

One of the issues that came up immediately was that the students wanted some feedback about what we had been finding in their journal entries to that point in the semester. The group considered the possibility of duplicating the journal entries and placing a set in the library, but there was some discussion about the fact that everyone would have to agree to this because the initial understanding had been that the journals would not be public documents in that way. Aside from the legitimate privacy issue, the time it would take for the class members to read through even a limited set of journals would preclude the serious undertaking and documenting of the individual research projects. The students seemed to agree that they wanted everything: to do the research projects, to get some feedback from the journals, and to hear the reports of the campus researchers. I hit upon what I hoped would be a reasonable solution, knowing that it would require some intensive work for Sharon Pugh and myself. "Here's what occurs to me, and that is that I think that occasionally Sharon and I should remember that we're parts of this community as well. . . . What we can do is go back and look over representative samples of the journals and try to list some of the range of strategies that seem to be related to each of these topics and maybe bring into you what we would call a preliminary working sheet." I also suggested that we invite the speakers in for the latter half of the subsequent class meetings. So it was agreed that Sharon Pugh and I would alternately make preliminary reports for the first half of each class meeting and then the speakers would be invited to share their research in the second part. The students would continue with their research projects and the documentation in the journals. The only other change that was decided on was that the students would review their own journal entries for the last two class meetings, and, instead of reporting to each other on the substantive content of their research papers, they would provide overviews for each other on what they had learned about their own approaches to reading and writing tasks.

We gave them further guidelines for what they should note in their journal entries on their self-designed tasks. We asked them to pursue the task in as natural a way as possible, even with the understanding that, some weeks, they might not work on this particular project because they had other priorities. But they were to describe in the journal whatever it was they had done in a given week and what they were thinking about as they were doing it. So, if their focus was changing or they were asking themselves new questions or they were looking for additional sources, we wanted them to note those things. Our intention was not to interfere with the process itself but to have them try to capture an ongoing description of the process as it actually was occurring.

The Role of the Journals

The journals had come to play an important role in the experience of the students in the course. I asked the students at the thirteenth class meeting "whether knowing that you would be able to write in the journals some explanation or account of how you interpreted the task, whether that affected the interpretation of the task that you came up with." Robin felt that it was always possible to "explain in the journal what you did. In a sense it gave you more freedom to do anything you wanted because you could explain why you did it in another separate form." Topaz reacted similarly, but felt she didn't *need* the journal to make her feel free: "It gave me the same feeling of freedom it gave you," she said to Robin, "to be able to do this; however, even without the journal, I still would have felt the same thing exactly." (But, as the analysis of Topaz's papers and journal entries for the first half of the semester will show (in Chapter 5), she was more concerned about her evaluation in the course than any other student except Lionel.) For Jade, the journal outlet provided an opportunity for less commitment to the tasks because she could justify her responses: "I don't think I would have [felt freer]. I didn't have to come to terms with the tasks to nearly as great a degree because I could just do something. I didn't have to come to terms with a task that I didn't want to do." This comment was consistent with her other remarks in the course about her lack of commitment to the entire enterprise. The journal writing provided opportunities to anticipate objections by the instructors and provide explanations, e.g., about why a paper wasn't extensively rewritten ("the assignment doesn't require that I go back and make this perfect") or why someone decided not to pursue an area more fully in the library. As the semester progressed, students noted that they were writing the journals less "after the fact," i.e., after the assignment was completed, and more often while the assignment was in process, thus more effectively recording their "heeded" experiences.

Student–Instructor Relationships

By the time the students were working on their self-selected projects, there had developed a history of the types of responses that Sharon Pugh and I had provided as the students had undertaken the assigned tasks. For Pearl, the non-committal stance we had taken ("Sharon and Marilyn both saying, 'Hum, so you did that.' ") had given her the confidence that she could interpret the assignments to suit herself. She said in class,

> And so this week I thought, well, what would be helpful to me in this paper which is a big assignment. And by God, I'm going to write something that will be kind of useful to me, at least. And so I related these two articles to that prior knowledge that made me choose my topic and so it . . . could definitely be a step along the way to my eventual project. But that in part had to do with the history of the interaction that had gone on in here. Whereas, if I had a similar assignment that a teacher had said, "And this—" I thought they had a hidden agenda, I would have probably tried to find the hidden agenda and do it.

But, it must be remembered, early in the semester Pearl had indicated that she would construct her own agenda for the course. So it is unlikely that she is the type of person who would have seriously bent her own principles to satisfy an instructor.

Ruby saw the stance we had taken as one in which she "consistently felt more freedom in interpreting the assignment because I felt like some of what you wanted to do was look at how people interpreted the assignment." In other classes, even graduate classes, she noted that "there are professors and you agree with them or you're wrong." What she is pointing out is that we were being given a broader range of interpretations of tasks than some other professors might receive, because we not only made it clear that we would tolerate such a range, but we overtly encouraged this. Thus, whatever responses we would receive would be as affected by our non-restrictive environment as others would be in a restricted environment. Neither could be said to be a "norm"; each was representative of its own context. We might wish to argue for the benefit of this non-restrictive environment, and I shall certainly do so in Chapter 6, but we cannot characterize it as "typical."

Pearl and Lila noted that, for them, the issue had been more that they wanted to be respected as graduate students. Pearl also noted that, even though she had not been concerned about the grade evaluation in the course:

> the first little bit is always kind of tense because you are trying to figure out what are the rules here, what are the pragmatics that are operating? What sort of relationships are you going to have or what am I expected to do? And I think

the anxiety for me comes from figuring that out in this case instead of thinking that I was going to be evaluated negatively because I already decided I probably wasn't going to be.

As these descriptions imply, we were attempting to set up a classroom context that included representative tasks but no specific instructions about how they were to be defined or undertaken. One of the mutual topics for our exploration would be how individuals define tasks, discover purposes, and explore audiences. We knew that their instructional histories would affect the decisions they made, but we also knew that there would be effects of the specific instructional context that they were working in. One of the major characteristics of that context was that they received little individual feedback, and then only in the general classroom discussions.

EFFECT OF AUDIENCE AND FEEDBACK

One of the major issues in the class was that the students felt that they were not receiving "official" individual feedback to their work. Their papers were not commented on or returned, and their journals were also accepted without response. The only feedback that they received occurred during the class discussions. Some students found this freedom liberating, but others felt that, since they were not provided with either substantive comments or value judgments about the quality of their work, they were not really being challenged to perform to their highest level. Some were also likely responding to instructional histories in which evaluation was the primary motivating factor for high performance. Most responded to this non-judgmental environment by putting in the "typical" amount of effort they would expect to expend in such a course. Since we were hoping to have them examine their work habits and processes under such a condition, we felt that the level of work that was received was satisfactory for the purposes of the course. But, of course, "typical" standards of graduate students surpass greater efforts by many undergraduates. And there was the additional factor of the public personas being revealed and scrutinized as part of the research component.

There were some individuals, most notably Lionel and Jade, who let us know their feelings of dissatisfaction about the lack of feedback. Lionel felt that he had pretty clearly understood his own processes before he started the course and so he had hoped to receive feedback about his own work and be able to compare it with the approaches of others. Most of the dissatisfaction, for him, seemed to center on his not knowing what he was going to be judged on and where he was headed. We explained that part of our plan was to reduce the role of authority on the part of the instructors and return authority to the students. Although he appeared mollified when we offered to share some preliminary findings from the journals toward the end of the semester, his final journal entry was a vituperative attack on the uselessness of the course to him. When commenting on the draft of this book, Crystal made a brief notation in relation to Lionel's attitude: "For whatever it's worth, he told me that he had only *one* worthwhile course in his entire year at I.U." So, perhaps, our course was not singled out for his displeasure.

Jade had had a different problem. She only felt satisfied when her work demanded that she have a real audience to convince about some issue and she felt a lack of that context in both the teacher-designed tasks and her own self-designed task. Thus, the writing was purposeless, although she acknowledged that she learned something from the inquiries she had undertaken. But without an audience to write to for some meaningful reason, the writing itself seemed like an artificial exercise. She explained this at the sixth class meeting when she said, "I wasn't arguing with anyone, so it was hard to write." She also missed the feeling of risk involved when a writer knows that a critical reader is just waiting to pounce on her arguments. As she noted at the eighth class meeting, "I haven't felt a lot of anxiety because there is no feedback from the papers. I can write something stupid and no one is going to write back and tell me." Chip, commenting on the manuscript, noted that he also missed the feedback because "a lot of the pleasure in school writing (or any writing) is in the response of a *particular* reader." As Sharon Pugh noted, the lack of feedback was a mixed blessing: they didn't have the anxiety they might have felt with a very critical response, but they did have the anxiety of not knowing how their work was being received. Amber also noted that, because short papers were due every week during the first half of the semester, their evaluation wasn't dependent on their performance on just one paper, as it often is in a graduate course. Jade's self-evaluation of her concern with audience came when she reported on her journal accounts at the fourteenth class meeting: "I also noticed in my journal my concern with context, audience, and purpose. And I always felt that way. I see that I'm almost obsessed by those things. It's really a neurotic kind of thing."

For others, like Heather and Pearl, the absence of a critical audience permitted the exploration of their own interests in a non-threatening and non-judgmental environment. Frequently, the students thought of themselves as the audience for their writing and used the writing as a way of trying out ideas and preparing materials that might be of use to them later.

Increasingly, though, it became apparent that the journals were the central focus of the class discussions, not the papers. Pearl had characterized the papers as the means for an "audit trail," to provide the mechanism for tracing their efforts in responding to these literacy tasks. And although we had not conceived of them in those research terms, in fact the papers were the impetus for requiring them to engage in the reading and writing tasks so that they would have a process to describe and investigate. In other words, we wanted them to be as much interested in *how* they came to produce the papers as *what* they decided to include. An analysis of the papers (in Chapter 5) reveals how the strategies documented in Chapters 3 and 4 culminated in the preferred approaches of interpreting and carrying out the tasks.

THE EFFECT OF RESEARCH SIMULTANEOUS
WITH INSTRUCTION

Researchers concerned with possible limitations of ethnographic research have raised the question of "how much should the researcher be a participant and how much an observer" (Kantor et al. 304). I have been trying throughout this book to describe the roles that Sharon Pugh and I played as instructors/researchers as fully as possible. However, another aspect of dual roles that is rarely raised in reviews of ethnographic studies is the effect that the dual role of student/research subject has on the decisions and processes being analyzed. For example, at the second class meeting, when the task was to write a reaction to the Valentine article, Heather commented, "I know that the two of you [the instructors] are being experimental, so I just removed myself from the evaluative mode. I, too, can be experimental." By these comments, Heather let us know that she did not believe her evaluation in the course depended upon her meeting whatever she perceived to be our expectations—she was free to follow her own inclinations. But this sense of total freedom proved to be somewhat illusory.

At the first class meeting, when we characterized the types of journal entries that we wanted, Sharon Pugh said: "What we don't want you to do is to take a lot of time and go back over it as you might a text that you're doing for a paper and really try to refine it and amplify it mainly because it would be a poor use of your time. We can find out what we need to know just from a regular journal-type record." Although she was trying to make the point that the journals were to be spontaneous rather than reworked, she unfortunately may have contributed to the impression that the journals were being written for us rather than for the students' own needs.

By the third class meeting, signs emerged that the dual activities of the course, pursuit of self-knowledge and research, were beginning to interfere with each other, particularly for a few of the reading students who seemed particularly sensitive to being research subjects. Jade noted that she hated to write summaries "but I really want to cooperate." By the fourth class meeting, Jade was more direct about the effect that the research component was having on her. When the class was asked how it was that they felt comfortable enough to tell us how much they disliked doing the synthesis assignment but not comfortable enough to deny doing the assignment, Jade responded quickly:

> I know why I do that. It is solely due to the fact that this is research. [I would do anything] to help somebody else's research. That's all there is to it. For that reason, I've been doing it. If this was a regular class, I wouldn't do some of these things. But if you see yourself as a researcher, you would obviously help anyone else who was a researcher.

(Only two years later, after she told me about her expectations for the course as a research course, did I fully understand these comments.) When Chip read the manuscript, he noted that he had similar feelings about wanting to help with the research, but at the time he "thought some of the others were over-reacting. Now I suspect that I was *under*-reacting, which is a habitual response for me." When she read the manuscript, Garnet also commented on the dual student/research subject roles the students had participated in. She noted that our not providing an initial overview of the course had made the students more dependent on us than was usual and had contributed to a research-type atmosphere in the course. She said,

> I know that a number of us did focus more on the class as research, as you needing to learn more about us, rather than we learning more our own processes . . . I think this was influenced by the way the course began. Only being told assignments one week in advance and not being able to talk to each other seemed like research manipulations and so I and others responded to it as research. I am still unsure whether the reason behind these two directives was based on the course learning goals or were due to research methodology. Either way, I do know that these directives focused my attention on the class as research rather than on it as a way to learn more about myself. As time went on, my focus did shift to what I was learning about my own processing and the processing of others. However, I was always aware of the research focus.

Clearly, doctoral students who are soon to begin the first major research efforts of their careers have this rationale for cooperating in someone else's research efforts. I tried to explain to Jade in class that we had not had preconceptions about the responses to the tasks and that compliance and noncompliance were equally interesting to us, but this did not appear to reduce her resentment in having to carry out some of these tasks. Furthermore, Garnet later told me, some of the reading students did not think of themselves as "beginner researchers," but rather just as "researchers."

Pearl felt that the fact that she knew her work was going to be data in a study complicated everything for her although she quickly decided that she was allowed to shape the work to her own agenda. A number of the students commented that when they came to write the summary of the Dennett "story" they were perplexed as to how to handle the assignment. Garnet spoke for many when she said that she didn't want to summarize just the plot and be perceived of as a "dummy." In other words, the classroom setting seemed to demand that they "come up with the meaning." Although the research aspect did appear to increase the self-consciousness of the students, particularly at the beginning of the semester, their behavior as students in a graduate seminar did not appear to be especially affected. As I have pointed out earlier, and Robin said in one of his journal entries, they were always trying to be "good graduate students."

At the beginning of the fifth class meeting, Sharon Pugh presented some summarizing descriptive statements about what we had been finding in the journals thus far. She noted that there had been some journal entries geared very specifically to us in relation to our data-gathering attempts and other journal entries geared very much to the individual writers. For those who had decided that we were the primary audience for the journals, there was a sense that they were trying to provide us with what they thought would be useful to us. Stressing the descriptive nature of her report, Sharon Pugh said: "Nobody's [journal] is unacceptable at all. Nobody is not doing a good job on the journals. This is feedback. These are not prescriptions of what you should put in your journals." We tried to retain this neutral posture throughout the course, believing that whatever the students would decide to include in the journals would be more meaningful and truer than any type of accounts that we would specify that we wanted. Certainly, as the task descriptions have already made evident, we were specifying *what* we wanted in the journals, but not *how* these requests should be met.

THE ABSENCE OF COLLABORATION

A major restriction that we imposed on the students for the first half of the semester was "not to confer with each other on the assignments." The reason for our decision to impose the restriction was that we wanted each student to examine closely his or her own processes. That restriction turned out to be totally alien to the way the graduate students were accustomed to working and in some ways skewed their experiences away from their normally socially-interactive ways of working.

In her journal for the fourth class meeting, Pearl complained strongly that the lack of opportunity to collaborate was hindering her learning process although, as she acknowledged, it also gave her more opportunity for risk-taking:

> I felt it was permissible to produce a personal synthesis and take some risks on
> interpretation in areas that I am only beginning to explore. If this were more

than a class paper [i.e., one week paper] and if we hadn't been prohibited from discussing the assignment with peers, professors, etc. I would definitely have sought out other interpretations. Actually, this interaction with colleagues is one of the most valuable learning techniques I have in graduate school—a "thought collective." If I am to grow much further in my understanding of these issues, I will need to *discuss* them with classmates, etc. to see how *they* interpret these articles.

Although, clearly, these topics would be discussed during our formal class sessions, Pearl was responding to the loss of the informal talk that goes on among classmates who are pursuing a new area together. The richness of this talk, she was maintaining, is essential to the trying out and sharing of new ideas and interpretations.

Robin reiterated this point in the fifth class meeting, when he described the frustration of not being able to call people on the phone. He said, "This injunction not to talk is really difficult for me. I learn a lot from talking to other people about articles. What he thinks, how does he feel about this . . . I do that with every other thing. This is the only time I haven't talked to people."

Although we had conceived the injunction not to talk to other people as a way of ensuring that the students would get a "pure" look at their own processes, such a restriction often has another genesis. Too often, instructors shy away from encouraging or even permitting collaborative work because they are afraid that a few students will do "all" the work or will be the source of the most insightful ideas. Violet noted, on reading this manuscript, that, even when not expressly prohibited, undergraduates frequently feel isolated because they find themselves in classes where they don't know anyone and the context neither facilities nor encourages collaboration. Thus, particular individuals interpreted the instructional context in ways that supported their analysis of the setting within which they found themselves working. But an injunction forbidding collaboration, even when motivated by "noble" reasons (as in our case!), disturbs the natural social nature of interchange that leads to the most productive learning. Jade later told me that she had interpreted the injunction not to collaborate as a part of our research design, intended to keep the responses controlled. This was another example of her interpreting the experience of the seminar from her particular research-centered perspective. Garnet, in commenting on the manuscript, also indicated that she believed that, at the time, our research orientation had precipitated this injunction. Two years later, Crystal noted that the injunction against collaboration "bothered some people more than others." She felt that simple personality differences might account for different attitudes, with more gregarious people upset by the injunction. The corollary, of course, is that other personality types might prefer to work alone, at least in some phase of their projects. This was later borne out by the differing attitudes and perspectives among the students in regard to their writing strategies in particular, although the vast majority seemed to feel that a more natural environment invited the opportunity for interaction.

THE SOCIAL DYNAMICS OF THE CLASS

Since the course was being offered in two departments, Language Education and English, it was possible for the students to enroll under either course number and receive credit. Two classrooms had also been scheduled, and Sharon Pugh and I decided that we would meet in the English seminar room that had been assigned, so at the first class meeting she met the students enrolled under the Language Education rubric and brought them over to the building where the English Department and most of its classes were housed and where our class would then meet on a regular basis. Since the English-enrolled students were already there (and sitting together at one end of the table), the Language-Education students sat at the other end. This "grouping" persisted for several weeks as people who knew each other better naturally gravitated together.

However, there was another kind of social dynamic going on that went beyond the initial seating arrangements. At the ninth class meeting, Garnet, a reading student, shared her perception of the early class meetings. She pointed out that at the second class meeting, when the assignment of the reaction paper to the Valentine article was being discussed, she had felt intimidated by the discussion of the English students:

> I remember the first time that we wrote the reaction paper and then we discussed it in class. People had such specific definitions and had really worked that out. I felt really concerned because I hadn't, so I started doing it. . . . There was this huge discussion and it was obvious particularly the English people from their past experience with writing certain things had really defined that out. It kind of shook me up.

As was noted earlier, Garnet was the student who had raised the issue as to whether they were to focus on writing strategies rather than reading strategies and had expressed her discomfort at having to do that. She was not accustomed to defining genre types and the English students had made her self-conscious about such writing.

When he was reporting to the class on his journal accounts of his processes at the thirteenth class meeting, Robin described his mixed emotions in responding to the early teacher-designed tasks. He had felt responsibility to the instructors who had been nice to him in the past, but he felt that the assignments had been pointless. So he had tried to balance his feelings by writing in his journal that he knew he shouldn't be complaining so much. He went on:

So that represents how context influenced not only the content of what I did but also the way I responded to the class situation. About the time we read the British people, these comments dropped out. And I think there are two reasons for that. One, we talked about it in class and I was really happy we did because I felt that other people felt like I did. It wasn't strange and I remember I went up to [Jade] and [Pearl] after class because I thought it was really great that you brought it up and I was feeling the same way. So, all those comments dropped out. I don't know whether I was just used to it or whether talking about it helped. I have a feeling that talking about it helped. The other thing that happened at the very same time was that I became interested in the subject matter.

The social dynamics of instructor–student relationships had been further complicated for Robin by his previous satisfactory relationships with the instructors whom he truly did not wish to offend. But, because of his straightforward and honest personality, he had to convey somehow his "irritation" at activities that had initially seemed pointless to him. Now his action of tacking on two paragraphs to his non-synthesis paper to produce a synthesis so that he could demonstrate that he was a serious student takes on a new light. He had also felt responsibility toward his instructors.

When Robin finished his report, and it was Daisy's (a reading student's) turn, Amber (an English student) interjected a comment, "Now we're going to find out how people read." Daisy quickly responded, "No, you're not," and then began her report about her organizational structures and other matters. Amber's assumption apparently had been that the reading students would focus primarily on the reading experiences, and examination of writing would be explored by the English students. At the following class meeting, when Garnet was giving her report, she alluded to Amber's comment:

One of the comments that was made last week was—most of the people who were talking [at the beginning of the period] were English majors. And when [Daisy] started talking, you [Amber] said, "Now we're going to hear about reading." And it took me aback because I had written about writing. And so I tried to think why it was that my introspections—most of the things that were in my journal felt to me like they were about writing. And then I realized that at least for me that it was the context of the wording of those assignments again.

But when she had gone back and looked at her journal she discovered that there was a great deal about her reading there, but, since it was in relationship to her writing, she hadn't realized how much about reading there had been. Because of the integrated nature of the tasks, the reading and English students discovered that they had inescapably focused on both reading and writing in their journals.

Just as Garnet had not recognized the interrelationship between her reading and writing activities until she reviewed her journal, so the social dynamics between the "reading students" and the "writing students" gradually grew until, as Amber said to me, about a year after the course was over,
if I wanted to note anything about how the seating arrangements had
changed over the semester, I might notice that, as the semester went on, the
"older, single women" tended to sit together and that had little to do with
their academic departments. But, in fact, that was not so. When I studied
the seating arrangements for the six classes that were video-taped, it was
apparent that the initial seating arrangements had persisted throughout the
semester, perhaps merely out of habit, as Chip suggested when he read this
description. Certainly, there had been exceptions. Amber herself had sat
with the "reading" group at three of the six video-taped sessions. But no one
else had violated that "territoriality" more than once, and in only one class
meeting had more than one English student sat at the "reading" end of the
table. Lionel and Jay occupied varying seats during the semester, but they
were both "different" from the other Language Education reading students
who were all women. Lionel was an English Education student and Jay the
only foreign student in the group. Among the reading students, Jade, Pearl,
and Garnet often sat together, as did Opal, Ruby, Topaz, and Daisy. Among
the English students, Crystal and Rose, literature majors minoring in composition, often sat together, as sometimes did Chip, Heather, and Amber, the
three composition majors. So, although there were open and friendly dialogues among the participants, they obviously remained most comfortable
sitting with their established colleagues who would more likely share their
frame of reference. These initial connections in our seminar did grow,
though, as Heather noted that when she later took a course in the Language
Education Department, she became quite friendly with Garnet and Jade.
And Jade later told me that the reading students had come to think of Robin
as more a colleague of theirs than of his fellow English students, a characterization which Robin told me he also shared.

THE EFFECT OF CONTEXT

I have tried thus to describe the contextual factors within which the reading
and writing strategies that will be depicted in Chapters 3 and 4, and the texts
that will be described in Chapter 5, were produced. Some of these contextual features were facilitating and some were inhibiting. But it is essential to
be honest about what the conditions actually were and what the effect of
these conditions was on the student participants. Only then is it possible to

evaluate the usefulness of the coping strategies that the students employed to respond to the specific features of the instructional context. Only then can we begin to evaluate the role that context plays in shaping decisions and begin to make recommendations about shaping contexts in the future that will draw on the strengths that we can identify and decrease the impact of the limiting factors.

CHAPTER 3

Reading in Relation to Writing

In presenting a theoretical model linking reading and writing as parallel processes, Kucer notes that, although students are often exposed to activities in both reading and writing, "each process is usually presented as if it were cognitively and linguistically unrelated to the other" (332). In our course, we consciously designed each reading activity so that it had a writing activity cognitively and linguistically associated with it. By this design, we intended our students to become conscious of the reading and writing relationships intrinsic to each task and of how each aspect would help "fine tune" the use of the language in the other aspect (Kucer 332).

Although this chapter and the next will each focus more directly on one process than the other, reading in this chapter and writing in Chapter 4, each is carefully designed to reflect the relationships *between* the two processes. Since our intention was to highlight this relationship and we designed tasks to foster it, it would be undermining our own goal to try to separate them. However, to organize the presentation, I have chosen to "focus" on one process in each of the two chapters.

Any analysis of introspective accounts of reading has to acknowledge the importance of research on metacognition on accounts of reading comprehension. Brown explains that the "problem of ascertaining the state of one's own ignorance or enlightenment is one of metacomprehension. . . . In reading, understanding the text content would be an example of reading comprehension; understanding that one has done so, metacomprehension" ("Metacognitive Development" 458). Metacomprehension in this study would arise from attention to heeded information that serves as the access point for later recall in the retrospective reports. It is, of course, the case that not all metacognitive knowledge will be accessible. Brown and Campione have noted that metacognitive skills are "not necessarily statable as a great deal of selecting, monitoring, inferring, etc. must go on at a level below conscious awareness" (3 quoted in Bracewell, 181). Not surprisingly, many of the events that trigger attention and bring them to conscious awareness are events that in some way disrupt the normal, smooth reading process.

Tierney and Pearson have proposed a composing model of reading with five components: planning, drafting, aligning, revising, and monitoring (34). Planning includes goal-setting and knowledge mobilization. Drafting refers to the refinement of meaning as readers deal directly with the print on the page. Aligning deals with the stance a reader assumes in collaboration with an author and roles within which a reader is immersed as he or she proceeds with the topic. In revision, a reader examines developing interpretations and leaves them open for reconsideration. Monitoring resembles the "executive functioning" of distancing oneself from the text the reader has created in order to evaluate what has been developed. Although this chapter is not set up explicitly to substantiate this model of reading, many of its aspects are examined and corroborated. In particular, the chapter addresses itself to Tierney and Pearson's call for studies to examine "how these composing behaviors manifest themselves in the various contexts of reading and writing" (44).

BUILDING KNOWLEDGE

One of the commonplaces of reading theory today is that reading requires more than contact with information on a printed page. The reader brings prior knowledge and experience to a text and utilizes that knowledge to make sense of new information. When appropriate knowledge is missing, the reader is said to lack "schema" to relate the new information to. So the issue of how a reader builds schema in a new area becomes a crucial one to understand.

Schema Building

The notion of schema originated with Kant, in 1781, who found it necessary to devise a mediating representation between abstract thought and sensory experience. This mental representation was directly activated by sensory experience, but it also provided an interpretation of that experience (Gardner 58). The term *schema* was introduced into psychology by Bartlett, in 1932, who believed that the human memory system involved the formation of abstract cognitive structures or schemas. These schemas developed from prior experiences with the environment and caused information to be organized in specific ways. Thus where new information was consistent with previous experience, recall would be helped and would prove to be accurate. But if there were divergences between prior schemas and new events, the possibility existed that the new event could be distorted or else the schema would have to be revised.

For our students, the term schema served as the level of generalization to which particulars could be fitted, while at the same time the generalization was always susceptible to modifications as new particulars might warrant. Because our students were familiar with the jargon of current reading research, the term schema came easily to them and they consciously reflected on how the presence or absence of prior knowledge affected their making sense of the readings assigned to them. Thus, they were an unusually aware and sophisticated group of language users to observe themselves as they were attempting to construct knowledge in a new field, the field of introspection itself.

Brown has pointed out that understanding a text is not an all-or-nothing phenomenon. The reader sets a goal of the level of understanding required within any activity. As readers' purposes vary, the criteria of comprehension will change as a function of the particular reading task. Brown notes that the "decision to process deeply and actively or merely to skim the surface will determine not only the strategies necessary for the task but also the reader's tolerance for intrusive feelings of failure to understand. In short, the reader's purpose determines how he or she sets about reading and how closely he or she monitors the purpose of reading, that is, understanding of the text" ("Theories of Memory" 454–55).

Sometimes, when students lacked schemas, they fell back on tried and true methods for analyzing reading materials. So, for example, Opal, who probably had more frustration than any of the other participants in the seminar in the early part of the semester, noted in her journal, when she had to write a summary of the Hebb article, that she "picked the ideas to be included simply by clues and repetitions in the paragraphs," since she was having difficulty understanding the article. But she acknowledged that she had an advantage over less experienced students because "instinct also probably played a part; if you're a student long enough, you begin to sense the presence of an idea even if you are unsure of its location or its meaning." Such a strategy in a different context, when the student would not be revealing this to the instructor, could easily lead the instructor to believe that understanding has been achieved while in reality it has not. From a different perspective, Pearl felt her limitations in synthesizing the Dennett and Hebb articles arose from her lack of appropriate background in the sources referred to by the authors. She commented in her journal,

> I note Hebb refers to "Cartesian ideas" and Dennett also refers to this. Obviously it is historically relevant. I don't really understand these references. To me, "Cartesian" goes with geometry. Both authors also refer to Locke and his position in this issue. I see they are referencing the same issue from different points of view. Without more background I can only see the *big* issue, but these nuances are still unclear.

As these two examples illustrate, lack of sufficient background impedes a full understanding of text being contemplated, but experienced readers have strategies for identifying major points and putting them into some kind of format for others, even if the readers themselves do not have a precise understanding of the material. And such sophisticated readers are likely to be more sensitive and honest about their limitations in their interpretations of new-topic source materials than are less experienced readers. The context would play a central role in the willingness to expose lack of understanding: Are there penalties for acknowledging the failure to understand?

The students also understood that schema-building is an ongoing process, and that as they read more, talked with others more, and learned more about the new area of investigation, their knowledge would gradually build to a more sophisticated schema for interpreting materials in the area. We had clear documentation of the development of such processes from the reading and writing activities that our graduate students undertook and from the sequence of papers they wrote.

For some students, there was a conscious awareness that this schema-building was going on at two levels simultaneously. When writing the summary of the Dennett story, Crystal noted in her journal that she was aware of multi-level attention: "one was reading [the Dennett story] in a sort of cumulative process so that as I read I 'added' the new material to what I'd already read. But the other process seems to be one of constant 'overview,' that is, while I was reading it I was trying to fit it into a framework of some kind." This back-and-forth movement between generalization and specifics was frequently noted by our students and is central to the formulation and reformulation of schemas.

But for other students, their strategies for building schemas seemed dysfunctional at first. For example, Rose reported in class that, when she first started to read new material, she would "skim through it cold" and then have to go back to reread. She had blamed herself for not paying attention and for not reading every word carefully. As she thought about this strategy, she realized that she went about writing in just the same way, sitting down and writing a complete draft of whatever she was working on, even if it was only "sort of a skeleton—really brief with the middle left out." But the feeling of wholeness was essential for her as she noted, in reading as well as in writing. So, although Rose initially thought of herself as inefficient for her preliminary skim-through of a text she was reading, she came to see this strategy as compatible with the writing strategy that she felt she used effectively. In commenting on this approach to reading, Heather felt that it was also possible that this approach was an artifact of prior instruction, an approach taught as the way one *should* read. Overviewing the whole is actually quite similar to the multi-level strategy described by Crystal. Both begin with a framework and then fill in the details while simultaneously altering the framework as necessary.

Using Schemas

The experiences in the course naturally created a set of expectations for the students as they read further into the package of materials we had prepared on the topic of introspection. By the time she came to the four articles in the *British Journal of Psychology*, Pearl not only knew that the articles would relate to the topic of introspection, but she could already anticipate what the major issues would be, for her whether introspection was a direct or inferred process. (It is interesting to note that these predictions varied among the students, evidence of the transactional notion of reading proposed by Rosenblatt (*The Reader, The Text, The Poem*) and Bleich (*Subjective Criticism*).) Pearl felt that her prediction was confirmed when she did the reading and she "got out that schema and tested the rest of my reading against that idea for confirmation or disconfirmation."

After reading through the four articles in the *British Journal of Psychology*, Chip felt that he had not been as efficient as he could have been had he used standard previewing strategies before reading through all the articles in detail. He discovered, at the end of the first article, a long one by Quinton and Fellows, that the key to the relationships among the four articles came on the last page of this first article. As soon as he came to the crucial sentence, he wrote in his journal:

> At this point I have formed a hypothesis that the articles will differ on the issue of introspection as a tool in research.

But he had learned something from his experience:

> The reason I wish I'd planned ahead is that the time I spent reading the first article was essentially wasted. There was a lot of info in that article I didn't need to read. I was just floundering around in a detailed research study. A much more efficient approach would be to scout ahead and discover my "purpose" first, and then read what I need to of the first essay.

Daisy had had an experience somewhat similar to Chip's in that as soon as she saw that same sentence in the Quinton and Fellows' article she knew that it was the key point. But because she had read the abstracts and introductory statements of all four articles before beginning to read through any of them, she recognized the key sentence in the Quinton and Fellows article because it looked familiar to her. She had seen it earlier in her previewing of the four articles because Evans had cited it initially in his article of refutation. She was thus prepared to anticipate the nature of the dispute in the sequence of articles assigned when she recognized the statement.

Recognizing Learning

The most dramatic breakthrough in building schema came when the students prepared to write their position papers. (In Chapter 5, the position papers are used as the basis for tracing the information and perspectives taken on the issue of introspection through all the prior papers and journal reports.) They had been asked to reread the earlier articles to discover support for their positions, and when they went back to the very first article they had read [by Valentine], they were frequently astonished at what they now understood *in that article* as a result of having read the subsequently assigned materials. They were, of course, experiencing the results of the schema they had been building. The information had become embedded with rich associations, thus permitting a deeper level of processing (Gardner 127). When reading this manuscript, Violet commented that she remembered being surprised at how much easier Valentine was to understand, and being surprised, too, at how much she had learned about introspection without realizing it as she went along. But, as Tierney and Pearson point out, the students were also experiencing the process of "revision" in reading; i.e., they were examining their developing interpretations, viewing the models they had built as draft-like in quality, and thus subject to revision (41). Tierney and Pearson also maintain that the pursuit of a second draft of reading requires a purpose, and that this purpose can be stimulated by discussions with a teacher who can provide a reason and a functional context (42).

Daisy noted that, in rereading the articles, "I became aware that I was building (though very slowly!) some background in the area of introspection which made some of the material more comprehensible. . . . The Valentine article was not as obtuse as I had thought in the first reading. Names are recurring in all the articles." Violet felt that the ongoing writing tasks associated with each reading had helped her build her understanding:

> I reread all the articles and realized that I had somehow been learning from them all along. When I reread the Valentine article, for instance, it made sense to me. Familiarity, it seems, is essential for understanding. Not just familiarity through reading, however, but that gained through writing. This confirms my belief that writing—putting into one's own words—is the best way to learn about anything. And the unfamiliar subject matter of this course makes the point clearly, at least as far as I'm concerned. If I had simply read the articles, I'm quite sure that I would have retained little or nothing about them. I know I'm self hypothesizing, but do you know how sometimes you can almost "feel" your brain working? There's a very distinct hard mental effort involved in reading and then putting the material in your own words on paper.

Langer ("Learning") has noted that "writing can lead to extensive rethinking, revising and reformulating of what one knows. It can make a person aware of what is known, what is unknown, and even what needs to be known" (400). By raising the issue of translating concepts into one's own language, Violet illustrates the importance of the process of moving from generalized thought to its specific formulation in language, a process necessitating greater understanding and analysis.

In class, the students reiterated the confidence they had gained in knowledge of the topic of introspection over the period of the semester thus far. Rose stated that she didn't think she was becoming a better reader in the sense of being a more careful reader, but she was becoming a reader who brought more to the reading experience. She said, "I think at the beginning I didn't feel I was a careful reader, but I was wrong. . . . Since the articles are starting to echo each other, I'm identifying positions now because I have a background." Robin pointed out that he no longer felt text dependent: "I felt like it was easy to summarize their positions without having to look back and see if I was really accurate enough. I felt that way because of knowledge, not because of skill of writing. I felt like I know more about the field, the ideas."

The major insight that developed through the rereading of the articles was that understanding of the topic of introspection itself had been growing all along. But not until the students were asked to reread the previously obtuse materials did they recognize themselves how much they had been learning. This seems, then, a useful strategy to apply to instructional settings: periodically require students to reread materials that had been difficult for them at earlier times. This experience will have three positive effects: it will consolidate materials and information explored earlier; it will provide opportunities to gain greater knowledge from the materials experienced earlier because the readers will now be bringing fuller schema to the earlier textual materials; and it will demonstrate the efficacy of knowledge-building through a series of coordinated reading–writing activities centered on a specific topic. For example, Opal's experience, two years later, when studying for her qualifying doctoral exam, was made less traumatic for her by the prior experience of knowledge-building in our course. She commented, "This time the frustration was less because from this experience [in the introspection course] I knew it would fall together even if I didn't understand in the initial stages. Ideas that were incomprehensible in a text revealed themselves as understandable as I read about them in other texts and I knew that I would eventually fit it together."

Approaches to the Self-Selected Topic

When it came time to select their own topics, the issue of knowledge-building was still present for the students although in a somewhat modified form. They knew something about their topics, either that they comprised areas about which they wanted to learn more, or they were areas that were extensions of knowledge that they already possessed and they wanted either to deepen their knowledge or apply it in a way that they had not done in the past. (A partial exception to this pattern was the decision made by Chip shortly after his initial exploration of his "topic" to create a science-fiction story, but in this enterprise he had to incorporate the new knowledge on brain hemispherity that he was investigating. He was also applying this knowledge through a genre new to him, fiction writing.) Since this was a more familiar enterprise for the students, studying in depth an academic area and being responsible for locating and evaluating the sources for themselves, it was not surprising that many of them had schemas for this kind of activity, i.e., a process-schema. Topaz's plan determined how she decided on the order in which she would read her source texts.

> I began with recent articles and worked chronologically backwards. I always do this because the most recent articles are usually the most valid because they are based on a larger body of research. By working backwards through time, I feel I am working inductively; hence, first I create a global schema (which is usually fairly intact by the time I have read five articles), and then I fill in the slots in the schema with specifics. However, the process is a great deal like the chicken and the egg: the global structure grows out of the specifics I read too. I'm not sure if it is a spiraling process or an intermingling of specifics and generalizations that layer. I do know, however, that both specifics and generalities are involved in forming my schema into which—later—more specifics are filed. This schema is not rigid—it also changes as I read, write, and mentally "file."

This comment on the levels of generality and specificity intermingling is reminiscent of earlier observations about details fitting into and simultaneously modifying the framework that is being created. It also fits into the structured approach that Topaz feels most comfortable with (which is described fully in Chapter 5). When reading this description, Heather noted the frequent use of the "file storing knowledge" as a metaphor. She felt that this indicated a concept of knowledge as being quite compartmentalized. Although the items of information may be "slotted" into the files, most students described a fluid, easily modified over-all schema.

In class, the students discussed further the differences between approaching their own topics and the earlier analyses they had done on the articles on the topic of introspection. Chip immediately pointed out that, now, he had control of the selection of the texts to be read. Pearl noted that, for her, the difference was that she already had a framework to hold onto, and, thus, new information that she acquired could be integrated into that framework. In the earlier assignments, information had come in in much more fragmented forms and she had not known how to integrate it initially. Jade, who had resisted many of the earlier readings, now commented that, with her self-selected material, she was in a better position to assess its importance and value. She had had no emotional or intellectual investment in the earlier readings, and, for her, it had been impossible to divorce these two negative assessments from her responses. But, under the conditions of self-selection, she and the other students were free to utilize their prior knowledge to make their own assessments about the usefulness and value of the materials they were reading, and adapt their strategies accordingly.

Unfortunately, we short-circuited this new decision-making ability briefly, particularly in relation to the amount of time and level of engagement that should be spent in preliminary explorations. We had asked the students to select two articles related to their self-selected topic and to summarize them. Many of the students felt that the summary writing task committed them to a depth of engagement with these articles that was unjustified because they had not yet decided whether these particular articles would be relevant to their final conception of their topics. Jade summed up the objection in class when she noted, "I wouldn't spend time poring over these two articles because I really don't know the literature in this area and these two articles might be worthless and so I read to understand them and as I continue reading, then I'll be able to see which ones are worthwhile." (She noted that to fulfill the summary task, for one of the articles, she cut out the abstract and turned that in.) Thus, the students felt that, although they probably understood these articles better than they might have without the summarizing task, this was not really the appropriate level of commitment in this preliminary stage of research on their topics.

In a manner similar to their original difficulty with the materials on introspection, some of the students found the reading on their new self-selected topics initially puzzling. This experience suddenly removed them from reading on an unconscious plane to the realization that they were having processing problems. Brown notes that "the difference in time and effort between the normal *automatic pilot* and the laborious activity in the *debugging state* is the difference between the subconscious and conscious level" ("Metacognitive Development" 455). The necessity for debugging stops the smooth flow of reading and forces the reader to concentrate on the debugging activities themselves. It also brings the reading process itself to conscious attention so that it is heeded (as Ericsson and Simon have pointed out) and can thus be available for description.

Garnet had taken on a very abstract topic, abduction, for her self-selected research and noted that "I hadn't felt at the beginning that I was moving in a fog but the grasp I had of the area and the issues was definitely stronger by the end of my reading and I could tell by the kinds of connections I was making as I read and the decisions I was making about what to use and not use and what to connect to what." She described this as a realization that occurred to her near the end of her reading, "how much more I was understanding of what I was reading now than at the beginning." What is interesting about these comments is that this examination of their own reading and writing processes seems to be leading these sophisticated language users and *experts* in reading and writing to realizations that they had not had before. If members of such a group had not previously consciously experienced learning as a result of building up expertise over time by concentrating in a specific area of content, how much less likely it is that undergraduate students would *consciously* know the usefulness of such strategies.

Some of the participants in the seminar saw that they could apply this insight, not only to their own experiences in the self-designed tasks, but to teaching strategies for their students. Crystal, reading widely on the poet whose work she hoped to analyze in her dissertation, made the associations explicit:

> Like the Valentine article, "Perchings and Flights," which was almost incomprehensible to me at first but which somehow "settled in" with other subsequent material and began to make sense, my recent reading about [my poet] is somehow—I wish I knew how—merging with the other information I already had. Perhaps there is no way to de-mystify the process of assimilation. Even so, its relevance to the teaching of composition seems vital. How often, for example, are students asked to read and almost immediately "react" to material by writing about it? It seems to me that this might be a good teaching tactic in that the students are forced to think in order to write, and in that they "learn" by writing. But it also seems that they then ought to be given a chance to go back to that material at some later date—perhaps after they have read supplementary material—and to write about it again.

Heather, responding later to Crystal's comment, heartily agreed with this teaching recommendation.

The opportunity to learn about an area through sequential reading and writing tasks rarely occurs in composition classes where skills and processes are the central concerns of instruction. But these examples of the building of schema through engaging in sequenced reading and writing tasks illustrate how students need to have demonstrated for them the value of close engagement with materials centered on one topic which they can examine and reexamine as their expertise in the area grows. "Names" that are referred to in research that is cited become familiar as do the principal concepts and/or experiments that are described. When they reread the earlier texts, they see the growth of the depth of their knowledge. These descriptions of schema-building in process confirm the theoretical perspectives on which models of learning are built. They also demonstrate that it is possible to design sequences of activities that will foster conscious recognition of the ways in which knowledge is constructed so that both teachers and students can apply this understanding to subsequent tasks that they undertake.

READING STRATEGIES

Williams has suggested that reading strategies fall into three categories: 1) Receiving Sense, 2) Finding Sense, and 3) Making Sense (33). Receiving Sense is a passive activity, requiring the reader only to receive the message already written on the page. Finding Sense requires the reader to search for a meaning hidden just beneath the surface of a text and is most commonly applied to critical readings of literature. Making Sense views reading as an experience or event that occurs with the participation of the reader, analogous to reader-response views of literary theorists such as Bleich (*Subjective*) or transactional models of Rosenblatt and psycholinguistic researchers such as Tierney and Harste. Although Making Sense models of reading were utilized by our students most of the time, when they had difficulty with the texts they were encountering, they fell back occasionally on a Finding Sense strategy.

Underlining

Reading and study-skills courses have established many tried-and-true methodologies for helping less successful readers achieve reading proficiency. Because several of the participants in our seminar were instructors of such courses, it became doubly interesting to observe whether they followed the practices they taught or whether they had developed different strategies for themselves. As has been pointed out earlier, most of the students experienced severe dissonance when they tried to make sense of the initial article in our sequence (the one by Valentine). Their difficulty was compounded by the first in-class writing task, because such a task required decisions in addition to comprehension issues, questions about what should legitimately be included in a summary. (This latter issue has been considered previously in an article that Sharon Pugh and I wrote (Sternglass and Pugh 1986) and will be discussed briefly in Chapter 4.) Garnet applied the strategies she knew to her first reading of the Valentine article in hope of making some sense of it.

> On the first reading, even though I was having difficulty following the author, I still underlined what appeared to be important points and topic sentences so that I could go back to these later in writing the summary. I looked for topic sentences at beginning[s] of sections and paragraphs and ideas which he [she was apparently unaware at that time that Valentine was a woman] appeared to be organizing with examples. On the second reading, when I was feeling more successful in gaining meaning from the article, I was surprised to note that the points I had underlined were the main points to the article and there was very little that I underlined the second time through in order to draw my attention to it in writing the summary.

As an example of how previous experience and/or instructional histories can affect strategies for learning, Chip noted when he read this manuscript that he has "never liked to mark up books in any way. I do it some, but it bothers me at (I guess) an aesthetic level. I feel like I'm defacing something." Perhaps his undergraduate background as a student of literature had influenced his attitude toward texts as artifacts. In any event, underlining was a much less comfortable strategy for him than for others.

DiVesta and Gray have suggested that underlining serves two purposes, as an encoding mechanism and as an external storage mechanism (cited in Blanchard 199). In the encoding stage, a search and selection process is being carried out "with the object of the search being information which the student feels is important" (Blanchard 199). Blanchard suggests that underlining becomes an external storage mechanism when students review for a test, but this use occurred for our students when they were preparing their formal written responses. He also notes that if students are underlining with clear-cut goals, more information will be remembered (200-01). Thus, Garnet's process schema for reading strategies stood her in good stead while she was coping with this difficult task. In addition to what might appear to be rote techniques of underlining topic sentences in paragraphs and sections, Garnet realized that a second reading was essential to gaining any foothold on comprehension. This might appear to be an obvious strategy, but it is likely that many less motivated students would simply acknowledge frustration and omit the essential second reading. But it is in this second reading that the reader can take from the overall framework perceived from the first reading and try to fit the details into the larger scheme. It is at this point that the two levels of reading described earlier can operate most effectively.

Finding a Less Difficult Source

Another strategy for coping with a difficult text is to find a less complex text on the same general topic to read first. This encounter with the less difficult text can help the reader establish an overall conceptual framework within which the more difficult or technical text can fit. This technique has often been mentioned as an effective strategy for writers. Beach and Liebman-Klein note that "[e]ffective writers use information or experiences that are familiar to readers in order to introduce less familiar ideas" (68). But it has less frequently been cited as a strategy that readers consciously adopt. Daisy described this approach as a strategy she frequently used: "This is an important technique—find a less theoretical text to redefine a concept in simpler terms." This strategy then helps her to explain the more difficult text to herself. In his self-designed project, Chip found the material on brain hemisphericity that he was reading too technical, preventing him from identifying a specific aspect to concentrate on. He noted:

I need to get more of an overview of brain research. In order to get such an
overview, I have turned to a couple of less traditional sources—books written
on the brain for a popular audience . . . They were "easy reads" for the most
part; indeed, I have in the past read quite a few similar popular science books
on different subjects. . . . So now I have a more detailed knowledge of brain
structure. Terms such as "neuron," "neurontransmitter," "brain stem," etc.
have begun to acquire a functional meaning for me. I have also acquired a
bibliography of the most important names in the field.

A particularly dramatic example of this strategy occurred when I taught a
course similar to the one at Indiana at City College in New York in 1986.
One of my Chinese graduate students told me that after the first week of the
course he read a book on psychology in Chinese to prepare himself for the
subsequent readings. This is another strategy, reading an introductory book
to get an overview of a new field, that is extremely useful and probably
widely used by proficient readers, not only by second language students,
but rarely suggested by instructors.

Tierney and Pearson have proposed a set of readers' goals that parallel
the set of writing goals (procedural, substantive, or intentional) suggested by
Flower and Hayes. They suggest that a reader may have procedural goals (I
want to get a sense of this topic overall), substantive goals (I need to find out
the relationship between one thing and another), or intentional goals (I wonder what this author is trying to say) or some combination of all three. They
note that these goals "can be embedded in one another or addressed concurrently; they may be conflicting or complementary. As a reader reads (just
as when a writer writes) goals may emerge, be discovered, or change. For
example, a reader or writer may broaden, fine tune, redefine, delete, or replace goals" (34).

Previewing

The value of previewing strategies was most strongly felt by our students
when they were reading the four articles from the British Journal of Psychology. Many realized that they could have skimmed the first of the four articles
much more rapidly when they reached the last page and discovered the sentence stating that the study had demonstrated the value of introspective
techniques as a research methodology. The other articles in the series debated the efficacy of such a research methodology. The fact that most of
them plowed systematically through the article without any previewing especially made the reading majors very uncomfortable. They recognized that
they had not utilized a strategy they promoted very strongly among their
own students, and learned firsthand its real usefulness.

But previewing turned out to be complex when the students confronted the Dennett story. Brown points out that "one commonly experienced triggering event [of comprehension failure] is the realization that an expectation we have been entertaining about the text is not to be confirmed" ("Metacognitive Development" 455). At the first encounter with the Dennett story, several students were perplexed and uncertain how to approach it. Robin started out by assuming that it was a conventional article, but "a clever article or something like that." As he was taking notes, he became irritated by the content and finally concluded that it was not an article at all but a story. When reading a draft of this chapter two years later, Robin recalled that he had had three successive rapidly changing schemas as he had read the Dennett piece. Initially, he treated it like a conventional article. When that approach didn't work, he flirted with the idea that the article was written from a deconstructionist perspective (thus employing his literary theorist schema), i.e., playing with language at the expense of a point of view. The third approach was a story schema, but he was still bothered by this as he waited for the story to make a point. When it failed to do that for him, he resisted writing about it, seeing this resistance as an appropriate moral stance. Daisy reported in class that she didn't take any notes at all. Although she started out by underlining, after the first two paragraphs she stopped underlining and decided she was "just going to read this." Chip said that his original impression was that it would start out as a story and then "talk about it," ostensibly in a more conventional analytic way, as Robin had expected. But Ruby pointed out that the prior readings and course expectations were what had "tied" the participants to their original perspectives on what such a reading assignment would be like. Rose confirmed this expectation, saying that the text had had a name, "Brainstorms," and this was a class and she had been assigned the task of writing a summary, so the conclusion was that this had to be an article. Of course, all the students realized eventually that it was a story and they then had to grapple with the way in which they could produce a "serious, academic summary," but their initial reading strategies had been thrown off markedly by the expectations of the academic setting within which the assignment had been made. Only slowly could they allow themselves to relax enough to enjoy the story before they had to take on the academic role again.

This disjuncture in their reading suggests the danger of being too readily locked into expectations when beginning any reading, thus potentially short-circuiting the intended manipulation of the reader by the writer, particularly in the reading of fiction. There must be a balance between expectations and openness, a stance that permits free transaction with any text on any level, even while the critical apparatus is operating, but not stifling initial responses.

Varied Uses of Note-Taking

Another reading strategy, traditional note-taking, was used and valued by some, but eschewed by others as the availability of the xeroxing process seems to have affected ways in which materials are gathered and analyzed. Tierney and Leys have observed that

> often a reader will respond to a reading assignment with a marginal notation, summary or some other form of reflective comment intended as an aid to staying on task or as a critical reaction to the author's ideas . . . Not surprisingly, the research suggests that if students are capable note takers or summary writers and if the purpose for reading the text warrants this type of response, such activities are worthwhile (20).

Here they are emphasizing the evaluative role in note-taking.

For those who "took notes" on their reading, the notes seemed to fulfill multiple functions. For example, when Robin was reading a particularly complicated text which he felt he needed to be familiar with in preparation for his doctoral oral exam, he noted that he took "copious reading notes—24 pages of them!" He went on in his journal to describe the role of reading notes in his approach to learning.

> I've thought about these reading notes—I always use them—they are my treasures. For my written [doctoral] exams I have over 200 pages of reading notes. When writing these notes I want to A) try to get terminology down in a way that I remember it—not just write down the definitions, but I usually copy the author's usage—a sentence or two of the word in the author's context. B) I try to summarize the point of a particular passage, and this part of my reading notes is more openly opinionated. . . . These summaries, interestingly enough, are not along the lines of the summaries we wrote for class where I tried not to put in my personal opinion. C) Often, when I read, I get the germs of ideas, usually for a writing project of some sort and this is why I treasure my reading notes. I usually can recover a train of thought from my reading notes which leads to an original (whatever that may mean!) idea. When I read for my written exams, I often got ideas for articles and got enthusiastic about exploring an idea of some sort.

Thus, these multiple functions of note-taking serve complex purposes for Robin. He recognizes that he needs to understand others' perspectives, but he is equally committed to evaluating the ideas he is exploring and establishing new and meaningful "original" connections for himself. This is an extremely sophisticated use of note-taking, yet one that could be encouraged for students at any level of expertise on topics that they are learning about. Their evaluative and original perspectives will become more insightful as their knowledge grows and permits their more critical examination of information and viewpoints.

Yet Robin had denied this evaluative perspective when he had written the summaries for our course. Admittedly, the function of summaries is not the same as note-taking, but several of the students found themselves "needing" to make their summaries evaluative so that they could later be useful for themselves. In Chapter 5, Violet and Topaz are shown to explore the conflict between evaluation and summary in their textual writings. For Robin, though, in this instance, the instructional setting appeared to stifle his use of a critical perspective either through the nature of the task as he had defined it for himself or through his interpretation of the demands of the context. If our goal in teaching is to encourage critical reading and writing, then both tasks and contexts must be designed to foster critical stances.

Using Research Materials

But such complex uses of note-taking directly from source materials such as those undertaken by Robin for his own purposes were far less frequent than might have been supposed from a group like the participants in our course. Rarely did anyone mention going to the library and remaining there to elaborately copy notes or quotations onto note cards. The students cited long hours that they spent in the library, but the time was almost always spent locating materials that could be taken out or xeroxed. They went through traditional bibliographic searches. They spent time scanning articles or chapters of books, deciding on "first cuts" of materials that would be useful to them. But then these materials were taken home where they could be worked on in patterns of time available or planned out. Almost universally, the students described scanning and reading these materials, underlining and annotating them extensively. The ability to write directly on the materials in margins or tops or bottoms of pages seemed to fill the response need suggested by Robin who used his more formal notes to record his reactions and critiques. So this group of students performed the same cognitive and affective strategies as traditional note-takers might, but often they put these responses directly on to the source materials which they "owned" and could personally mark up. Two years later, Heather still noted her strong feelings about this both for herself ("If I can't write on it, it doesn't belong to me") and for her students ("It makes me angry to read some texts on writing and research [that] actually state, 'don't xerox'").

When they came to organize their materials for writing, the students followed rather traditional formats in that they made general plans, sometimes in the form of sparse or elaborated outlines, but instead of referring to notes in filling out their plans, they referred back to the source documents which they still retained and which they had marked up with their evaluative comments. The students were very conscious of taking evaluative stances toward their material in their self-selected research papers and eschewed any notion of mere information transfer, the stance often taken by freshman students asked to complete conventional research papers.

I will more fully describe the students' writing strategies in Chapter 4, but these procedures for annotating and utilizing reading materials in preparation for writing are far removed from the traditional procedures recommended to students who are undertaking the proverbial "research paper." Many instructors of freshman composition classes, and probably instructors of upper level "content" courses, are sending their students to the library and instructing them to assiduously copy out the information they will need for their projects through procedures delineated in their textbooks or research paper guides. I am sensitive to my own eclectic procedures in preparing to write this book. I read carefully through all the journal accounts and papers and transcriptions of the class meetings and made detailed notes on increasingly elaborated topic areas that developed from the examination of the source materials themselves and my own philosophical perspectives on reading and writing processes. I made tentative outlines of topics that would be addressed in the individual chapters and then went through each topical area again to work out the ordering of the presentation within that area. But, when it came time to write the drafts of the chapters, I returned endlessly to the original documents of the students, searching out appropriate quotations and citations to support perspectives I wanted to discuss. The use of source materials in writing can be seen to be entirely analogous to the creation of schema in reading: a back-and forth movement between the creation of conceptual frameworks and the fitting in of details to support and illustrate those understandings. The specific techniques of note-taking, underlining, or annotating seem less critical than the realization that they all contribute in significant ways to the back-and-forth movement central to both reading comprehension and the creation of text. As in so many other issues related to teaching, it seems crucial that students be brought to recognize the central conceptual activities they must undertake rather than having their attention focused on any dogmatic procedures for accomplishing these goals.

Use of Time

Because our students had eight weeks in which to undertake and complete their self-designed projects, we had the opportunity to observe how they partitioned out their time. Not surprisingly, most of them scheduled their work on "our" paper in relation to their other commitments and responsibilities. For most, this meant blocking out chunks of time for going to the library, reading through the materials they gathered, talking with others, writing drafts, and writing final products. None of these activities occurred linearly; talk could lead to another trip to the library, writing a draft could lead to further talk, reading through materials could lead to further searches for sources mentioned, and so on, every possible permutation of recursive behavior occurring. Because there was a large enough group to describe this range of behaviors, it is possible to assert on the basis of real behaviors that there is no specific ordering of activities that will lead most directly to success in learning tasks having literacy components. In fact, it seems clear that, if this same group of individuals had different types of tasks to undertake, they would alter their strategies on an individual basis to fit the demands of the new tasks as they envisioned them.

One of the strategies described, particularly in relation to reading the materials that had been collected, combined two processes rarely discussed in the literature about reading: "marathoning" and "burn out." In her journal, Topaz described how these two activities occurred during her reading periods and how they were related to each other:

> Whenever I "marathon" through readings for a paper—which I always do!—I burn out briefly. After about three spaced marathons—sometimes five—I'm ready to write. I seem to process/integrate material better if I read it in large chunks of 11 articles or four books, one right after the other. Not only is the information processed better, but also I am better able to rank the articles more readily from "valid and reliable" to "slick." I think basically it is a holistic approach to integrating and evaluating readings. . . . I may have programmed myself to burn out at specific intervals to allow "thought time." Or it may be that I expect too much of myself (which I do) and thus push my natural brain capacity to the limit, forcing it to short-circuit in a burnout. Or, burnout may be a device my unconscious uses to terminate my compulsive reading: I never think I have read enough to write a paper so I go on reading anything I can put my hands on. If I didn't burn out, I'd never get to the writing event. OR, it may be all of the above.

In this excerpt, Topaz highlights important components of any extended reading–writing–learning activity.

Such activities, central to learning, could never be discovered through a short-term protocol of an individual responding to a demand requiring instant reaction and writing. First, the whole notion of "marathoning" implies an extended period of reading and conscious deliberation about a topic for which an individual has specifically selected and collected materials. The process of selecting and collecting materials already implies a level of engagement with the topic that has allowed the individual to make choices among many possible competing materials. By "chunking" the reading, as Topaz describes, her critical apparatus is brought to bear as she evaluates the importance of the materials being perused. And she also realizes the importance of time for reflection. Wallas has called this period *incubation*, a part of the creative process. Bruner has said that "discovery, like surprise, favors the well-prepared mind" (401). But central to both of these points is that time must be available for reflection between the input of ideas from reading, talking, writing, thinking, and the creation of an original perspective. Durkin has maintained that it would be possible to retrace the origin of a new synthesis from a detailed protocol, but it is uncertain whether such protocols can be produced with the detail required. It is also uncertain whether all of the unconscious linkages are retrievable. In arguing for the validity of protocol accounts, Ericsson and Simon in "Verbal Reports" have argued that it is not essential to have a complete account for one to consider the data that is produced valid.

In relation to the shorter one-week, teacher-designed tasks, the students also commented extensively on the value of having incubation time between the time of the assignment and its due date. As I have suggested earlier, one of the advantages that retrospective journals has over other types of information gathering is that they allow the students to record and report what happened to them over real time. Whether we or they characterize these time intervals in negative or positive terms—as delaying tactics or incubation periods where ideas "soak in"—it becomes clear that time is an ally. It allows individuals to think through their problems, accept or reject initial ideas, rethink and reanalyze their own responses, and produce more considered thinking and reading and writing than would have been available had an immediate response been demanded. Often students reported that they were doing their writing at the last minute, but this writing came only after prolonged periods of mulling and thinking that had begun as soon as the tasks had been announced. (This topic is developed more fully in Chapter 4.)

The delaying tactics were varied, yet possessed similar characteristics. Chip noted that he "started thinking about a synthesizing idea for this essay right after class last Wednesday. I was walking home from class and tried out a couple of possibilities in my head, which were similar to what I ended with but maybe better. I'm not sure because I didn't write them down." When he read this manuscript two years later, Chip commented: "It is amazing how soon I forget ideas if I don't write them down! It's like they aren't in my mind so much as the place where I'm thinking." This appears to be an example of thought not being translated specifically into language and thus not being placed through short-term memory into long-term memory, resulting in it not being accessible for retrieval and retrospection. Putting off writing something down can, for some individuals, represent serious losses of their ideas. But for others, like Jade, who noted this after she read this manuscript, writing down her ideas never became a part of her learning strategies; she relied on her memory and it mostly served her well. Perhaps individuals, through repeated practice, can learn to translate their ideas into language that is easily retrievable from memory.

In her journal, Garnet described her frustration with the definition of a key term in one of the articles:

> I was really bothered by my lack of understanding of [the term] physicalist. I hadn't attended to it when writing my summary and it had bothered me when several people in class mentioned looking the word up. I tried to gather clues as I reread the article and noted a number of things. My dictionary was no help and so I was very frustrated. At that point it was time for me to leave for class in Indy [Indianapolis] so I took off thinking I could think through some of the issues on the way there. However, as I drove, my mind went to everything else but that paper. I was again trying to postpone a task I was finding difficult to pull together.

This working and worrying emerged as a pattern for many of the students in the class who were often frustrated by the weekly assignments. Daisy noted that after a period of time in which nothing tenable was developing, she

> put the material aside to come back to later. I found myself thinking about how I could come up with something. This occurred while I was driving, cooking, eating, and going to sleep. I would think of something, go to my desk, re-examine the articles, and throw out the idea.

But these students recognized the value of having time to sort out their thinking, and apparently, the more difficult the task for them, the more valuable it was to have that time.

Just as it became apparent that time was a liberating factor, in relative terms that is, giving the students a week to complete each of the teacher-designed tasks and eight weeks to complete their self-designed tasks, so was it a limiting factor. Not surprisingly, our students were very pragmatic about what could be accomplished in one week's time when they were doing the initial set of tasks, especially in relation to the other demands simultaneously being made on them. In commenting on how the time limit affected her work, Amber raised an issue that our retrospective reports could not account for, the issue of what does *not* appear in the students' papers. Whereas Ericsson and Simon had inferred that the individuals producing the reports were likely unaware for the most part about what was omitted from their accounts, Amber indicated that she was aware that many of her initial thoughts were recorded neither in her paper nor in her journal account. Sometimes our students shared their preliminary and speculative thoughts with us as they appeared, particularly in relation to their reading notes (often recorded in their journals), but we are sure that a great deal of this type of thinking was not captured in the material that we have. We can only say, along with Ericsson and Simon, that although we would wish for the fullest possible accounts, their incompleteness does not invalidate the information that we have been given.

There was an extreme desire to know every possible thing that could be known about the topic being investigated. Topaz's solution to this dilemma was "burn out." Garnet noted her desire to be extremely thorough when she went into a new area. She reported in class that she felt a compulsion to read everything that had been written on a topic. And if she didn't do this, she had strong guilt feelings, with the result that most of the time she was investigating a topic, she had these strong guilt feelings. Only when the information in the readings began to become redundant did she begin to feel fairly safe. But, at that point, she is willing to take risks in expressing her own opinion on the topic because she feels confident that she knows what other people have said on the topic and so she is prepared to defend her position. Heather later commented that she called this the "enough, move on" stage for her students.

For others, like Pearl, more pragmatic strategies were devised. Pearl reported in her journal that on Saturday and Sunday,

> I began to tackle the giant stack of articles and books I had collected. I began underlining and making notes on another sheet of paper as I read. These notes gave a brief idea of what the article described and noted sections that were important for the paper. I also noted my personal thoughts, concerns and points of relation with other articles. [These uses of notes are reminiscent of Robin's comments on his more extensive note-taking.] After spending half a day reading articles thoroughly and carefully, I realized I would never get through at this rate. This is a situation that always drives me nuts! When there is a subject I want to really know a lot about, I would like to read everything thoroughly and feel like an "expert" in the area. However, time constraints, now (as always) cause me to skim for the necessary information for the task at hand. So, at this point, I made a decision to begin a new strategy—read intro, procedures, and discussion thoroughly and only skim the statistical analysis sections. I feel somewhat guilty doing this, because I feel I should evaluate this for myself to decide whether their analysis was sound—and whether the study really has internal validity. But a brief reading will have to do [emphasis in original].

Being forced by inevitable time constraints, the students thus had to make pragmatic decisions about the use of their time in relation to the goals they had set for themselves and their other concurrent obligations. All too rarely do such examinations of tasks take into account concurrent obligations which must necessarily affect the amount of time and energy an individual can devote to any specific task.

Unassigned Additional Research

For the weekly assigned tasks, another issue related to the amount of time to be spent on the tasks was the extent to which it might be expected that students would pursue the topics in the readings in additional library research. In designing the tasks, Sharon Pugh and I planned one set that would have benefitted from outside research and we were interested in seeing whether any of the students would pursue such additional reading. In fact, none of them did, but several noted in their journals that they were sensitive to the fact that they were lacking important information. Thus, they felt obligated to construct explanations in their journals for failing to search for further information. Ruby's comments in her journal were typical of those who noted the need:

> As I previewed the four articles [in the *British Journal of Psychology*] about the value of introspective research, I thought responding to the assignment would be pretty cut and dried. There seemed to be 2 articles for and 2 against. However, as I read the 3rd piece, things didn't mesh. Some of the ideas to which Morris was responding had not been expressed in the preceding Evans article. Checking the dates, I realized that a lot had gone on in the five years since the 1976 articles and those of 1981. To really do justice in responding to the ideas in the 4 articles, I would have had to read the work Evans had done during the intervening five years. Morris' 1981 rebuttal is based mostly on that work and not on what Evans had said in 1976. As of 1976, Evans had not ruled out introspection as a means of observing conscious strategies, but by 1981 he seemed to have discarded the method totally. I did not, however, read all of Evans' work (*it wasn't in the assignment*). Were I more fascinated by the assignment, I might have [emphasis in original].

In the subsequent class meeting when the question of possible library research was raised in connection with that week's assignment, many students acknowledged that they had considered but rejected the possibility of going to the library. They maintained that the primary reason they had not done so was the time limitation for the task, a single week in which they also had many additional responsibilities. But, interestingly enough, Jay, the sole foreign student in the class buttressed his paper for the following class meeting with substantial library research materials. Perhaps the discussion made him feel that we as the instructors would value this, or perhaps his insecurity with the topic of introspection led him to seek additional help, and we had legitimized this process through the class discussions.

CONNECTIONS TO OTHER KNOWLEDGE

One strategy that the students employed to help them make sense of new materials was to search for connections with concepts and materials that they already had some familiarity with. Tierney and Pearson have noted that "readers, depending on their level of topic knowledge and what they want to learn from their reading vary the goals they initiate and pursue" (35). We would have expected our students to search for connections with prior knowledge and value them highly, but to our surprise, some students seemed to fear that making connections to previously known or thoughabout materials might prejudice their responses or lead them to unproductive side issues.

Inter-textuality

In a sea of unfamiliarity, Chip derived comfort from coming across a name he had encountered in the past. Thus, he noted that his interest in the reading grew when he saw a familiar name in the article by Valentine:

> It's odd, but if there's a name or term in the text that I'm already familiar with (for example, Wundt), then I tend to be interested in that part and read it attentively the first time through. But if a section is full of unfamiliar names and terms, I want to skip it at least the first time through. (I can remember the first time I ever heard of Wundt—it was in Professor _____'s course here . . . Whenever I come across Wundt's name, I think of that course.)

Two years later, Chip commented, "I think this wording is exactly right here. It is comforting to see a familiar name—just like seeing an old friend in a far away place." What is odd about his comment is not that Chip's interest is heightened by this connection, but that he is surprised by this. Just as in the earlier discussion of schema building, Chip is attempting to make connections to prior knowledge that will help him formulate a conceptual framework within which he can place the ideas of Wundt and Valentine so that they can be compared or contrasted and assessed.

But this familiarity also led to a problem for Chip. He explained at the class meeting when he was turning in his journal account that after he had seen a familiar name in the reading, he had assumed that he could "go quickly" through this section of the text (although he had maintained in his journal entry that a familiar name led to attentive reading), but then later he discovered that he had missed something very important in that paragraph. Later he had to go back to discover the definition of a key term that had been presented in that section. So his original decision that he "didn't need to read that paragraph too closely" had not served him well. Chip's comment two years later was, "Yeah, but the nice thing about reading is that you can go back." His experience is just another example of how the balance between expectations based on prior knowledge and the openness required for new learning must always be delicately preserved.

Earlier personal philosophical perspectives on the relation of mind to body were evoked by some of the readings, particularly the Dennett story. Lionel was concerned though that his earlier philosophizing might have influenced his interpretation of the reading (as if to suggest that it would be possible and desirable to eliminate personal interpretation while reading is going on):

> . . . it seemed to me that the heart of the article (or brain) of the article was the author's speculation about the relationship of mind to body and the location of the essential self. So I decided to organize my summary around the specula-tions, but mention the farcical situations to at least suggest by reporting that there was some humor in the original. . . . It is possible, too, that because I have often mused about the relationship between mind and body and self, that I have biased myself in this reading and am reading only what I wanted to see or would readily recognize.

Clearly there is a danger of willful misinterpretation in reading, but in this situation it is more likely that previous musings on these philosophical issues would heighten rather than detract from the response to the material. Ruby felt that her past musings in these issues had prepared her to interact more thoughtfully with the philosophical issues raised by the story. She noted in her journal:

> As I read, it [Dennett's story] evoked memories of past concerns with the ideas of connections between body, brain, and "mind." I remember how, in my youth, I had wondered about the mind. Was it simply the content of the brain, or was it some sort of essence of an integration between brain and body? If there were an afterlife, what lived on? It must be the mind or intellectual es-sence of the person that was. (Wasn't it lovely how, in our youth, we assumed that answers to such questions must exist.)

This journal entry, then, allows Ruby to continue her musing, for herself, but also possibly for us. Here was an opportunity for dialogue that we clearly missed by failing to respond to the journal entries.

Testing New Knowledge

Amber noted that she was surprised about the extent to which she refused to trust flat statements that she found in the reading. She reported in class that she felt a strong need to test everything against her personal experience and knowledge. She acknowledged that she rejected things out of hand if they didn't fit with something she was convinced of. Background knowledge and belief systems had different effects on different students as they read, but they always affected the transactions that took place. Amber's belief system, in particular, affected the stance she took in the texts she wrote (as is developed in the analysis of her papers in Chapter 5.) In other words, there could never be a purely objective reading of anything because no reader exists who brings no belief system to reading.

One student who almost seemed to "apologize" for making connections to other texts and knowledge was Violet who noted in her journal that since

> all the two readings [Dennett and Hebb] had done was raise some general thoughts for me, I found I had trouble keeping other related (and some unrelated) thoughts out of my essay. The Hebb chapter had gotten me thinking about studies that try to account for some sort of genetically based mental abilities, like the recent study that claims to have discovered some link among maleness, left-handedness, allergies and mathematical ability. (My many allergies have never helped me with math, but then I'm missing the other three components.) I've also just begun to look at Gould's *Mismeasure of Man*, and I found that not only was I creeping into the essay, so was Stephen Jay Gould.

In her paper, she had discussed studies of the physiological properties of the brain and cited Gould's study in which he raised the implications of trying to weigh and measure brains as an example of the limitations of such approaches. Thus, her outside reading and knowledge provided her with appropriate insights and interpretations to bring to bear on her synthesis, yet surprisingly she felt apologetic about these connections when she discussed them in her journal. Two years later, in commenting on this manuscript, Violet said:

> I think one reason I may have seemed apologetic is that this was one of the first times I consciously thought about how much "outside" things affected what I was working on. Of course, they weren't really outside—they *were* connected. I had just realized that even when I wasn't consciously trying to draw information from different sources, somehow the connections got made—almost as if by themselves or without my control.

So, what we had seen in her journal entry was perhaps her initial conscious realization of how inter-textuality and associations with prior knowledge necessarily influence current activities, an example again of a present moment being cumulative of all prior moments.

Reactions to Prior Knowledge

Sometimes the associations to prior knowledge generated negative reactions to the work being examined, even if there were substantial differences between the current texts and the previous experience in the field. One of the students, Lila, seemed to have been permanently antagonized about experimental research in psychology by an experience she had had many years earlier in a freshman psychology course. She wrote in her journal:

> When I think of classic methodology, I am constantly reminded of the Milgram experiments where the scientist conspires against the participant, and based on this authoritative position, forces the participant to administer lethal dosages of electric shock to a stooge/patient who gives "wrong" answers to questions. Naturally, the patient/stooge and researcher are in cahoots and the real person who suffers is the innocent participant who experiences trauma, guilt, and is manipulated into a terribly compromising position by these jerky and sneaky experimenters. I read about these experiments when I was a first year college student taking an intro psych class, and I have never gotten over my fear, anger, and suspicion of psychologists ever since. Certainly, this experience is the source of my hostility to them.

Such a strong affective response made it impossible for Lila to evaluate in a neutral manner the studies she was reading about in the field of introspection, which were all carried out by psychologists, even though they represented a range of theoretical perspectives. The effects of this perspective on her evolving texts for the course are described in Chapter 5.

When reading this manuscript, Chip speculated that Lila's reaction to Milgram itself may have been rooted in some still earlier affective experience. It is interesting that even though Lila was sensitive to the origin of her deeply held feelings, she could not overcome the precipitating distrusts enough to examine the readings objectively. Looking back at her journal entries and papers, it is possible to see evidence of her antipathy toward experimental studies, but not until the last task in the sequence on introspection does she acknowledge the basis for her responses. Often, such causes remain submerged or completely hidden so that readers of students' writing have no insight into the perspectives and biases that their students may bring to certain areas. We may believe that our students are intransigent and closed to new ideas, but the source of their difficulties may instead be deeply ingrained in affective experiences that they find impossible to discard. There are no magic answers for overcoming such feelings (nor perhaps should there be), but at least bringing them to the surface (as reader-response theorists in literary criticism do) can make the individual aware of how these feelings are shaping the responses they are making. Heather felt that such an insight was particularly important for college teachers who she felt often characterized their students negatively without trying to understand the source of their difficulties.

Another type of relationship to prior knowledge does not have to do with specific content or affective relationships, but it has to do with processes and procedures for carrying out tasks. Just as students were shown to have process schemas in relation to carrying out the reading tasks, some students drew on previous courses or knowledge of genres to affect how they carried out or chose the format for writing tasks. Thus, Topaz drew on a course in which she had been required to map grounds, claims, warrants, and modalities as the source for her approach to writing the position paper. She noted that the course had trained her "to be more organized, more structured, in my approach. It also trained me to be more suspicious, and thus, not accept stated claims at face value until I had explored implied claims." A part of this analytic stance toward the texts she was reviewing in preparing to write the position paper was her realization that there was a similarity between Evans' attitude toward introspection and experimental researchers' attitude toward ethnographic studies which she clearly admired. Because she could adopt a historical stance and see how research methodologies are often a product of the socio-cultural period in which they exist, she was less critical of Evans' views than she might otherwise have been:

> Another aspect of the reading that influenced my perception of Evans' claims was that I viewed his treatment of introspection as similar to the treatment ethnographic studies had received for years. This helped me place his objections in a historic framework rather than to view them as the subjective complaints of one man. Building this type of schema seems to really help me read or write: it allows me to stand outside the argument.

So, unlike Lila, who cannot remove the shell that constricts her, Topaz is able to take advantage of this historical perspective to be more tolerant of views that she disagrees with than she might otherwise have been able to.

Another methodological process that was called upon was an attempt to imitate a genre. When Jade approached the task of writing her position paper, she noted:

> The idea of a dialogue occurred to me as I was reacting in the margins. Evans is staunchly defending the scientific paradigm while Morris seems to be aware of its limitations. (Morris does not go far enough, in my opinion, but that's another issue.) It seemed to make sense to have these two men talk to each other.

With that idea as a starting point, Jade then decided to use the format of Plato's dialogues and unsuccessfully searched for a copy of *Cratylus*. Even though she couldn't find the copy, she felt that she had sufficiently internalized the genre to attempt to imitate it and she gave her "characters" impressive Greek names.

ASSOCIATIONS WITH OTHER ON-GOING ACTIVITIES

In addition to building connections with prior knowledge, students, particularly in their work on their self-designed projects, consistently built connections to other tasks that they were undertaking simultaneously. In fact, several of the students selected topics that would be directly related to other tasks for which they had responsibility so that they could be channeling their energies into related areas, deepening their knowledge, and constructing relationships among the areas of their interest.

At the same time that she was working on the paper for our course, Pearl was working on a research project with one of the professors in the Language Education Department. She reported in her journal that working on the two projects simultaneously was enhancing both:

> I have not read any articles, etc. I specifically looked up related to this project. However, I did find as I read research articles for my research internship (working with _____ on the comprehension grant), several of them seemed to be at least tangentially related. When I work on one project, I look at all my other reading with "new eyes," focusing in on aspects that I might not have particularly noticed otherwise.

Similarly, Ruby noted how she consciously strove to build connections among her interests and her projects:

> I find that one of the reasons I read slowly is that, as I read, I apply the information to several things I am working on at the same time, stop and take notes, and often open bibliographic cards during the reading process. For instance, while reading *Discourse Analysis: What's That?* I came across the concept that, while there may be universal communication system constraints, there are also ritual constraints in the application of the communication system and these vary greatly across cultures. This is an aside from foreigner talk [her topic for our course], but is vitally important in developing my theoretical rationale for the alteration of what we teach in ESL [English as a Second Language] programs. It also ties in with an idea I have about counselling foreign students [part of her job at the Learning Skills Center] for consultation with their professors. . . . So I guess what I am saying is that when I am reading, I don't stick to just my original interest or reason for reading, but go in more than one direction at once.

As these examples illustrate, students are enriched by working on related projects simultaneously because such overlapping activities encourage and facilitate the consideration of multiple perspectives and the creation of new relationships that might not otherwise develop. It also encourages the likelihood of looking at an old and familiar problem or issue from an unexpected perspective. Insights "pop up" as individuals suddenly find themselves thinking of an application to another problem that they likely never considered to be related to their present exploration until the insight occurs.

CONCLUSION

The information in this chapter has revealed a range of strategies competent readers and writers use to acquire comprehension and to learn. The strategies are not always efficient, easy, or enjoyable; often they appear dysfunctional at first to the user, but for a variety of reasons individual learners have adopted patterns that appear to work for them.

Schema-building appears to be central to the building of knowledge. When readers start with a mass of what appear to be unrelated facts without a framework to attach them to, they are often overwhelmed by the facts which frequently appear incomprehensible. As a framework is built over time, these facts both fit into and modify the framework.

A range of strategies existed for this group of learners in building essential schema in a new area. Skimming through an entire text to get an overview, previewing beginnings and sometimes endings, using more accessible materials to gain access to a new field, underlining even on an initial reading when materials appeared largely incomprehensible, making connections to already existing knowledge, and rereading materials all helped readers gain entry. But, most importantly, having to write something (almost anything!) about the readings forced a level of engagement beyond any reading strategy or combination of reading strategies. The requirement to put something about the reading text in one's own language seemed to be the most crucial component that contributed to learning through reading. (Semioticians might argue that similar engagement is possible through other sign systems such as art, music, or drama, but as has been previously pointed out, those forms have not been explored in this study.) In the next chapter, I will describe the approaches and responses to the reading tasks that were carried through in the writing tasks and demonstrate how learning through reading is learning through writing.

CHAPTER 4

Writing in Relation to Reading

As noted earlier, all of the reading tasks had writing assignments associated with them. In this chapter, the strategies used to respond to the readings through writing will be explored in detail. The readings served as precipitating stimuli, but the students often went far beyond the external stimulus to make sense of their own thoughts, to interpret the information in the source texts for their own purposes, to relate the information to their own knowledge, and to learn new material.

We had specifically designed a range of writing tasks to accompany the reading tasks because we believed writing would foster the use of more complex reasoning strategies than any other type of accompanying task. In a study of secondary students, comparing reasoning strategies used in responding to study questions, notetaking, and essay writing, Langer ("Learning") found that "the greatest variety of reasoning operations occurred during essay writing, suggesting that this type of activity provides time for students to think and ponder their growing ideas" (405). In terms of learning, she found that "topic knowledge increased most from essay writing, next from notetaking, and least from answering the study questions . . . This suggests that the extended writing activity gave the students the opportunity not only to think about the information in the passages they had read, but also to integrate it into more highly organized units of knowledge" (405). Similarly, we found that, although the notetaking took on highly sophisticated forms for some of our students, the writing of the full paper responses was the most important contributor to serious engagement with the reading materials, exploratory thinking, and subsequent learning.

INTEGRATING READING MATERIALS INTO WRITING

Before discussing the composing processes that were revealed through these retrospective accounts, I want to describe the ways in which writing and reading enriched each other. In Chapter 3, I noted that knowledge was built through extended reading in a specific area allowing for the construction of more and more sophisticated schemas. Often, the students noted in their journals that the closer engagement demanded by writing something in response to the reading aided their learning process. When writing her position paper, Pearl commented that "having to write made me pin down my thoughts, clarify and analyze them." However, there have rarely been examinations of the effects that different types and levels demand (by types I mean genre types—summary, reaction, synthesis; by level I mean informal notes, annotations, jottings, in contrast to the writing of a formal paper). The experience of our students forces us to confront the issue of when the appropriate time exists to write a formal paper for learning to take place. Pearl notes that she has already written in the journal her understandings, "so my purposes for formalizing the format and language into an essay is to complete a class assignment." She thus distinguishes between learning for herself and the demonstration to her instructors that she feels the formal paper will represent. Later in the semester, when working on the summaries of the self-selected articles, she reiterates the same point in her journal:

> I decided I would write my summaries directly from the highlighted articles, so I didn't make any more notes. Actually, such note taking is my *usual* procedure when synthesizing articles, books, etc. rather than writing a summary. I never write a summary because the time and effort needed to put it into complete sentences and formal paragraphs is wasted at this point. The writing of notes serves for me the function of noting important features that I think will be important in an overall sense . . . and also my own comments, conjectures and hypotheses. I usually bracket my own comments to separate them from the authors.
>
> Interesting, now that I have written the summaries, I see that I have left out *most* of these notes to myself about how I feel these studies will fit in, what I think of their methodology, etc. Somehow, the assignment of "summary" didn't allow me these types of comments. However, if these two documents are to really be useful to me, I will have to jot these comments on the bottom.

Thus summary seems to preclude analysis, evaluation and hypothesis formation, the means by which active rather than rote learning occurs. But, as will be noted in Chapter 5, some of the students found themselves so frustrated by the constraints of summary writing, they either wrote evaluative paragraphs following their summary paragraphs in their formal papers or in their journal entries. For these sophisticated language users, Pearl notes that "summary is mainly tied to my construction of the author's text," a neat phrase suggesting reading from a transactional perspective. In this situation, the reading and the evaluative notetaking appear to be more functional then the writing of the formal response because the constraints of the genre are so limiting and the functional usefulness of the summary is unclear to the writer.

Jade had feelings similar to Pearl's later in the semester in regard to the writing of the final research paper. Although she had indicated enthusiasm early in her journal toward the topic and pleasure that she had really identified the crucial ideas in the field, the writing of the actual formal paper seemed pointless to her. She had previously felt the lack of feedback in the course and now believed that this final paper would receive the same treatment. She noted, "I never write a paper just for the fun of it, in my spare time. This is almost what this was, only I didn't have the spare time." For her, the writing process was not seen as part of the learning process that could deepen her understanding. She also seems once again to have abdicated the responsibility for the depth of engagement required to her instructors.

These comments do not diminish the contribution of writing to the learning experience, but they do raise the issues of types of writing assignments and their timing to facilitate learning. Some kinds of writing tasks can be dysfunctional if they are too limiting in their constraints. If summary for many students precludes analysis, evaluation, or speculation, it might discourage "well-behaving" students from taking risks in their thinking or in their responses to such tasks. (The issue of risk-taking in writing is discussed in another section of this chapter.) Furthermore, as has been frequently discussed in the literature on composing processes, when not constrained, writing has the potential to lead to discovery of new ideas, a topic that will also be discussed further in the section on Drafting in this chapter.

However, the act of writing anything, for some even a summary, has the potential to contribute to greater understanding of material that has been read. For example, Robin noted that after he had read his self-selected articles for the beginning of his research paper, "I felt that the summary helped me a great deal. I feel I understand [the chapter] more after I had to write something about it. The chapter and the summary were hard to read/write. Some of it I actually read out loud to try to figure it out." These comments suggest a sensitivity to the fact that writing demands more direct confrontation with one's own thinking than simply reading, and furthermore, that learning can be facilitated through the reinforcing processes of writing. These different reactions to the writing tasks suggest that it might be wise to ask for written responses to reading materials, but to leave open the form in which these responses might be developed.

The fact that the writing tasks were all based on reading materials also forced a level of organization and consolidation in the writing process that was consciously monitored by our students. As was described in Chapter 3, many of them read copiously in preparation for the self-designed project paper and then had to confront what to do with the mass of information they had gathered. Although they often began with highly structured plans, it quickly became apparent that this order was easily subject to change. Daisy, for example, classified the materials she had already read and summarized into categories related to their usability in the final paper as either "applicable" or "not applicable." But as she developed the categories, she "realized that the 'not applicable' list was applicable" too. Pearl described her organizing efforts over a week's time, thus presenting a picture of plans as they emerged and were altered. Her early plan was to jot down a tentative outline of the various papers she had to write for her courses (since several of the topics were related). She noted of her outline that she "wanted to try to jot this down below before I go on to other things because I feel it is only partially formed and will be lost otherwise." She reported that the previous evening she had sorted all her articles into piles and folders by the topic she saw emerging as important. But when her journal account continued several days later, she wrote that she had not followed her plan of the previous Sunday. "Instead I read two articles that were not filed into a folder yet because they looked interesting and then an article . . . because it was in a book instead of a xerox copy. I decided it would be easier to take notes on it while I am at home with the computer." These kinds of influences, being distracted by something that looks interesting, or taking notes from a book that has to be returned to a library, or, as Heather later pointed out, the availability of a computer, are commonplace elements of the context of composing that are never reported in the studies gathered through protocol analysis or stimulated recall because they do not *appear* in the composing sessions that are monitored through these approaches. Yet, they are as much a part of composing as planning, drafting, editing, and reviewing (the recursive processes reported by Berkenkotter in her study of Donald Murray). The invisible elements in the composing process that deal with changes *within* planning periods are difficult to locate and document unless the information is gathered under conditions that reflect natural times and places, allowing the elements of the context that influence behavior to emerge.

PURPOSES FOR WRITING

I have been suggesting throughout this book that the reports gathered through the retrospective accounts were more natural than accounts typically gathered through protocol analysis because the retrospective reports capture reading and writing processes over time in the complex settings in which they actually occur. Hillocks has also criticized the sterility of accounts of the composing process gathered through laboratory settings: "Nearly every study of the composing process gathered for this review asked the young people to write one composition at a time and to write in a limited time period—not to develop plans for several approaches to the same topic. Should we be surprised when the subjects do what the researchers have requested?" (42). It thus seems appropriate to compare the views of composing generated through the retrospective reports with the cognitive processes model proposed by Flower and Hayes ("Cognitive Process Theory"), based on their protocol analysis reports. It would, of course, not be surprising to find many overlapping features. However, because of the nature of the tasks described in this study and the contexts within which they were performed, it would also not be surprising to find some differences. Although it is not my intention to come up with a model of the composing process (in fact, the major intent of this book is to show the variability in composing strategies), I will be describing aspects of composing as they emerged from the student writers' experiences with the intent of showing that there are additional aspects of composing that are not revealed in the sterile laboratory setting in which most of the composing process descriptions have been elicited.

Similarly, in arguing for an ecological model of writing, Cooper believes that a purely cognitive model of writing "obscures many aspects of writing we have come to see as not peripheral" (365). She criticizes the study of the "solitary author" who, she contends, is unnaturally separated from the social world (365). Cooper proposes instead that writing be viewed as "an activity through which a person is continually engaged with a variety of socially constituted systems" (367). Chip later commented that this would be the case whether the individual was aware of it or not.

In their studies, Flower and Hayes did not base the writing tasks on reading materials (except in their study of revision ("Detection, Diagnosis"), and the reading there is of a single letter that has been manipulated to have stylistic and grammatical infelicities), so their writers would not likely comment on incorporating immediate reading sources into their writing, although, of course, they could draw on previous information, some from prior reading, stored in their long-term memory.

Flower and Hayes describe composing as a "goal-directed thinking process, guided by the writer's own growing network of goals" ("Cognitive Process Theory" 366). They see these goals as consisting of both high-level and supporting sub-goals which may be changed or added to as the writing proceeds.

What Flower and Hayes refer to as goals, I have been calling "purposes" in writing. One of the difficulties in our course was the purposelessness which many of the students felt about some of the assigned tasks. This was truer of the initial summarizing tasks than the reaction statements and synthesis papers. In the early summarizing tasks, viewed as requiring less complex thinking than tasks of analysis and synthesis on most taxonomies of cognitive complexity, the students surprised us by having difficulty with task definition. First, the summarizing tasks were seen as artificial because the students had difficulty in locating both audiences and purposes. They pointed out that summarizing was not a meaningful activity for students at their level because it served no functional purpose. The note-taking activities described in Chapter 3 illustrated their customary approaches to recording information from written source texts. The students grappled with what was "allowed" to be in a summary: Must it be controlled entirely by the information and the language of the source text? Was any interpretation permitted? Another dilemma, especially at first, was that the materials were difficult for them to understand. Garnet acknowledged in class that she relied completely on the author's structure in one of the early assignments. In fact, she engaged in a strategy often employed by students who are uncertain that they have understood a complex text adequately. "I quoted it," she reported to her classmates' understanding laughter. The students were caught between two equally unattractive responses: a relatively rote recounting or an evaluation which they felt might not be responsive to the assignment they had been given.

I have no intention of defending the design of these tasks, but I do hope that it is possible to learn something from responses to tasks in which students do not have a high degree of commitment. On those occasions, the goal-seeking need which Flower and Hayes propose is subverted by the exigencies of the task conditions. Writers certainly construct goals so that they can complete their assignments, but these goals are of less value than the kinds of goals writers would create under conditions of real need and interest. Chip agreed with this analysis and noted that "Flower and Hayes seem to confuse 'goals' with 'needs.' We set goals to satisfy our needs, and our needs emerge from the full human context—which is a matter of psychological *content*, not just *structure*."

Writers are also impeded in their analysis of the audience, often the abstract academic audience characterized by Rubin and Rafoth as a fictionalized or constructed audience, one that has no tangible identity that the writer can perceive. In such cases, writing does not manifest a clear socially instrumental or manipulative intent (10). Thus, the lack of a clear audience can combine with the lack of a real purpose for the writing to lead students to the typical perfunctory passionless paper so often seen in writing courses. In a preliminary review of the journal accounts with the students, Sharon Pugh commented in class,

> There was a certain amount of floundering [in the initial tasks]—you felt you were doing a certain amount of floundering either because the assignment wasn't clear or because it wasn't being read and responded to critically, or because it was making you do something that you didn't want to do and didn't see any purpose in it yourself. But you were willing to do it because you were

told to do it. So that's interesting. The whole idea that you are willing as a student for the purpose to reside in the assignment or in the instructor.

Flower and Hayes do not report on their informants complaining about the meaninglessness of the tasks they are engaged in, but the few excerpts they cite suggest no enthusiasm for the task at hand (usually a description of the protocoled writer's job for a reader of *Seventeen Magazine*).

Because we had two types of tasks, those designed by the instructors, and those chosen by the students themselves, it is possible to examine the students' comments when they compare their sense of purpose under these two conditions. Garnet clearly articulated the contrast in her journal after she wrote the summaries of the two articles she had selected to begin her research on her self-selected topic:

> A comment about writing the summaries: These summaries were much easier for me to write and I felt that this was true because I was more familiar with the topic being discussed and because I had a "real" purpose in summarizing them. I did not stop to think what was meant by a summary or wonder what the teachers were looking for. Instead I saw the activity as one that was helpful for me in gathering together some information that I could use later on in a paper. I was really surprised at how the change in purpose and context affected the ease with which I could write the summaries and attend to my own purposes rather than the teachers! There was not a debate about what I should write. I chose both the main points in the articles and the points that I was particularly interested in.

In this shift, the self-defined goals determine the selection of materials to meet the self-identified needs. Furthermore, Garnet points out that she is not distracted by having to figure out her instructors' goals and perhaps consciously or subconsciously subverting her own goals to those of others. It would be impossible to see this type of contrast if we did not have reports from students participating in a variety of types of tasks over time who had become accustomed to examining their own processes and thus sensitized to reporting the differences in their experiences.

But even when selecting topics for themselves, the pragmatics of their lives heavily influenced and limited the choices the students could make. We had as participants in our study a group of advanced graduate students who were almost all near the end of their course work and thus very close to the selection of dissertation topics. This exigency made itself felt for many of the students: Robin selected a topic for an upcoming oral examination; Garnet needed to understand a particularly difficult concept (abduction) in preparation for writing her dissertation proposal; and most particularly, Crystal had telescoped her course work into a frantic academic year and had developed a carefully planned timetable for the completion of her degree. She pictured her decision-making process in her journal:

> My first inclination was to pick something that would be fun—I tossed around such things as Baroque music, TM, Italian Opera or some way to combine research with a creative paper. I know that I have to be practical, though, because I want to stick to the time schedule I've set for myself regarding this degree. Since I'll probably write a dissertation on _____'s poetry, therefore, I decided to pick a related topic for this paper. [This poem] is one of her important later works, and since I haven't even read it yet, I thought it would qualify. Once I'd decided on [the poem] as the topic and a literary research paper as the project, I was perfectly happy with it, even excited about it because it would fit so well into my long-range plans.

However, this project led Crystal into a succession of highs and lows as she worked on it. More than the completion of a paper for our course was at stake for her. She commented later, after a series of frustrating writin g blocks, that if the project did not work out for her, she might not have a dissertation topic at all and this was extremely frightening. She felt i n fact that her blocks were caused by her anxieties and she could acknowledge their cause only after she had resolved her difficulties with the paper.

One other student, Jade, who had been most resistant to the teacher-designed tasks, suddenly used the word "liberation" in her journal to describe her exhilaration when the work on the self-designed tasks began. She could set her own goals and envision a purpose for herself. She wrote in her journal:

> Liberation at last! Now decisions made during writing are based on functional needs as opposed to constructed ambiguity.
>
> My decision to write about ESL [English as a Second Language] is based on having felt a need to become familiar with that literature. I really hate the thought of reading that stuff as I'm fairly confident it is pretty awful but I should know what is there. I've put this off for quite some time—since there is plenty of good stuff to read as opposed to this bad stuff—so it's about time I got to it.
>
> The other reason for my reading this literature is that I hope to someday do some work in ESL. While whole language methods have had an impact in many other areas of language education, ESL seems to have remained untouched. I believe that socio-psycholinguistic theories have a lot to offer in this area.

Her enthusiasm was sustained throughout the research process, but as has already been mentioned, Jade felt that her learning had been accomplished through the research process itself, and the writing of the paper became merely an exercise to be endured because of the course demands. She had also been revealing gradually in her journal that writing was an excruciating and demanding activity for her, and that realization may have influenced her attitude toward the writing of the final paper, although she later told me that writing had always been difficult for her, not just in our course.

In class, the students described to each other the varied reasons why they had selected their topics for their final research papers: some people were using the opportunity to fill in gaps in their knowledge; some were looking ahead to dissertations, oral exams, and other kinds of specific responsibilities in their own fields that they wanted to concentrate on ; still others were responding to more immediate demands being made on them. Amber's interest in examining the concept of validity within experimental and naturalistic models of research had come out of her earlier background i n testing and measurement and her interest in concepts of metaphor, but it had also been stimulated by discussions in our course on the concept of multiple realities. This topic had piqued her interest "because I am just convinced that there are realities that are more valid than other ones." So she wanted to examine how validity is evaluated or established or argued for within a non-quantitative model. Daisy similarly wanted to investigate methods of analyzing qualitative data because "I'm trying to analyze some data I have and I thought this might help me and give me a background." Prior or prospective teaching experiences influenced the choices of some student s. For Violet, the opportunity to have an open choice of topic led her to decide to read about schema theory "because I don't know very much about it and I am not likely to take another course, so this is a good chance." She had spent the past two years helping to develop basic skills reading-writing courses and had in separate semesters taught both the reading and writing components. Lila chose to look at "business writing texts because I'm teaching business writing this term [and] most of the texts I've looked at are real deserts as far as theory is concerned."

Lionel asked in class why everyone had come up with "meaty" topics and "no one wanted to find the origin of Mickey Mouse ears." He wanted to know whether the choices had really been motivated by serious concerns or whether people "wanted to look like graduate students." He doubted that, in a similar situation, freshman composition students would have made the same kinds of choices. Jade argued that freshman composition students do have areas that they are "incredibly interested in," the implication being that somehow instructors or contexts don't encourage a strong level of commitment. Robin felt that freshmen would try to pick a topic "that is good for you, teacher, that I can write about." The consensus was that our graduate students were trying to pick topics to explore that would lead to the creation of something they could use later and that playing a role for a teacher had not been a conscious factor in their decisions. The open question remained of how to establish comparable purposes for freshmen who likely have not identified future needs so clearly at that point in their education.

After reading this section, Crystal wrote to me that she had tried open-ended tasks in a research writing course she had taught that had drawn students from the freshman through the senior year. She found that her students, like her former graduate student colleagues in our class, had made "overwhelmingly practical" choices of topics to write about. "Freshmen and sophomores may not have had clear-cut career plans, but one, for example, knew that she would be taking an American History course and thus wrote about the Civil War. Another, a poly-sci major, wrote on illegal immigration." In a freshman composition course, she found, that given free choice, many students "chose topics that they thought would help them in future courses . . . interestingly—almost all of these freshmen (1 had 48 the first semester and 22 the second semester) ended up choosing something they thought would be *helpful* to them, just as we did in your course." Heather also commented that her students would select topics related to their major *if* they trusted the instructor. Upper-class students, she found, would select functional topics that they could use later on or on the job in the present. It may well be the case that composition instructors have erroneously made the assumption that the majority of freshmen and other undergraduates will not be knowledgeable or sophisticated enough to make either appropriately practical decisions or decisions on topics that will at least engage their interest and commitment.

As these few examples illustrate, the nature of goal-setting is a much more complex enterprise than simply taking the assignment a teacher hands you and trying to figure out how to respond to the needs of an audience. Goal-setting, when it is meaningful, is influenced, perhaps even controlled by, the complex interpretations of the demands being made on the individual at a given time and fits into that individual's present life in a particular way. It cannot be explored under laboratory conditions, wherein none of the important constraints of the individual's environment exist. Particularly in the case of teacher-designed tasks, the goals may be simply to finish the task, and no individual interpretive goals may be set. To understand what types of goals are being set, all aspects of the composing process must be viewed in their larger context to be sensitive to the multiple influences that affect the writing that is being undertaken.

Although I will be describing the various processes often mentioned in recursive models of the composing process in the next few sections, I hope to be able to highlight aspects of these processes that have not hitherto been considered. I will also be adding elements that have not been previously included in descriptions of the composing process.

PLANNING

Planning or pre-writing activities are usually the first aspect of the composing process considered. This, of course, makes sense, since it represents the

initial foray into the investigation of a topic. As recursive models of composing suggest, planning is an activity that can also take place at later stages of
the composing process as the development of the topic requires rethinking,
reformulating and/or revision. Bracewell has noted that writing is a type of
problem-solving in that the solution to the problem does not yield to routine
procedures. He notes that, in constructing solutions to writing problems,
"the writer must have conscious access to writing subskills that range from
vocabulary to genre levels" (183). Because the students in our study were
sophisticated language users, the majority of subskills associated with writing were handled through automatic procedures (accounting for little attention in the journals to their editing processes). Therefore, the more complex
issues related to composing were the ones likely to be raised to a conscious
level and discussed in the journals.

One of the aspects of planning that emerged from our students' journals
was their contemplation of the appropriate genre for their writing and their
familiarity with the conventions of that genre. In reviewing research
on the composing process, Hillocks was concerned with understanding how
knowledge affects process. One question he posed had to do with genre
type: "To what extent . . . is the discourse type selected for a given task
dependent on knowledge available to the writer?" (234). When the genre
was specified by the instructors, as in the summary writing, reaction, and
synthesis tasks, questions of definition arose either as problems or, as in the
case of Violet's response to the summary task, a simple reaffirmation of her
concept of what summary properly included. What is interesting in Violet's
comments is that she grappled with the odd demand of writing a summary of
the Dennett science-fiction story (in this clearly academic setting) and then
decided that she should fall back on the conventions of this genre (her
schema for summary writing) that had worked for her in the past:

> I finally tried to analyze how I normally write summaries of readings in litera-
> ture or composition that I want to use for future reference [she has identified
> the audience as herself]. I normally try to identify the main point or thesis of
> the work and briefly outline its general argument. If I'm reading the work for a
> particular purpose, I then also include notes on how the work relates to that
> purpose. I nearly always include some evaluation of my own, since I
> want to remember how I reacted to ideas that the author has raised. If I have
> questions—critical or informational—I include them. I try to include every-
> thing that could be helpful to me if I come back to the summary at some later
> time. I decided to approach the summary of Dennett's article the same way
> . . . At the end I added some comments of my own reaction to the chapter,
> since that would be important to me if I ever needed to decide about the future
> usefulness of the chapter to me.

In this example, the genre conventions prescribe and proscribe what will be
permitted in the summary. That they are far looser and more interpretive

than the rules decided on by other students does not diminish the fact that they do set out a set of rules for the writer.

When Crystal began to write her proposal on her self-selected research project, she described it as almost an automatic act which she accounted for through her "familiarity with a task genre." She wrote in her journal:

> I can't point to any specific, conscious steps as I could regarding assignments which called for a "summary" or a "synthesis." I think it's a good example of the kind of "assimilation of previous knowledge" which makes it easy to write when one has been reading and thinking about a specific subject over an extended period of time.

Clearly, the experience and fluency of the graduate students in our class could not be assumed for beginning undergraduates, the population most frequently enrolled in writing classes. But, what is suggested by these observations of experienced language users is that concentrated, repeated experiences in reading and writing are the means by which automatic literate responses can be developed. Only through the doing, and perhaps as Crystal has mentioned, the thinking about a specific subject over an extended period of time, can increasing expertise be gained. The fragmentation of topics and assignments so frequently found in writing courses does not permit expertise in content to develop over time. It is only with security in the knowledge base that a writer can gain confidence that he or she has something important to say and will become committed to its competent expression (Sternglass 77).

The Evolution of Decisions

An aspect of the planning process that is only artificially represented in protocol analysis accounts or stimulated recall accounts is how the available time span affects thinking and writing. In relation to the acquisition of a knowledge base, as just mentioned, our students were able to describe the tentativeness of their thinking at the beginning of their self-designed research project and even to speculate about how their "early ignorance" would compare with their "later knowledge." For example, when Chip was starting his research on brain localization (and just before he decided to turn his paper into a creative effort), he described the writing of his prospectus for the project:

> Our assignment was to write a proposal this week. I spent only half an hour at this, describing my present understanding of the localization theory and indicating what my general approach to it would be. Right now, I see myself doing a lot of fairly difficult reading and learning in order to write a fairly simple paper. My proposal will be interesting to look back on in a month or so when I

have built up a network of ideas on the subject. I'm sure it will seem both inaccurate and superficial.

Shortly thereafter, Chip made the shift to writing a creative paper. He documented his changing thinking in his next journal entry:

> What I am considering is a paper that will draw on my research, but that won't be a traditional sort of research paper. I may do something in a satirical view. One idea I have is a dialogue between a "left" and "right" brain in which the applicability of psychobiology to the classroom is debated. Or—a more complicated idea—I could write a fantasy or science fiction story revolving around some issue of brain research. What if there were a virus that impaired or destroyed the functioning of a part of the brain?

It is possible to see the evolution of thinking as it is occurring, perhaps something that could similarly be reported through a protocol analysis, but because these thoughts have evolved over several weeks time, the evolving changes are captured in the journal entries as they are occurring and maturing.

When Crystal, who had written several creative pieces in the course, read Chip's comment about the science fiction story being more complex than the dialogue he considered earlier, she registered surprise because for her the writing of "a straight forward dialogue" would be much more difficult. She was interested that for some the writing of creative responses seemed more complex than straightforward analysis. For her, the opposite seemed to be true. An analysis of her papers and journals in Chapter Five reveals the basis for these judgments: that creative writing responses do not seem to demand the same logical rigor for Crystal that straight academic papers do. Since both approaches, when handled competently, actually do require complex thinking about complex topics, both should be nurtured and students encouraged to select the genre forms through which to express their ideas.

Another shift in planning is described by Hillocks reviewing a protocol description by Flower and Hayes:

> They quote parts of a protocol from Roger, a competent college writer who is planning aloud a paper on Boethius. Roger is doing this for a course, not simply for a researcher. He develops one plan to write about how he himself became convinced of the logic in *The Consolations of Philosophy*. (He had previously had objections to Boethius' logic.) However, Roger rejects that plan when he realizes it will produce a narrative—not the kind of thesis and support paper his professors will expect. His second plan is to develop the paper as a dialogue between himself and Boethius, a plan which allows for thesis, antithesis, analysis and support—a true text level revision—but one that occurs during prewriting" ("Plans That Guide" quoted in Hillocks 42).

This report of a protocol obtained from Flower and Hayes work differs in substantial ways from their other protocols: The work reported here by Roger allows for enough time for evaluation and revision at the planning stage, and the work is intended for a "real" audience in a course, not "simply for a researcher."

In Chip's further journal entry for the week describing the change in his thinking, he also clearly documents the effect of the immediate instructional context on his decision as well as the self-knowledge to be gained by trying this risky new type of venture:

> I guess in a "normal" seminar I wouldn't be considering [these possibilities]. But, then, I wouldn't have picked this particular topic either. Writing some sort of satire or fantasy story would solve the problem of narrowing my research. I could use a lot of things in a peripheral way. It would be fun, too. The question is, if I decide to write a story, how would that change the research/ writing process? Since I have written a great many traditional research papers, I would certainly be able to introspect about the differences involved in doing research for a fictional narrative. I think I will take a couple of hours and work up some extensive notes on my ideas and then see what I've got. . . . I think I will read for a few days before deciding.

Here again, time and a perceived supportive context are allies in the decision-making process involved in Chip's planning.

The dramatic shift in genre for Chip's final paper reflects that on one level the most important kinds of revision are taking place before the writing actually occurs. Certainly the evolving text will be revised, but the fundamental decisions are occurring during the planning period itself. This pattern has also been noted by Hillocks when he reviewed many studies of revising by elementary, high school, and college students and found very few revisions reported at the text level. Hillocks speculates: "Perhaps such revisions go on during a prewriting phase when a writer considers a variety of topics" (42). As Chip's experience suggests, the decisions may involve not only choices of topics but also choices of vantage points and genres.

Scheduling Time While Planning

The importance of scheduling time in relation to their multiple responsibilities was a common theme in the students' journals, particularly toward the end of the semester when they also had papers due in other classes. The students frequently mentioned that the papers they were working on in various courses were related to each other, not so surprising since they were often taking courses that dealt with related issues, and particularly in the case of the topics that they selected for our course where they had a free choice and thus could build such connections intentionally. The issue also arose that they were exploring topics that were parts of a larger whole in relation to their major areas of interest. For this reason, some recognized that the work done on any individual paper was only part of a larger process of learning in a wide field they were beginning to explore. Ruby, for example, noted her difficulty in starting to write her paper because she saw its planning as only the first stage toward greater understanding:

> I have read all the things I was able to find and I'm ready to start working. It is difficult to get started writing because the information I have found is far from conclusive in relation to two of my questions. This is to be expected in such a slippery subject and the only way I can work toward my goal of building a rationale for the way I think a beginning ESL level should be is to gather enough data to lend credence to a set of theoretical assumptions. The reading I have done has helped me find the directions to take in developing an argument. At this point I will consider my paper as a precursor to something larger, perhaps eventually to be worked into the monograph I am attempting to write.

Because she could set her own purposes, such planning has no conflict with expectations of outsiders. Furthermore, her paper is seen as one piece fitting into a larger mosaic of goals.

Topaz, whose marathoning strategies in reading were described in Chapter 3, told in her journal how important structuring time for writing was to her so that she would not have to marathon through writing:

> I began reading my Xeroxed materials last night and making listings of contents for comparative purposes. . . . I have gone through four authors this way so far. The purpose is to tell at a glance where integration of the material is possible for a rough draft. On a rational (left brain!) level, I was planning to put this off until right before the final draft. However, on an intuitive level ("gut" level), I felt compelled to do this now because I have read so much that my mind needs to structure it all. Also, I have my weeks planned out up to April 18, and I felt this step might help keep me on schedule.
>
> Creating a weekly schedule of activity is something I always do because it gives me a sense of "being in control" which is necessary both to good writing and to my mental health! (I don't like coming down to the wire and "marathoning" through a paper.) I have to have my priorities in order.

This structuring of time fits well with Topaz's need for structure both in reading and writing. The analysis of her papers on introspection in Chapter 5 shows the compatibility of strategies with outcomes.

Anxiety

A relationship between planning time and level of anxiety emerged in a class discussion following the students relating the first set of selected articles for their final research topics to their prior knowledge in the field. Several students noted that the numbers of papers due in a course affected their level of commitment to each one. Pearl commented,

> I felt like I could deal with some of that anxiety by adjusting the [weekly] assignment to an acceptable level that I could manage to get done and in which I was guessing would be acceptable to you. Where some of the topics could possibly have . . . taken some library research, my assumption was, "Well, yeah, I could go to the library to understand this more, but on the other hand they are giving us an assignment every [week]" . . . it was one of those sorts of "This is all I really have time for and this will suffice for this assignment."

Lionel noted that there was a fine line between "a little pressure mak[ing] me work more efficiently . . . without that anxiety, I get a little bit lazy." He also reported that too much anxiety had produced writer's block for him on another project he was working on. Effects of audience on anxiety were brought up by Chip, who noted that he worried "a lot more about writing something for a professor I don't know very well," and by Jade, who commented that, in our course, she hadn't "felt a lot of anxiety because there is no feedback for the papers." Apparently the context of our class provided low anxiety for all the reasons mentioned: high frequency of papers due, thus diminishing the importance of any single paper; familiarity and comfort with the instructors; and little apprehension about negative feedback from the instructors. These conditions are not necessarily the ones which will stimulate the highest possible level of work from students. As is discussed later in this chapter in the section on Audience, it is clear that more feedback on the teacher-designed tasks would have stimulated, for some at least, a greater commitment to the tasks. The trick is to find the optimal balance between productive pressure and anxiety for each context or what Carolyn Burke has called the difference between tension and stress. In commenting on the manuscript, Garnet noted that "tension is crucial to moving learning along, but stress is counterproductive and produces blocks and dependent behavior."

The Effect of Removing Pressure

Another aspect of the use of planning time emerged when eight weeks became available for work on the final research papers. The students were told that their only assignment for the weekly class meetings would be to record in their journals what, if anything, they had done on the research project for our course during that week. That "if anything" turned out to be a factor influencing their efforts during those eight weeks. Because most of the students were working simultaneously on several long papers for different courses, we were interested in how they would break up their time in undertaking these activities. Opal reported in her journal, "I wish that I could record that I am spending the majority of my time working on this paper but alas, it is not the case. Dr. _____'s paper had priority this week." Others reported that although they were reading on several topics (often related) simultaneously, they attempted to undertake the writing of each paper sequentially rather than simultaneously, thus suggesting the need to concentrate their energies on one formal writing task at a time. The choices for sequence were frequently determined by the harsh due dates on the calendar. Garnet described the effects of such constraints on her work:

> Well this is my "I feel guilty" entry. [It is interesting to note that even though we anticipated *with* the students that there might be weeks when they could have other priorities over the paper for our course, guilt still reigns supreme in the student–instructor academic relationship.] I have done very little since my last entry two weeks ago and I not only feel guilt but I am also worried. After my last journal entry, I decided to spend part of an evening working on a schedule to try and budget out my time. I decided to work on the papers in blocks rather than doing a little bit on each paper every week. On major papers like this, I have found in the past that I do much better if I can concentrate on it in one block of time rather than spreading it out in small parts over a longer period of time. I have a major paper due next Monday so that has been the topic that I have been concentrating on.

When reading the manuscript two years later, Garnet noted that her guilt had been directed more at herself than at us as her instructors. She said, "I had set up goals for how far I wanted to be, and when I didn't reach them, I was worried and felt guilt that I was not going to complete the project on time or at the level of quality that I demanded for myself. Having to write a journal entry made that realization more conscious whereas [at] other times, the time just sort of slipped away without my realizing that I was behind." Since we were asking the students to document and explore their own real-context strategies, we were quite interested to receive such descriptions telling of the factors in their contexts that affected their working habits. But, as Garnet's later comment reveals, we were not the only ones making discoveries about their processes; the students were observing their own behavior more consciously than they had before.

Other elements of their lives and personalities also affected their use of time. Rose described her drained feeling after taking her oral examination for the Ph.D.:

> Remember when both of you said that there would be some weeks when we probably wouldn't be able to do much. Well, this has been one of those weeks. I took my last Ph.D. exam on Monday, and it took me all yesterday to

find my desk, my kitchen table and the surface of my library carrel. I have good intentions for next week.

Crystal also described the effect of having the weekly assignment pressure taken from her:

> Sorry, journal. All my good intentions about taking notes every day of spring break came to nil. Now, however, with spring break over and three other papers that I had to complete, completed—I can get back to you. It's interesting to me, though, that as soon as the "required" weekly assignments in this course were suspended in favor of an independent project, I immediately did nothing. No, that's not quite true; I've done some more reading and I had pressing assignments in other courses which had to be finished.Nevertheless, I'm convinced that even the most conscientious students need to have consistent "required" writing assignments.

Again, a facet of the writing process emerges that would be hidden in a restricted episode of writing. Perhaps these comments suggest that there needs to be a balance between frequently demanded, short-term assignments and longer ones that will respect students' needs to juggle their own time, decide on their priorities, and develop the strategies to undertake multiple tasks simultaneously. The longer tasks also obviously require a deeper level of reflection and preparation that can demonstrate to students the importance of having the time to rethink and reshape their thoughts.

Thus, although planning in its broadest sense, encompasses the initial thinking and preparation for writing, it also draws on the prior experience and knowledge the writer has, both in terms of information and knowledge about composing conventions. Genre conventions may be known or unknown or require redefinition. The amount of time available for a task affects every aspect of its undertaking from the thinking and rethinking to the formulation and reformulation. The use of time (carefully planned or the alteration of careful plans) varies with the individual's style of working, the other demands being made simultaneously, and the commitment to the task at hand. The context of composing influences what is perceived to be permitted or not permitted. But the writer's pragmatic choices can overrule all other constraints.

INCUBATION

Just as time is crucial in the planning process, so is it central to the notion of incubation. Incubation can hardly be said to exist under conditions of immediate response, but it can be seen as a crucial component within planning when conditions allow it to emerge. Ericsson and Simon note that incubation is often described as an insight or illumination of a creative idea as the result of a period of unconscious work following preliminary work in becoming familiar with a problem ("Verbal Reports" 238). However, Ericsson and Simon cite several studies that suggest that "subjects are not aware of [their] unplanned episodes of thought on the problem" (238). They also note that such unanticipated thought processes will be very difficult to retrieve in introspection.

For some of our students, descriptions of incubation seemed to be almost of the "textbook" variety wherein descriptions of the unconscious at work were presented. Topaz, for example, wrote in her journal that "after I reread the chapters, took notes, made an outline and thought about where the paper was going, I went to bed." She continued in her journal to describe what she said was a common phenomenon for her: "If I sleep at this point in my organization, my subconscious continues to process material and synthesize it. I went to sleep thinking about it, and when I woke up Saturday morning, my mind was doing a dialogue between Dennett and Hebb. I was ready to write." Of course it is impossible to document the contributions of the subconscious processing she claims, but once again the importance of time for reflection is revealed. In a strikingly similar manner, Lionel depicts an episode of incubation that occurred to him along with the emergence of an "ah-ha" phenomenon:

> I began this [position] paper by asking myself what I really thought about introspection at this point in time. There were aspects or issues that I didn't even want to think about, because I had dismissed them as unsubstantial, or perhaps because I don't see their significance yet.
>
> Right away it became clear that I know very little about introspection and because of it, I felt unwilling to take a position and staunchly support it. Instead, a voice began to materialize in my imagination, a sort of Platonic voice playing devil's advocate to my questions about what seems true to me about introspection. Truth itself is an issue—in fact, a bigger one in my pre-writing thought than is represented in my paper. However, I considered writing the paper in the form of a dialogue.
>
> I slept on the whole thing and let my unconscious work on it. In the morning, as I became gradually conscious (standing in the shower), the thought came to me—emerged, really—to present the dialogue not with a Plato character, but my own voice in its split state as Jekyl/Hyde. Jekyl I took to be the rational and Hyde the emotional, instinctive, romantic aspects of my own thoughts.

In this excerpt, Lionel reveals the tracing of an "ah-ha" phenomenon as it gradually emerged as Durkin maintained could be done. The attractiveness of the dialogue as a form in which multiple perspectives can be presented is examined further in Chapter 5.

A somewhat different aspect of the incubation period is revealed by Chip who treats a part of planning as rehearsing. He notes that when he came to write the first paragraph of his reaction statement to the Valentine article, "I drew pretty heavily on my 'mental notes' or 'rehearsing.' I'd thought of many of the points I made there much earlier than the moment of composing." It was also the case for other students at other times that such mental notes acted more like the transitory "flights" noted by Valentine and that they were not retrievable. As Chip points out, an element of rehearsal is probably required to place these thoughts in long term memory from which they can be retrieved through appropriate connections at appropriate times.

"Mulling" Periods

At the eighth class meeting, the students described a wide range of approaches they took to the drafting of their papers over the semester. Several described an intensive period of reading followed by a "mulling" period, the length of time determined by the amount of time available. Amber noted that she preferred to just start writing (after the reading was completed). Once she formulated the first sentence, the organization of the paper would be apparent to her. But if she found the task difficult, she needed to allow for time "to sit down and do notes or just sort of mess around and stuff." She said that she left time for this reflection on purpose, and noted, "Mulling is one of my better activities. Rumination, A+." Robin built in a shorter reflection period to his writing, usually a half hour. "I look [at my reading notes] and I sit and think and then because all the papers are pretty short, I think is why I don't need any outline or anything like that."

Lionel felt the need for an organizational pattern before he could begin any formal writing, although that could variously take the form of notes or outlines or a first draft. Pearl felt the first necessity was the identification of a goal and that would dictate the procedures to follow. If it were a paper based on other than her opinion, she would read and prepare an organizational structure. If the paper was to be totally her opinion, she would go directly to writing. Chip noted that for complex papers he had to leave time for false starts. His mulling thus took the form of these false starts which he described as "obvious and boring." Chip stated, "If I don't write, I figure I'm not doing anything. I know I have to go through that stage usually to get anywhere." Conversely, Jade felt that the "mulling is probably more important than the writing," consistent with her belief that once understanding was achieved, it was not essential to convey this understanding in writing. For Lila, the mulling occurred as she was doing other activities and an idea would occur to her that she would note down.

There seemed thus to be a conscious directed mulling of the type that Amber, Robin, and Chip describe and an "incubation-type" of mulling on a more unconscious level that Jade and Lila described. Pearl noted that she could only "mull unconsciously" and described how ideas came to her when she was driving or swimming. Sharon Pugh noted that individuals seemed to build in mulling breaks in characteristic ways. Amber noted that her schedule was organized because it was "the only way I know to deal with my anxiety."

These few examples illustrate the role of an incubation period in the planning process even though it may be difficult to describe its operation fully. Its role is simply another support for the necessity of examining composing processes over real time in complex settings.

DRAFTING

Some models of composing have postulated that shaping of thoughts occurs at the point of utterance (Britton et al.; Flower and Hayes on the "linguistic hypothesis" ("Pregnant Pause")). Closely related to this notion, of course, is the idea of discovery while drafting and the importance of translating concepts into language. Examples of all of these phenomena were present in the journals of our students, lending credence to the existence of these aspects of composing while, of course, not limiting what occurs in the drafting process to them.

In his reaction to the Valentine article, Chip provides a full example of "shaping at the point of utterance," discovering both ideas and the language in which to express them:

> As I got down toward the end of the first paragraph, I began to worry about where to go next. I knew in general terms where to go—to the content—but I still didn't know exactly what content I wanted to discuss and I didn't have a good idea for a transition. I didn't get an idea until I started composing the first sentence of the second paragraph. I saw then that I could repeat the "echoes" idea from the end of the previous paragraph. That gave me a transition. But it also helped limit what I was going to talk about in the rest of the "essay." I started out with one of the echoes—the mentalist/behaviorist debate that I had encountered in linguistics—and after writing about that for a bit I saw that another of my echoes—the issue of "thinking aloud protocols" and their validity was actually the other end of the spectrum. My reaction thus ended up focussing on the extremes of opinion regarding introspection. But I didn't start with that focus. Rather I was looking for ideas in the text that connected to things I knew about. The structure of my reaction is accidental though by the end I was quite aware of it.

His use of the word "accidental" to describe the evolution of his discoveries while writing does not diminish the detailed trail that he provides and the links to previously known materials that he makes to the emerging text which provide the basis for the approach he presents. Or, as Chip later noted, "It was only accidental from the point of view of my *conscious* mind." It is the identification of the focus that bridges the gap "between generating ideas and turning them into a paper" (Flower and Hayes, "Plans That Guide" 45).

Reacting to the Context

In contrast to Jade's perspective that the most meaningful learning has taken place in the reading/note-taking period, Violet describes how she at one time subscribed to this belief, but changed her views because of her experiences with writing. She also highlights another aspect of the composing environment that bears crucially on students' decisions as they proceed with tasks. Violet writes in her journal:

> Through the years, it has been difficult for me to actually *write* papers because the act of writing them seemed almost a waste of time; all of the construction had already been worked out mentally. That may be true for very short papers (say 3 pages or so), but it's certainly not true for larger projects. I generally do have a good notion of what I'm going to write, I find, but in the actual writing I make specific decisions, changes, etc. I even have new insights—often prompted by what I've already written, or by rereading notes or sources.

She then goes on to describe how the specific constraints a student *feels* in an academic environment affect the way in which a response to a task is shaped:

> I feel much freer about this assignment than I normally do. You've both said that you want the class to feel free to interpret assignments, and I feel secure taking you at your word. In contrast, I *don't* feel very free about the _____ project. At this school at least (and probably elsewhere) one doesn't mess around with literature seminar papers. The lack of pressure in this class is refreshing, and it seems to add to the feeling that I'm accomplishing something that *I* want to do.

(This comment supports Garnet's observation that the English students did perceive our course as operating in a less restrictive environment than some of their other courses, particularly literature seminars.) The ability to make decisions while planning and drafting are affected not only by what goes on *during* the writing process, but by what the student perceives is permitted within the constraints of the context.

The shaping that occurs during writing often leads to perceptions that, through the evolution of a draft, such important insights have been achieved that it would be best to rework a paper, often to take the needs of a reader into consideration (see Flower "Writer-Based Prose"). Even though time constraints may not always permit such extensive revision, nevertheless writers often recognize that the understandings acquired during writing should lead to such reformulations. Topaz pictured such a process in her journal when she was writing her summary of the Dennett science-fiction story:

> As a revisionist personality, I wanted to rewrite my summary. I did not have a full sense of structure until I finished writing and realized that what I had written last (not the words but the meaning) should have been used to structure the beginning. I felt I had moved inductively as I wrote, letting the meaning fully come to me as I wrote; if I revised, I would restructure to move deductively to make my meaning clear to the reader.

Restructuring then can be seen as the writer's obligation to the reader.

A rather full picture of the drafting process emerged from Garnet's description of a paper she was writing for another course at the same time she was enrolled in our course. In her journal, she first described a false start where she tried to write directly from underlines and brief marginal notes she had made on her source materials. When that process was unsuccessful in generating a satisfactory draft, she threw it out and began a more formal pattern of organization, making an outline and then going through the articles to identify salient points which she noted on appropriate sections of the outline. She noted the difference in her composing processes on the two drafts:

> The first draft I had written and given up on had very little of me in it. I felt like I was just paraphrasing different articles and readings. However, by the time I started on the second draft, I had a broad enough knowledge base on the topic that I could easily put my own thoughts and words into the paper and still pull in appropriate references at the right time. Normally when I need to write a second draft, I do so by going back through the first draft and adding inserts, making crossouts, and perhaps totally rewriting or adding certain sections. This time, however, I began over and referred only occasionally to the first draft. I think that I tried to start writing the paper too soon. I should have spent more time on developing an outline and going back through my readings before I ever did that first draft but I felt pressed for time and so spent all morning composing a paper on the computer that I had to throw out.

If we could share experiences like these with our students more frequently, or ask them to share their composing experiences with each other, it might be possible to convince them of the value of preparation before writing begins, although we would not of course demand adherence to any particular approach (such as outlining) or demean the discoveries that take place during the writing process itself. But cursory preparation leads writers, neither to discoveries, as Bruner has suggested, nor to structures that are satisfying to themselves or their readers.

Writing Without Clear Comprehension

Although it might appear that this group of doctoral students would always be fluent in their reading and writing, the particular readings on the topic of introspection were often difficult for them and they sometimes noted that they reverted to basic strategies in trying to fulfill their writing tasks. Pearl gave a rather full description of her strategy in class when she described writing the summary of the Hebb article:

> . . . I saw myself as a fairly incompetent reader of this text . . . But I assumed that I didn't know much about this topic and therefore it made sense. I knew it made sense so I just wasn't understanding. I really assumed that I was fairly incompetent in getting his point and so I really did what I kind of see basic skills writers do which is to go down and really try to pull out—not in his words—I tried to put them into my own words, but I did try to pull out his major points right out of the article. Then I tried to make them hang together, but still that was definitely my strategy because I didn't understand a lot of it or I thought I didn't.

Other students who had difficulty understanding the Hebb article reacted differently. Amber said she "finally decided I'm a good enough reader to lay the blame on the writing," while Jade announced that if there was something she didn't understand in the reading, she just didn't care. She maintained that rereading hadn't helped her in the past, so she just kept going on. Garnet used her knowledge of organization to help her write the summary, quoting directly from the article when she didn't have enough understanding to paraphrase. Rose solved her writing problem by only writing on what she was sure about, "not dealing with what I couldn't deal with."

This range of responses to writing about a difficult article suggests that writers revert to safe strategies when they feel inadequate to the task or they search for reasons why they should not feel responsibility or guilt. Perhaps we can learn from these responses that there is a level of uncertainty so basic that writers cannot just write themselves out of it. Greater preparation would seem to be called for prior to the reading of these materials so that a level of frustration is replaced by a level of challenge. We could have mitigated this frustration by initially, at least, providing a basic framework for the students or a historical perspective on introspection. But we made the decision (perhaps unwisely) that it would be valuable for the students to experience knowledge-building from the very outset. We may have confounded the experience for them by replacing challenge with too high a level of frustration.

Sharon Pugh noted in class that the students had been invoking rules to support their decisions. They by no means shared the same rules, but they felt a need to establish rules (e.g., definitions of summary, reaction, etc.) and then in some instances break the rules. The journal provided an outlet so that students could explain when they stayed within the bounds of their rules and when they were stepping out of them.

Effect of Deadlines

Pragmatic conditions exist in academic situations for students who are undertaking writing activities that affect their responses. One obvious constraint is the imposition of deadlines; semesters end, papers are due. For some the pressure of deadlines is not necessarily conceived of as a negative factor. Robin, for example, noted in his journal:

> Deadlines actually do help me get things done and even though I hate the pressure I am always glad to produce something. I don't think I always have to have deadlines, but when I have deadlines I almost always produce something. I am sometimes amazed that the quality of what I write under pressure isn't any worse than what I write at leisure. Sometimes the typing is quite a bit worse, but I don't think that the quality of thought, or the quality of the style differs much.

But, as Crystal noted two years later when reading this manuscript, such competent responses are more likely to emerge from experienced writers for whom most of the composing skills are automatic. The issue of deadlines may not just be an abstract artifact; it can be linked with internal pressures that are brought to the surface by the deadline, but not actually caused by it. For example, Crystal, who had such difficulties working on her critical paper on the poet she planned to study for her dissertation, imposed new complications on her life when she decided to use her paper for our course as the basis for a conference presentation. The deadline for the conference abstract came before the final paper was due, and Crystal agonized over the abstract. When she reflected on her problem with meeting this deadline, she indicated her recognition of the complexity of her response to this normally automatic academic endeavor: "The point is that I am trying to figure out why, since writing to meet deadlines is something I'm used to, this particular deadline posed such problems. My conclusion is that I unconsciously projected onto this paper all the fears that are connected in my mind with 'dissertation.'" So, although the deadline did energize her into producing an acceptable abstract, it had been a particularly agonizing experience for her, one that would be repeated as she worked on the final paper for our course because, of course, all of the tensions affecting her continued to exist.

Just a week after Robin discussed in his journal the effect of deadlines on his writing, he described the conditions under which he "spontaneously" writes:

> When I have time, and when I'm interested in my subject, and when I really want to be able to recall my thoughts or stabilize them, and when I think that I'm going to eventually write anyway (end of conditions), I spontaneously write. With so many conditions on the context, you may wonder about my use of "spontaneous." But really—the last 3 (interest, recall and plan to write) are usual with me. So when I'm studying or thinking, I often write out my ideas. This is much different than taking notes because I leave off the book and write in paragraphs and complete sentences. I even look up appropriate quotations, etc.

This kind of drafting is obviously exploratory, but it also fulfills the function of keeping a record of important thoughts so that they will be available for whatever future needs may arise. Crucial to this experience is the sense that the writer is recording his own ideas, ideas that he deems worthy of preserving and reflecting on. This observation by Robin reminds us that writers produce drafts for their own purposes, even if such drafts do not fit neatly into models of composing at appropriate "stages."

At the sixth class meeting, the first class in which "creative" responses to the tasks appeared, a discussion developed about the relationship between such responses and conventional academic papers. Crystal, who along with Lionel, Jade, and Chip were the only students to attempt creative responses during the semester, provided the rationale for her first fable: "I didn't feel adequate to any kind of examination of this kind of material—and so I handled it the only way I could handle it fairly competently and that is creatively." When challenged by her classmates to articulate the distinction she was making, Crystal explained:

> I guess I'm opposing creative writing and academic writing. Creative writing gives free rein, in my definition anyway. There can be connections of one kind or another, but there is no judge as far as to say your argument isn't logical here or your sources aren't adequate. Whereas in academic and scholarly writing, writing does require logical development and adequate support for points made.

I had believed that Crystal and Jade, who had written a dialogue-response, were asking for a more tolerant mind-set and stance from their readers than they would expect for straight academic prose. The freedom to take risks (and offer creative renderings) had been encouraged by the previous week's class discussion in which Sharon Pugh had raised the possibility of alternative modes of responses to the tasks. But Jade, on reading the manuscript, noted that, for her, writing the dialogue was a riskier enterprise than writing a straight academic piece. It was the first time she had attempted such a genre, and she was more unsure about her readers' responses. Believing, though, that such writing had been "cued" in the earlier class, she decided to attempt the risk.

Drafting of text is seen as a complicated enterprise wherein it is possible to trace the origin of complex ideas and accompanying genres while they are emerging. This picture of drafting shows the dissatisfaction that writers can feel at this stage in the process. They often know that they could formulate better (i.e., more satisfying to themselves) responses to the tasks, but frequently the constraints of time and other responsibilities preclude the reworking they wish to undertake. The drafting stage is seen as a way stop to a more final, acceptable piece of writing. A great deal has been learned through the drafting process that prepares the writer to undertake further rethinking and reformulation that will lead to successively more satisfying drafts. Thus, drafting and revision can be seen to be one and the same thing; it does not seem productive to think of them as separate entities.

MAKING MEANING

The issue of making meaning has already been touched on in discussions of planning and drafting, but its importance to the writing process demands that it be examined further. Collins and Seidman have explained that "[m]aking meaning requires that students connect their inner personal world of motivation and thought with the outer social world which they perceive and experience. Learning requires that, in the end, students make meaning for themselves" (5 quoted in Kantor et al 298). One of the central issues raised by the nature of the writing tasks that were assigned is the degree to which individual writers were free to construct meanings of their own, or whether they would be "boxed-in" by what they perceived to be the constraints of the tasks. Because the participants in this study were familiar with transactional models of reading and understood that all reading was constructive, they were unlikely candidates to limit themselves to simple retellings of the readings even when the task (e.g., of summary) might have led to such a definition. We have already seen examples of constructed summary writing, but these examples were augmented by descriptions of constructive reading of the source materials. Ruby described clearly the synthesis of transactional reading with the requirement of summary writing: "I guess what I am trying to say is that any act of summarizing what another has said or written is, in truth, an act of interpretation and will be influenced by my own schema for dealing with the information summarized. Thus, there is no such thing as a totally, text-dependent summary." In other words, any reader brings personal experience and knowledge to a reading task, filtering the reading through that experience so that any writing that emerges will be a product of the ensuing interpretation. The reader has had to construct meaning, and that meaning will be reflected in even a summary.

The task of summarizing the Dennett piece proved to be the most problematic for the students in deciding what appropriately belonged in a summary. For those who believed that interpretation was not "permitted" in a summary, a retelling of the narrative often emerged. But the journal served its safety-valve function for these students who could then announce that they understood that the piece operated on more than one level, but that they had restricted themselves to the retelling because that was how they defined the assignment. For such students, interpretation was seen as a discrete process. Thus, Chip explains in his journal why he limited his summary to a retelling of the narrative: "That is what my summary is—the plot. Were I to go beyond the main elements of the plot, I think I could convey Dennett's piece better, but I would be writing an interpretation then and not a straight summary."

Although, for the most part, there did not seem to be significant differences between the reading and English students in their responses to the reading and writing tasks, these last two examples do point out one contrast that may be accounted for by their backgrounds. Ruby, a reading student, had been as firmly "schooled" in the models of transactional reading as Chip, an English major (concentrating in language and composition), had been in literary criticism, leading him to definite ideas about what interpretation of literary texts involved. Thus, from their differing perspectives, a summary of a literary text (such as Dennett's science-fiction story) engendered different possibilities. Ruby was free to construct her own meaning; in fact, she believed it was impossible not to do so. Chip, on the other hand, took to heart the classical components from literary criticism of a summary of a story and explained in his journal: "So my summary has the form of a story—introduction of characters and setting, complications and resolution." But he felt troubled by this decision and went on to explain: " . . . but [my summary] lacks the details that convey the real meaning in the original. That is, the significance of the original is in its speculative spirit and its fanciful style, and these things aren't in my summary except insofar as they are conveyed by the plot." Thus the formal response to the assignment follows the schema each finds appropriate for writing a summary, while the journal opens up the task definition for analysis and criticism.

Making meaning can be a risky enterprise, though, and less self-confident students avoided providing their own interpretations even when the task specifically seemed to demand this. When the students were asked to review the reading they had done and take a position on one of the issues raised, most found this to be a rewarding experience through which they could come to realize and then acknowledge to others what they had learned, and, thus, what they now believed. But, even at this point in the semester, Jay, the sole foreign student in the class, did not feel confident enough about his knowledge to try out his own ideas. Instead, he chose to go to the library to seek out further research materials on the topic of introspection so that he could cite them in his paper. (He may certainly have been picking up on a comment we had made a few weeks earlier in class when we noted that the students in our course did not seem to be frequenting the library for further information to help them understand the complex readings we had been assigning.) But it seems more likely that he simply felt too insecure to believe that his own interpretations and evaluations were worthy of formulating and sharing.

Thus, the making of meaning calls upon prior knowledge as transactional/constructive reading is transformed into writing. The interpretation of a task may limit what is "allowed" to be presented as the formal response, but the meaning that is created will remain with the writer whether or not it is shared. Environments need to be created wherein it is safe to take risks so that writing can fulfill its most important dimension, the exploration of the writer's new ideas as they are emerging, are being formulated, and later reflected on.

RISK-TAKING

The degree of risk-taking the students were willing to engage in influenced their responses to the range of tasks as they interpreted the contextual factors around themselves. Amber, certainly one of the more self-confident students in the class, was not troubled by taking risks. In writing the summary of the Hebb article, she commented in her journal, "It doesn't really matter to me if I'm wrong—what matters is not feeling certain. But I'd rather be insecure than bored." And then she noted wryly, "There's a certain amount of fiction writing in this summary." Pearl made a distinction between the kind of summary she had written initially on the Valentine article (what she called a student summary designed for recall of facts) and the executive summary she was writing on the Hebb article, in which she committed herself to "boiling down to key concepts and relationships." In this latter type, she noted, "it is necessary to take risks to interpret the author's meaning from my own understanding—this was more difficult because of my lack of background in the discussions of such philosophical questions." She makes a major point about the amount of time required to handle the complex thinking she has demanded of herself: "I could never have even begun to produce the 'executive summary' within the confines of one class period, as much more time for reading, rereading, thinking and writing was required." This comment is one which illustrates the point, made earlier, that our tasks scheduled over a minimum of a week's time could furnish us with retrospective accounts of more natural approaches to complex reading and writing tasks. It would have been impossible for Pearl to approach this reading material, analyze it adequately, and produce a written response under artificial, single-episode composing conditions. Perhaps this is why so few protocol-analysis studies have examined the relationship between reading and writing.

Interpreting Tasks

The specific wording of the assignments often had effects upon the students' responses beyond anything we could have anticipated. A particularly dramatic example of this is two opposite decisions made by the same student on two tasks in relation to the extent to which she was willing to take risks. Garnet, who was cited as carefully "quoting" from source texts when she was not confident about her understanding, was quite conservative in her summary of the Dennett science-fiction story. She wrote in her journal:

> I did not feel that I had to draw an interpretation of the issues raised by the article to the topic of introspection although I knew that there were definitely some to make. Another reason I made this decision was that it was much less risky to try and stay more closely to the text and not put too much of my own interpretation of the article into the summary. I really was not too confident in how well I had really dealt with the issues the author thought he had raised in the article even though I knew that there was no way that I could get all of the author's text. Even though I accept the concept of multiple realities and therefore multiple reactions to a text, I still find myself anxious that I will not get the meaning the "teacher" wanted me to. All of these thoughts (plus others I'm sure) led me to decide to stay closely to the actual text.

If such a sophisticated student as this feels so constrained to figure out and produce what she believes the teacher wants, we can only speculate with anguish about how less confident students' responses are shaped by these feelings. Reading this manuscript two years later, Garnet commented that "staying close to the text was a normal response for me until I felt I had familiarity with the material rather than a response to the 'teacher.' " Nevertheless, at the time of the seminar, there must have been some influence of the "teacher"; otherwise, she would not have mentioned it in her journal.

At the next assignment, to our astonishment, this same student was suddenly liberated from all these constraints simply by her interpretation of the wording of the task. When she went back to her notes to check the exact wording of the assignment, Garnet found "they said 'synthesis essay' and this stopped me. Synthesis essay had a different meaning for me than synthesis paper although I can't really explain what I saw as the difference except that an essay seemed to be more open to reader interpretation and not as much of synthesis . . . As I glanced over the points I had made [in my notes], the transaction point stood out and I decided to stick my neck out and make that my synthesizing idea. The word essay allowed me to do that because it seemed to indicate risk-taking and my own thoughts . . . When I finished, I wasn't sure that I totally agreed with myself but felt it was an interesting argument and had been very productive for me in that it had helped me to take a different perspective of the article and so might also stimulate the thoughts of others about these articles even if they don't agree." The little word "essay" had produced this massive shift in her willingness to explore her own thinking in a way far more productive than her previously restricted approaches had permitted. (Garnet later commented that her attention to the specific wording of the assignments had been influenced by two factors: the previous attention to the definitions of genres by the English students, and the fact that "the only place to gain cues was in the assignments themselves.")

But, whatever the cause, not only had her thinking been liberated, but her writing process itself had been dramatically altered so that it came to resemble what Britton has called "impelled writing":

> I have read authors who write about not knowing what's going to be written on the page until it's there and being surprised at what comes out in print and I had this sensation as I was writing this article. The line of reasoning I was pursuing seemed so productive at the time that I didn't really want to handle counterarguments until later (much later). It will be interesting to see if I still feel this way tomorrow when I reread the essay or if I feel it's junk.

It is difficult to believe that this is the voice of the same writer who wanted carefully to protect herself so that she would come as close as possible to the "teacher's meaning." What this suggests, of course, is that we must search for the means, whether through the task design or the atmosphere of acceptance that we create in the classroom, that will foster this willingness to explore one's own thinking and risk exposure of untested ideas.

Self-Confidence

Throughout the semester, it became clear who the more self-confident and less self-confident students were. Those who had decided from the very beginning that they were going to use the course to pursue their own agendas acted out that position throughout the semester. Others acquired the self-confidence, and perhaps the trust in us, to explore more gradually. A few, like Opal, remained more cautious throughout the period of the course when we had been giving the specific assignments. Opal had had a breakthrough in comprehension of the reading materials on the last weekly assignment as was described for other students in Chapter 3. But only when she was allowed to select a topic for herself did Opal finally take on what she perceived to be a genuine risk. She wrote in her journal:

> I'm probably going to get nailed on this one—it's the first time I've taken a risk in this class, but the worst that can happen is that you say no. (I still believe you when you say there's no right or wrong in here.) I've chosen to interpret this assignment very broadly and look at an issue within a topic; I realize that this is practical in nature rather than academic but nevertheless— . . . Everyone will be doing very scholarly research on academically appropriate topics. However, the reason for all this is practical application.

These comments suggest several changes in Opal's perspective. First, she is willing to designate her own interests and needs as primary in the selection of her topic. Secondly, she is willing to risk being seen as somehow less scholarly or intellectual than her classmates in order to achieve this. Thirdly, she has become trusting enough of her instructors to believe that their only agenda is the students' own agenda, and, at the least, she is willing to test this out openly. This kind of trust can only be built over time, by actions as well as by words. It provides another reason why it is so important to examine the reading and writing experiences of students over extended periods of time, rather than through study of excerpts from isolated pieces of writing collected under unnatural "laboratory" conditions.

Opal's response to my analysis of her behavior suggests that more personal factors may have played an important role in her changed stance. She said, "I'm not certain as to whether this change grew from gaining confidence or just deciding 'to hell with it' and deciding to risk it—probably a bit of both. My entire life at that time was topsy-turvy and this may have been an attempt at maintaining some control." But even these comments reveal positive changes during a personally stressful period for her, a gain in confidence and/or a willingness to take risks, both of which gave her a sense of the appropriateness of her own decision-making.

Trust

A discussion of the relationship of trust to risk-taking took place at one of the early class meetings. Pearl clearly put the issue of risk-taking into its contextual role when she responded to a comment of Jade's in which Jade maintained that she was trying to respond to the cues I see myself being given and so I feel I'm learning a lot about how students or research subjects or whatever you want to call them would respond. I'm seeing that they are looking at a lot of those cues and I have to be real careful [as a teacher] about what those cues are. I'm responding to what I see the cues as being and trying to stay within those cues and not say, 'I'm an adult; I'm going to do totally different.'

Pearl immediately related this point about responding to cues to assessing permissible levels of risk-taking in an academic setting. She said,

I think it makes a difference, too, the personal relationship you may or may not have in the course. In other words, I don't see the willingness to take risks or not take risks as a character trait. I see it being very different from class to class. I don't know Marilyn that well, I don't know Sharon that well. I know them well enough to guess, but on the other hand, professors who I've had a lot of exposure to, I know how far I can go with them. And I know what they think of me too. I know that they will know what my intentions were when I did what I did. But I think that it's not risks, the desire to take risks is a situation by situation and class by class [decision] for all students.

Again, the necessity to unpack dynamics of specific contexts is shown, as Spence has suggested, so that readers can understand the role of the context on the responses being made to tasks. Laboratory setting, free from real interpersonal relationships, could never provide pictures of decision-making as they are affected by the contexts.

In Chapter 2, I described briefly how Crystal had responded to several of the tasks by writing creative responses. She explained in her journal that these creative essays frequently developed out of her frustration with attempting to develop conventional responses, but she recognized that they involved an element of risk for her. And, in fact, when she turned in her first creative response to a task, she appended a short summary of the source essays to assure her instructors that she had known how to take the assignment seriously. Even when she produced her most satisfying creative response, the labyrinth story alluded to earlier, she still felt the need to mention her uncertainty about the appropriateness of this response in her journal: "I'm a little uneasy about it. Hope I'm not subverting the point of the assignment. In fact, when I was finishing it up this morning, I wondered if I shouldn't try to write a short, conventional paper." She resisted the impulse on this occasion, so perhaps this demonstrates that she had achieved some security in the setting since the time she had produced the earlier creative paper. In addition, by the time this paper was written, the discussions about trying something different had already occurred in the classroom.

Two years later, when Crystal read the draft of my manuscript, she still recalled the feelings she had had earlier. She wrote to me:

I'm intrigued by the far-reaching effects of introspecting as we did. In particular, one aspect that "stayed with me" relates to the element of risk-taking, an
element which I've tried to take into account in my own teaching. Remembering that I was so concerned with "over-stepping boundaries" by writing
creative responses to assignments, even though in a course which made it explicitly clear that there were not penalties or prohibitions whatsoever, I was
struck by the weight of inhibition my own students must feel. The dull, pro-
saic, wordy papers that we receive *must* be related to the students' fear of
doing something other than "what the teacher wants." Your manuscript
makes it perfectly clear that every teacher needs to consider this factor.

Most classes appear to students to be places where only conventional responses will be rewarded. The need is to facilitate learning while simultaneously making thinking exciting.

The elements of risk-taking can never emerge from a model of the type
that Flower and Hayes have proposed. It is an element of the writing process
that the writer is unlikely to mention in a protocol report because it probably
doesn't seem to fit with the exigencies of having to produce writing on demand. The expection is not only compliance but attention to the demands of
the moment, i.e., producing the document. As Chip later suggested, "When
you are given a very limited amount of time in which to write, you just go
ahead and do it and worry later (if at all)." As Ericsson and Simon point out,
protocol reports give us access to what the individual is attending to at the
moment, and although that is certainly central to understanding what is going on, that does not necessarily mean that the report is complete in that the
associations triggered in long-term memory may be not only substantive,
but affective as well. We need to be aware of this dimension and its effect on
the writing that is produced.

SELF-IMPOSED CONSTRAINTS

Another aspect of the composing process that emerged from the students'
journals was that individuals had particular requirements or restrictions that
affected their composing behaviors. Although it may appear that some of
these restrictions are idiosyncratic, the point is not that they are appropriate
or inappropriate for others, but rather that individuals do have strong prefer-
ences and needs. Thus, contexts for writing tasks must be flexible enough to
accomodate the particular strategies that individual writers find productive
for themselves.

In a time when the social dimension of composing has become so widely
discussed (see, e.g., Harste, Woodward, and Burke; Langer *Children*), one
of our students told of how essential initial solitary exploration was for her.
Only after she was able to produce something in writing could she "bear" to
discuss her ideas with anyone. Topaz described this need in her journal:

An interesting observation that I have made about my writing behavior is that I can *never* talk about what I *am going to write*; this has reached a "taboo" status with me. It's almost as though talking will destroy what is going on at a subconscious level, and I will end up with nothing to write. *After* I get the words on paper, I can talk about what I have written. I have a friend who is a professional writer, and he is just the opposite. I don't understand this, do you? [emphasis in original]

Although Topaz does not specify what kind of writing her friend does who is a "professional writer," it is interesting to speculate whether he is a creative writer. If so, his needs would approximate those which Chip describes (in the next section, on Audience) when he undertakes the writing of a piece of fiction. Topaz's taboo about talking with others also differed sharply from the feelings of many of her classmates who I have described in Chapter 2 as being frustrated by their inability to talk with their classmates when they were doing the initial tasks in the course. Nevertheless, it is essential to respect a strategy that is functional for an individual and not require that individual to participate in activities that would disturb his or her working habits. Although collaboration is a popular and useful activity in composition classrooms, it may be necessary to find out from individuals if there are legitimate reasons why they may not wish to participate in such approaches to writing. It may also be the case, as for Topaz, that initial collaboration is difficult but collaboration would be welcomed at a different point in the process.

Another widespread practice in the teaching of composition is to prepare students to do research work through and in the library. As was discussed in Chapter 3, many of our students preferred to made xerox copies of materials they wanted to use and work with them in their own settings. Jade was the most adamant about this and described in her journal the importance of choosing her own composing environment:

I found a couple of other sources [for my research paper] and began copying articles. I find myself unable to work on this stuff in the library and find I have to bring copies of the studies home. (Not a financially advantageous position to take.) I am unable to do anything productive in the library. This is something that probably should be remembered in terms of all students, as we all have our quirks.

Once again the point is made that individual differences must be respected.

Composition instructors have conscientiously tried to allow for individual differences in designing tasks, but they must also be sensitive to the range of strategies different students may wish to employ to carry them out. Naturally, what are generally known to be constructive strategies should be made known to students, as long as flexibility in the carrying out of tasks is built into the context.

AUDIENCE

There are many dimensions from which the effect of audience on the composing process can be examined. There is the personal decision made by each writer as to whether the audience for a specific piece is the writer or another. There is the dimension of whether the task appears to be severely constrained (e.g., summary writing) or more open-ended (reaction statement, position paper, self-designed task). There is the issue of whether the writer believes that new information will be made available to the reader or whether the writer believes the reader is more expert than the writer, in which case only information-transfer is being attempted. In other words, both the knowledge-base and the attitude of the prospective reader can affect the stance taken by the writer.

Self as Audience

There were occasions when our students chose themselves as the primary audience for their writing. On such occasions, they asserted that their needs (present or anticipated) had to be accounted for somehow in their writing, whether through the formal task or, in the context of our course, through the journal, or in some combination. Violet described a pattern in her writing that she generally followed in writing summaries, in which she described the evolution of her responses to the Dennett and Hebb assignments. (Ericsson and Simon have warned against the tendency of informants to describe "typical" rather than specific responses to tasks, but in the journal accounts our students often began with descriptions of a typical response and then described their specific activities in relation to the particular task they were undertaking.) Violet noted her concern for audience in her response to the Dennett summary writing task:

> I found it a little bit difficult to write a summary for the Dennett chapter because of its odd nature, and because I had difficulty deciding exactly what Dennett was getting at. I finally tried to analyze how I normally write summaries of readings in literature or composition that I want to use for future reference. I normally try to identify the main point or thesis of the work and briefly outline its general argument. If I'm reading the work for a particular purpose I then also include notes on how the work relates to that purpose. I nearly always include some evaluation of my own since I want to remember how I reacted to ideas that the author has raised. If I have questions—critical or informational—I include them. I try to include everything that could be helpful to me if I come back to the summary at some later time. I decided to approach the summary of Dennett's article the same way. . . . At the end I added some comments on my own reaction to the chapter, since that would be important

to me if I ever needed to decide about the future usefulness of the chapter to me.

From the very beginning, Violet's summary is generated in terms of how it meets her purposes, and this of necessity comes to include evaluative comments for her later recall. In writing the summary of the Hebb article, Violet remains with her own purposes, but she indicates her uncertainty about whether this is appropriate to fulfill the purported audience's (i.e., the instructors') expectations: "Again, I tried to identify the main point, his purpose, and the general outline of the argument. I found myself even more inclined to include some comments on my own thoughts about what he was saying. I'm not sure that that properly belongs in a summary, but it's the sort of information I would want to have if I were later going to need to recall what the chapter was about." Here Violet tries to balance the desires she perceives in her audience with her own needs, but ultimately she takes ownership of the task, asserting that she is the proper audience for her writing and she must thus tailor its content to her own needs. The evolution of this perspective is described in Chapter 5.

This felt need to be the audience for their own writing emerged, not surprisingly, in a much stronger form when the students undertook their self-designed tasks. The strongest expression of this feeling was expressed by Topaz in her journal as she was writing a draft of her final paper, in which she actually characterizes her reader as hypothetical (the real reader, of course, being herself):

> By page 20 (handwritten), I became very aware of how much I must be boring my hypothetical reader: Just because all these studies, articles, facts, and examples were interesting to me did not mean they would be to someone else. Briefly, I considered that I should have chosen another topic in which I was less interested but in which the reader could be more interested—a topic which had more flamboyance and less technical detail. However, I abruptly pulled myself out of this thought by reminding myself that *this topic and paper were for me*: I could be both selfish and, if unavoidable, *boring*!! Since an education allows for very little selfishness, I sat and relished this thought of self-centered freedom for a few minutes before resuming writing . . . It's the freedom of *being happy and knowing it* all at the same time—which is rare— usually happiness is recognized only in retrospect. Being able to write something for myself is so rare that it contains within the experience simple delight [emphasis in original].

It is certainly a sad commentary that writing for oneself and pursuing one's interests, even intellectual and academic ones, are perceived as being selfish rather than the properly pursued type of activity.

Rubin and Raforth noted, in their study of the relationship of social cognitive ability as a predictor of writing quality, that "social cognition played a more significant role in writing a persuasive message to a relatively determinate audience" than it did in expository writing (17–18). They found that social cognitive ability accounted for about 25 percent of the variance in the judged quality of persuasive writing. This finding can help explain the shift in the quality of their own work our students felt when they began to work on their self-selected topics. Regardless of whether they chose themselves or the instructors as their audience, they began to reason explicitly about others' thoughts and assumptions (18). For even the student who declares that she is "selfishly writing for herself" has had to report and explain her observations about these decisions (in our study in the journals rather than in the formal papers).

Others as Audience

Often, especially in the early tasks of the semester, when the students were "feeling out" both the constraints of the tasks and their relationship to the instructors, the students perceived "others" to be the audience for their writing. Even then, they sometimes had multiple audiences for their early experiences and tempered their responses to the particular audience. Since the students had been admonished not to consult with each other for the teacher-designed tasks, they sought out others to talk with, frequently sharing their experiences with family members. Daisy found herself summarizing the Dennett story for her adult son: "However, the oral summary to my son dealt more with the essay as a science fiction story rather than what the author was saying from a philosophical viewpoint. I, therefore, tried to formulate a thesis statement for the essay and outlined points made by the author to support it." Her language in this journal extract clearly delineates the two levels she sees in the piece: for her son, she treats it as a science fiction story, while for her instructors she is outlining points from an essay. She perceives that the academic setting wouldn't be relaxed enough for her just to have fun with the story.

Similarly, Garnet indicated in class that she was very concerned her instructors realize that she understood the Dennett piece operated on more than one level. She said, "I'm not going to just be a dummy and summarize the plot, because anyone would know that . . . " Her comment was interrupted by knowing laughter and a further comment, "I know I just can't put down the plot. I had to come up with some meaning." Thus the constraints of the academic setting forced an academic interpretation, and the serious-student role emerged triumphant.

Ruby decided that the purpose for her writing a summary of the Dennett piece would be "either to encourage people to read it or to discourage [them]." She notes that she had enjoyed reading the story and so decided to give it a favorable review. With this as a perspective, and the potential readership now clearly defined, she expresses some uncertainty as to whether what she is proposing to do falls within the task demands: "The problem with this was that I was not really following the assignment to summarize. However, since the wording of the assignment made it clear that I was to decide what to include in the summary, I decided that perhaps I was really doing OK." Thus, for her, content and purpose decisions included audience considerations, all being seen as a consistent organic whole.

Effect of Audience Response

Because the only feedback we had been providing the students with occurred in the classroom discussions and we had not been returning either their papers or journals with any specific comments, some of the students felt the lack of critical responses to their work. (Although about half-way through the semester Sharon Pugh and I started to provide feedback on our observations on the journals, there was no direct substantive feedback on the formal writing.)

The issue of audience also had an effect on the students' perception of ownership of the texts they were creating. For some, like Lionel, ownership of the texts was related to the care the writer took in creating it, not to the audience response. He noted in class, "If I had taken some care over words and struggled to be precise in the meaning or something like that . . . I do feel commitment, a kind of ownership to it." Amber commented that she felt liberated: "The stuff I'm doing for this class is much more my stuff because I'm not having to write to somebody else's beliefs." But, later at the same class meeting, she made a revelation that might appear to contradict this self-assurance: "The one place in my life where I've gotten some approval has been from teachers. And I still work for that. It still means a lot to me." For her, the solution was to explore her own beliefs whenever the context encouraged that, but not to do anything to jeopardize her diploma or career "unless it was so unethical."

Jade articulated the view that writing, for her, was virtually controlled by the nature of the responses she anticipated. She felt the lack of feedback more strongly than any of the other students, although later in the semester Lionel also raised the issue. When it came time to write her position paper on the readings on introspection, Jade noted in her journal how her motivation was influenced by her sense of no critical audience for her work:

> I decided that contextual variables in classrooms and research settings was
> something I could really get myself up to write about. The strange thing was,
> though, as I sat down to enthusiastically write, I realized there was no real
> issue, and I had no one to persuade. My bubble was burst . . . the wind was

knocked out of my sails . . . and all those other clichés. So what you get is pretty tame stuff. I wonder if this indicates what I have always thought of as my obsession with audience. I always write to an audience and I prefer writing to a critical audience. This pushes both my thinking and my writing. I find the challenge of producing persuasive discourse both fun and incredibly exciting. This context just doesn't do it.

She obviously did not consider the option that writing could ever be a means of pushing herself toward more critical understanding.

Because Jade's criticism was legitimate, I decided, when I taught a similar class called "Examining Your Own Reading and Writing Processes" to graduate students at City College of City University of New York in the spring of 1986, to write a "reply journal" to my students in response to their papers and their journals. In my journal replies, on a weekly basis for the first half of the semester, I commented on both the substantive aspects of their formal writing and their journal experience with the introspecting activities. What I came to see was that from an instructional perspective, consistent response was very helpful to the students, but, from a research perspective, it would muddy any analysis of their responses unless the study were designed to include the possibility of strong instructor influence on the description of the processes being examined. For example, I tried to urge the students at City College to pay attention to the "flights" of thought that Valentine described in her article and to annotate their readings and then "annotate their annotations" with their thoughts, feelings, and connections as they were reading. While these were the same kinds of things we wanted the students at Indiana to observe and describe, we intentionally gave them no directions, waiting to see what would emerge naturally. We wanted to let the introspection process develop without direction from us so that we could describe its strengths and limitations. This is just another dimension of the type of conflict, discussed in Chapter 2 that arises in an instructional setting where research is being undertaken. In neither case do I feel that the students suffered, since the purpose of both courses was to have the students observe their own reading and writing processes, but the amount of direction and support provided in the two instances differed considerably.

This is perhaps a long way to point out that the absence of a real audience from a writer's perspective has the potential to decrease substantially the commitment a writer puts into a piece of writing. As our research shows, the lack of a real audience will not necessarily inhibit or distort the writing process for all writers, but its impact must be honestly described on those students who are most strongly affected by this sense.

Audience as Evaluator

Another issue related to the lack of feedback in the course was the concern with evaluation. Lionel indicated his concern at the fourth class meeting by asking whether the writing assignments were going to be evaluated. In particular, he said, "I know at the end I'm going to get some kind of grade, some kind of credit; therefore, what am I going to be judged on? Where am I headed?" Sharon Pugh responded by telling him that, although we were required to assign grades, if we assessed their writing as an "A" synthesis or a "C" synthesis, "we would be stepping in as the authority in the way that we have tried not to do . . . and that would bring to a grinding halt the kind of discovery or learning that we are hoping is taking place here." She went on to explain that our only basis for evaluation could be the extent and depth of participation by the seminar students. It also became clear that, in the class discussions, we were focussing more on the processes whereby the students responded to the tasks than on the substantive content of the responses. For some, like Lionel and Jade, this continued to be a source of dissatisfaction, but most of the other students felt that this was a legitimate emphasis in light of the course's purpose, the examination of their own reading and writing processes. This issue was mitigated considerably when the students turned to the writing of their final papers on topics they selected for themselves.

Audiences for Creative Writing

The writing of fiction seemed to generate an even greater demand for an audience. Although several students wrote creative responses to the teacher-designed tasks, only one student, Chip, decided to write a piece of fiction as a final project paper. Writing fiction was a new experience for Chip, and he was interested in noting the differences in his own composing processes in comparison with his composing while writing more academic forms of discourse. One of the first and most important differences he discovered was in his relationship to audience. He noted in his journal:

> One thing I've been doing that I don't usually do in writing a paper is showing my work to a reader as I go along. I want to see the effect of the actual words on a reader. I need reassurance, I guess, not being very practiced in this sort of writing. My reader is _____—a pretty stern judge of fiction (she knows what she likes, anyway, and can talk about why she likes or doesn't like it).
>
> So far, she has reacted very positively to my drafts. She has found them readable, interesting, the characters plausible, etc. I have bounced ideas of where the story might go next off her, and in doing so have changed my perceptions somewhat.
>
> Also I think by letting her read my stuff I have gotten over the fear all fiction writers have—the fear of being laughed at. (Actually, maybe all kinds of writers have this fear when they attempt a kind of writing they aren't experienced at. It is a fear of personal rejection. This is *me* on the page.)

By the end of the semester, Chip's commitment to the piece of fiction he was writing (now growing almost exponentially out of his control toward the length of a novel) had developed so fully that he was extremely sensitive to the difference between his work on this piece and an assignment he had for another graduate course, a conventional research paper. He described this difference in his last journal entry for our course:

> This experience [of writing an expository paper for another course] stands in contrast to my struggle with the story [for this course]. First, in the expository piece, I had a clear pattern and purpose from the start. I also knew as I was writing how much detail I could afford to go into (i.e., not nearly enough!) and a better sense of how my words would affect a reader. Second, in my expository piece, I had the sense of making a very limited commitment. The topic interested me, to be sure, but there was no chance of being able to fully explore it in the time I had. Also, I felt only a marginal personal commitment to the teacher who was (is) my primary audience. It was, in contrast to my story, a perfunctory effort, something I did to get a grade in a class. To the extent that I was able to choose my own subject matter and do some reading and thinking that will be useful later on, it was a worthwhile project. But I feel only partial allegiance to the piece of writing itself.

He then went on in his journal to give a page-by-page description of how he came to write the three versions of his story that he was handing in, even though he knew that the story was not complete. He had concluded that he really had the makings of a 200–300 page novel.

When the writer identifies purposes for himself or herself, the audience serves as an energizing element. The writer may feel a communicative component to what is being written and in those instances consider appropriately the needs of a reader, or direct the writing to his/her own needs, immediate or long-range, But the chief determination of commitment appears to be the identification of a purpose that fits the context and meets the needs of the writer.

REVISING

In view of the extensive research literature on revising, it was somewhat surprising to find relatively little mention of revising in our students' journals. This paucity may be accounted for in part by the fact that the early teacher-designed tasks were so intensive and the deadlines so short (one week) that the students had little time to revise their efforts. In fact, there were comments in the journals bemoaning the fact that there was not time for further revising and rewriting, but the students had to make their peace with what could be accomplished within the limited time constraints. (In the section on drafting, for example, I noted the frustration which Topaz experienced in not being able to rewrite her paper after she completed a draft and recognized a new appropriate structure for it.) Other examples in the drafting section also illustrate ongoing revision while writing is occurring, an illustration of why it is fruitless to suggest that the components of composing can be neatly separated. Unfortunately, the artifact of identifying categories for discussion, as in this chapter, tends to perpetuate the discreteness of the elements of the process. Perhaps it is only through insisting on the overlapping qualities of the "categories" that we can demonstrate the wholeness of reading and writing processes. All of these aspects or categories might be thought of as threads interlocking in a weaving. Each strand may be pulled out for separate examination, but the significance of the pattern is only revealed through the effect created by the whole.

One of the few aspects related to revising that was raised in the journal accounts illustrated the practices of writing in different "media": handwriting, typewriting, word processing. Chip described an alternation between handwriting and typing that seemed to serve different needs, exploration or consolidation. When writing the Dennett and Hebb summaries, he described these processes in his journal:

> I made a decision on length based on how much time I had to write and type (i.e., a couple of hours). Then I wrote out a very rough draft that covered Dennett, stopped when I got revolted by what I had written, and couldn't think of what to do next (i.e., on Hebb). So I started to revise (on the typewriter). This is a standard pattern with me. There always comes a point where going on with the composing depends on reformulating what I've already done in long hand, adding things here and there and then stopping typing when the ideas get too hard to express the first time out. Then I write some more out in long hand before going on.

Thus, the two processes, what he calls "writing and typing," differ substantively for Chip. When ideas become too complex, he returns to handwriting, echoing the points made by Emig when she notes that "writing through its inherent reinforcing cycle involving hand, eye, and brain marks a uniquely multi-representational mode for learning" ("Writing and Learning" 124–125).

For another student, Garnet, the computer led to an alteration in her composing style that she found liberating and led to revision being an integral part of composing. In her journal, she described five axioms from naturalistic theory that served as the basis for her position paper:

> I began writing the papers using the 5 axioms to organize what I wanted to say. I used the notes on the axioms as an outline to go from and once I had completed the first draft of the paper I went back to my underlines and numbers in the articles to see what I needed to still include in the paper. I realized as I did this that this strategy was one that I had developed since I began composing on the computer. I find it easier to just sit down and type it into the computer with little reference back to my original sources and once it is there I go back to my

references and see what I need to go back and change. I think that this works because I usually have spent a lot of time reading and thinking for what I want to do and being able to just sit and compose without having to stop and refer back to my references doesn't break my train of thought and puts the article in my own words. Before I always wrote with my references right out in front of me and carefully referred to them as I wrote. The ease of revision has changed this strategy for me.

For Garnet, the opportunity to write and revise freely releases her from reliance on the source texts as she is organizing and expressing her own ideas. The computer allows her to insert documentation and support at any point in her writing process, rather than restricting her to full development of each point as she is writing, an element of composing on the typewriter for anyone who strives to avoid extensive retyping. But this form of composing at the computer did not come full-blown to Garnet; she describes in her journal how she started by writing her papers out and then copying them on the computer and only doing minor corrections at that point. She gradually developed the alternative method of composing on the computer, utilizing the flexibility it offered almost unconsciously at first.

The writing of creative responses to the tasks also offered opportunities to examine the revision process. When Crystal constructed her fable of the labyrinth, she felt as though the story almost wrote itself. But her journal description revealed that conscious reflection and revision played important roles in the writing:

> Finally last night (this is the only assignment in this course I've put off—and I did so this time because I couldn't seem to come up with an approach) I thought about writing a fable and from then on it practically wrote itself. It took a little while to come up with the labyrinth, though—at first I was going to have a giant, impenetrable meteor land at the door of the castle—the idea of the "subjects" being women didn't happen until I had written most of it. Then when I was looking back at it I thought, Damn! Why is everything we imagine automatically in the masculine gender?

So, although the story may have flowed easily once she conceived the idea of a fable, two central components, the labyrinth and the female protagonists, were components that replaced earlier ideas in the fable, another instance of drafting and revision occurring simultaneously. As writers read over their developing text to evaluate it, writers "construct a representation of [their] own text or text plan as a basis for comparing intention and text" (Flower et al. "Detection, Diagnosis" 31). This is clearly what happened to Crystal; as her intentions changed, she modified her text to make it meet her new objectives, which were primarily affective.

The fact that there was so little discussion of revision as a discrete entity in the journals of the graduate students suggests that revision was likely an on-

going activity for them, occurring simultaneously with planning and drafting. Similarly, editing was rarely mentioned as a separate activity, suggesting that it was not an element requiring much conscious attention but
rather handled automatically (therefore not being "heeded" in Ericsson and
Simon's terms).

EDITING

Virtually no attention was paid to the process of editing either in the students' journals or in their comments at the class meetings. This can probably
be accounted for by the fact that the participants in this study were an ex-
ceptionally literate group of doctoral students who would probably have felt
little need to comment on any infelicities in their writing that they might
have encountered. It probably was an issue that they "heeded" very little in
their writing. The sole comment even related to this area came from Chip's
final journal entry, in which he was reviewing what he had noted about his
composing process over the semester:

> I have a sense when a word, a phrase, a sentence, a passage, a paragraph isn't
> "right." I would call this a "stylistic" sense, yet often when I tinker with some-
> thing on a stylistic level, I end up adding or changing the content.

This is clearly a sophisticated interpretation of editing, and Chip recognizes
that what appear to be stylistic changes always cause changes in meaning.
Now that Hirsch has recanted his belief in "relative readability," there
seems to be no argument that style affects meaning in substantial ways.

CONCLUSION

Keeping in mind that all the writing tasks examined in this study were undertaken in connection with reading tasks, it is possible to make some observations about writing processes that reflect the importance of examining these
processes within their specific instructional contexts. Support was found for
Langer's idea ("Learning") that essay writing demands more intensive engagement and thought than note-taking, although it is important to notice
that specific genre types (such as summary writing) may constrain analysis
or interpretation and the making of meaning. Purposes for writing are
strongly affected by the demands of the context, the audience envisioned by
the writer (self or other), the amount of time allotted for carrying out the task,
and the degree of interest and commitment the writer has to the topic. Writers must decide where authority lies—in the assignment, the instructor, the
self, or some combination of these. When writers subvert their own goals to

what they perceive to be the goals of others, the writing becomes more per-functory. Self-selected topics and goals bring greater commitment, but also greater risk, as writers have much larger stakes in the outcome of their inves-tigations.

Planning and drafting are seen to overlap to such an extent that they be-come one process, and for our competent language users, also to subsume revision. Although these processes have often been described as recursive, it becomes extremely difficult and artificial to delineate them even as sepa-rate "stages" in a recursive model. Prior knowledge of writing conventions plays an important role, so that, for example, known genre conventions can be utilized when appropriate. The observation of the role of time constraints revealed that even a week's time between assignment of the reading and writing task and its due date allowed for some reflection, incubation, associ-ation with prior knowledge, and discussion with others (although, in our set-ting, initially not with others in the seminar itself). This time span encour-aged thinking and rethinking that took different forms for different writers: note taking; rereading; "daydreaming" while driving, swimming, cooking, or taking a shower; trying out ideas on friends and relatives. Whatever com-binations of activities took place, writers formulated and reformulated their ideas before writing, while writing, and/or after writing drafts. No single set pattern could be seen to emerge for individual writers or for groups of writ-ers, suggesting that the writing process is individualistic, but not so idiosyn-cratic that it could not be compared to the "community of readers" often posited by theorists of reader-response literary criticism. It thus becomes possible to posit a "community of writers" who share certain conventions and processes without demanding that each follow a prescribed composing model, even a recursive model. It also removes the need for the "black boxes" of the monitor so often called for in models of the writing process, because the processes can be attended to, "heeded" in Ericsson and Si-mon's term, and thus be accessible for inspection. This would be the case even more so for basic writers and freshman writers than for our graduate students, because one of the outcomes of this study is to note that the stu-dents were able to introspect more successfully about elements in the writ-ing process that gave them problems than those processes which they had control over and which proceeded more automatically for them. If, in fact, freshman writers have difficulties with basic elements of composing such as planning and drafting, it appears likely that asking them to introspect on their composing activities would help them to bring to the surface the partic-ular difficulties that they have.

The planning of longer self-designed projects reveals again the range of strategies employed by a group of competent language users. When stu-dents are given the option to plan their own time in relation to their other commitments, they are seen to make decisions that are realistic, assign priorities (frequently on the basis of the order of deadlines), plan and organize their reading and writing time so that they can work in the most conducive settings (xeroxing in the library but taking materials home, writing by hand, on the typewriter, or on the computer depending on their comfort and experience with each, some finding the different media appropriate for different aspects of the composing), to decide whether they prefer working concurrently on several projects or to concentrate solely on one project at a time, and to select the audience for the task as is permitted within the setting and functional for their needs.

Drafting emerges in different manifestations for different writers, some discovering meaning in the drafting process itself and others feeling that the writing is only a record of their thinking from the reading–note-taking stages. The extent to which students feel free to take risks in the specific environment will determine the amount of interpretation, analysis, and evaluation they will include in their written responses to the tasks. The degree of risk-taking is intimately connected with the confidence they have in the instructor's willingness to tolerate individual interpretation. The students' own confidence in their ability to make meaning from the reading naturally also influences how freely they will deviate from a strict following of what they believe are the task demands. In a paradoxical way, some of the creative responses to the tasks seem to emanate from a lack of confidence in writing a rigorous, analytical paper, although the use of the conceptual materials in the creative responses demands a highly sophisticated understanding of the material, as anyone who has attempted to write in an ironic vein knows.

Writers do have individual styles of working, though, and these must be respected and accommodated. The social nature of writing has been described often in recent years, and its many contributions to writing and learning are evident. We were painfully aware of how we had short-circuited that aspect of learning in the restrictions we imposed during the writing of the first set of tasks, as the students frequently vented their frustration in not being able to talk over the tasks with their fellow students *while* they were working on them. To overcome that limitation, when I taught a similar course at City College in 1986, I distributed to the students a list of all the seminar participants' names and home telephone numbers, since on a commuter campus telephone contacts replace the more likely get-togethers on a residential campus like Indiana University. These telephone connections proved to be of great importance to the students, especially early in the semester when many of them lacked confidence in their interpretations of the difficult articles on the introspection process. It seemed that they did not even share much interpretation with each other, but they provided reassurance to each other that they were not the only ones having difficulty with the assignments. Later in the course, when six of the eleven seminar participants decided to write short stories as their final project papers, the new fiction writers turned frequently to the more experienced writers for support both with their processes and their actual drafts. Their experiences provide support for the social nature of writing, but we must also keep in mind the feelings of individuals like Topaz, who found it impossible to share her thoughts until she had at least produced a draft for herself. Although such students may be rarer in number then those desiring and benefiting from social interactions while planning and composing, it is essential to remain sensitive to strong and important individual needs.

The need for feedback is a strong component of this social dimension. When we failed to provide significant individual feedback to our students, we distorted their commitment to producing the strongest intellectual response they were capable of. For some, feedback of an evaluative sort was sought, but most students really seemed to prefer responses to their ideas, a sense that an audience cared enough to reflect on their reflections. This difficulty with lack of feedback was partly mitigated by the serious group of students we had who undertook these tasks responsibly (taking into account their other simultaneous commitments), who came gradually to understand that the journals were the documents we would focus on in the class discussions, but that these journals could only describe their processes if they seriously engaged in the tasks, and by the final realization that the most serious and productive work would be undertaken when they identified their own needs and themselves as their audience.

This description of writing processes reveals that a range of complex factors come into play when students undertake complex reading and writing tasks. They incorporate similar processes in undertaking these tasks, thus constituting a community of writers, but they employ a range of strategies in a range of orders with a range of emphases depending upon the perceived needs of the individual writer and that writer's interpretation of the complex demands of the setting. These observations suggest that writing instruction must be sensitive to these factors and design tasks and contexts that will facilitate engagement with writing as a positive contributor to the learning process.

In the next chapter, we will examine the texts the students produced during the first half of the semester and the ways in which they built knowledge.

CHAPTER 5

Textual Origins: Building Knowledge Effectively and Affectively

Thus far, this book has dealt primarily with the journal descriptions of the students' reading and writing strategies. But it is also important to examine the major influences on the development of the texts that the students produced for the course. By the time they wrote their final position papers, it was clear that individuals had developed "preferred" orientations, preferred in the sense of genre, structure, or stance they wanted to take toward the topic of introspection. And these approaches can be seen to have evolved gradually over the first half of the semester as they grappled with a topic and research methodologies that most had little formal background in.

Not surprisingly, the different backgrounds that the students brought to the course influenced strongly what came to be central issues for them. But substantive issues were not the only concern or the only manifestation of the concerns that arose in the final position papers on introspection. Four major orientations appeared in the final position papers: (1) a concentration on substantive issues; (2) a concern with the formal structures for presentation; (3) the influence of prior knowledge both substantive and affective; and (4) the use of creative writing to explore substantive issues. Each of these approaches can be investigated by tracing back from the final position paper on the usefulness of introspective accounts the insights explored in the earlier papers and journal accounts and how they contributed both to the content and form of these papers. Case studies will illustrate each approach.

CONCENTRATION ON SUBSTANTIVE ISSUES

The substantive issue for the seminar, of course, was the validity and usefulness of introspective accounts in research. All students dealt with this question in some way in their final position papers, but some in particular saw their growing knowledge base affecting their interpretations and perspectives. As their substantive knowledge grew, they could "outgrow" affective responses and replace them with intellectual arguments.

Two students in particular, Violet, a literature student, and Garnet, a reading student, focused on substantive issues in their final position papers. Violet was conscious that she had been developing her position all along favoring the use of introspective reports under suitable conditions, but the final paper provided her with an opportunity to explore her thoughts more fully and consolidate her own thinking. She moved from over-generalized, charged language to more substantial and logical arguments. Garnet had been frustrated throughout the course, as she had felt that introspection was being "forced" into an empirical research methodology where it did not belong. Because of her growing knowledge about the naturalistic paradigm, she was finally ready to defend with evidence the position she sincerely, almost passionately, had believed in all along.

Violet

Violet notes in her journal that she realizes with this final position paper assignment that she has been developing a position all along. She says:

> As I looked back at the other assignments and journal entries I had written, I could see opinions creeping in here and there. My problem, then, was not so much to determine what my position was as to clarify it, and to "check" it against the readings again.

She reports that she then flipped through all the source readings except the Dennett piece.

In her paper, Violet explains that introspection is useful as a research tool, but it must be used in situations where subjects are not made to feel incompetent or silly. She acknowledges the limitations of introspective reports, but argues that "[e]ven if introspection cannot help us understand all the workings of the mind, it seems foolish to ignore the information it can give us." She, like several others, concludes that introspection can play a role in conjunction with more traditional experimental methodologies (a position Garnet comes to reject entirely).

This positive attitude toward introspection, and its possible suitability within experimental paradigms, begins with her response to the first article on introspection she read, the Valentine article. In her initial reaction statement, she notes:

> It seems only sensible to me that introspection is the most powerful method for investigating mental processes like reading and writing, as well as thinking

(How else can we get that information?) Therefore, some of the objections to introspection cited in the article seem extreme to me. Yet I am aware of certain doubts and potential problems associated with using introspection as a research tool.

Thus, in the very first "formal" paper written for the course, Violet has already staked out the position that she later explains she has only to "check" against the readings again. She has also already characterized the objections against introspection as "extreme," a strong indication of the mind set she is bringing to these readings, although she dutifully notes that she is willing to acknowledge that there are some problems.

In her summary paper on the Hebb article, Violet chooses to write one "legitimate" paragraph of summary and to follow that with an evaluative paragraph. In the summary paragraph, she notes Hebb's critical views on introspection and that he contends

> that our awareness of the existence of the mind is based on evidence from the outside world (including our own bodies); what we actually observe is not the mental processes we go through, but rather the sensory result of that process.

Violet knows that the explanatory paragraph, a succinct summary of Hebb's position, would have been sufficient for the assignment. But, consistent with her initial viewing of Valentine's objections to introspection as "extreme," she tags on an evaluative paragraph to her summary paper.

In this evaluative paragraph, Violet raises arguments to show the relevance of introspection to the kinds of studies she is interested in:

> Much of what Hebb claims actually makes sense, but to question the usefulness of introspection on the basis of his arguments would be self-defeating, *especially for certain kinds of studies*. Hebb's biological analogy narrows his approach to the question. It seems true that, when we introspect, we don't discover the physiological, chemical processes of thinking, and that knowledge would be fascinating and potentially very useful. However, a physiological understanding of mental process is not necessarily what we are always looking for *when we use introspection. If we use it to try to determine what readers and writers do, and our intention is to understand the processes better and to perhaps use that understanding to help less proficient readers and writers, then a chemical understanding of what is going on in the brain would be of very limited use* [emphasis added].

Two steps are taken in this critique beyond her earlier characterization of objections to introspection as "extreme": she acknowledges the validity of substantive objections to her own position, but redirects the discussion to a consideration of the *uses* of introspection, and particularly those uses she finds of greatest interest to herself.

In her journal entry on the Hebb article, Violet notes that her normal pattern of writing summaries includes "some evaluation of my own, since I want to remember how I reacted to ideas that the author has raised." Seen from this perspective, her paragraph of evaluation then takes on the role of a normal, habitual response Violet has to writing about work she has read. In her journal entry on the Dennett piece, though, she questions this habitual approach:

> I found myself even more inclined to include some comments on what he [Dennett] was saying. I'm not sure that that properly belongs in a summary, but it's the sort of information I would want to have if I were later going to need to recall what the chapter was about. As I was reading, I found myself jotting things down in the margin—not the sorts of things that would help me understand what he was saying, but rather reactions or objections to what I thought he was saying.

So it is clear that she has adopted a critical stance toward the readings from the very beginning, a stance from which she is viewing all the criticisms of introspection and this will lead her easily and consistently to the position she will develop in her position paper—an assignment that she does *not* know during these early weeks of the semester that she will have coming up. The position she is developing is arising out of her own experience with the readings as they are clearly interacting with her views about research and instruction.

Violet's synthesis of the Dennett and Hebb pieces breaks no new ground for her; she restates the dilemma of trying to understand one's own inner mental processes:

> We are . . . highly aware of our awareness, and we wonder how our minds work, what makes us think as we do, and what makes us think we are who we think we are. This self-conscious tendency to reflect on our own nature leads us to a circular kind of problem: we are trying to use our processes of understanding in order to understand those very processes, and so one of the things we may be most limited in understanding in any objective way is ourselves.

And, in this objective analysis, Violet removes herself from her critical stance to state the inherent problem of the validity of introspective accounts.

In the assignment to summarize the two basic positions of the researchers writing in the *British Journal of Psychology*, Violet writes a very short, barebones summary of the four articles assigned. Her topic sentence states almost everything: "The arguments in the Evans [two articles], Morris, and Quinton and Fellows articles divide basically into two opposing positions: one that does not accept the validity of introspective reports and one that does." This statement is followed by short descriptions of the positions of the various authors.

Although Violet's summary paper does not contain her "usual" evaluative comment, such a paragraph appears in her accompanying journal entry (dealing with substantive content and not with process accounts):

> One thing about my decision not to go very deeply into their arguments bothered me—Quinton and Fellows and Morris seemed to accept the notion that the ability to successfully describe and predict behavior based on introspective reports did imply causality for the processes reported. In keeping with his strict "experimental psychology" stance, Evans totally rejected that possibility. I thought that that was an interesting difference, and one basic to their opposing positions. After I had written the summary, I rather regretted not mentioning that difference, because I think it's an important reason why they will probably never be able to agree with each other in a very constructive way. Evans *seems to be clinging to strict scientific method with the same sort of fervor* with which a fundamentalist Christian *clings* to the literal word of the Bible, and his arguments with Morris don't seem to go any farther than arguments between creationists and evolutionists [emphasis added].

Although this paragraph continues to present substantive differences in the positions offered by the various researchers, the charged language of the last sentence attributes to Evans a stance far from the objective scientific one he would doubtless characterize his own work with. In relation to her earlier summary statement of Dennett's piece, Violet had noted in her journal the possible inappropriateness of her including an evaluative stance in the formal summary paper itself. So it may be possible now to interpret her ongoing discussion in her journal entry about Evans as, not merely the result of "a decision not to go very deeply into their arguments" in the formal paper, but, perhaps on an unconscious level, a decision to delay this discussion until the writing of the journal entry so that it could be followed by an evaluative stance including highly charged language.

In the final position paper itself, Violet immediately goes on the offensive, setting out the issue, acknowledging a series of criticisms, but immediately refuting each one. Her opening paragraph gives a sense of this:

> Most opponents to the use of introspection as a research tool seem to object mainly on the issues of subjectivity and control. Traditional empiricists, like J. St B.T. Evans, tend to refuse to acknowledge the value of data collected under circumstances in which the experimenter must trust the responses of the subjects instead of his or her own observations. *However*, not all information may be accessible to an outside, objective observer, especially in investigations of human processes that do not have many outward, physical manifestations—like thought. *If we limit* investigations to only those areas that can be explored by traditional scientific means, *then we must limit inquiry* into the world around us, and into ourselves. *If, however, we want to attempt to understand* "unseen" processes like the function of the mind, *we may have to ac-*

cept less traditionally objective methods of investigation like introspection. *Moreover,* . . . [emphasis added].

As this excerpt demonstrates, Violet has become confident that she has acquired the substantive knowledge to refute the positions and arguments that she could only label "extreme" at the beginning of her reading in this topic area. She had staked out a position for herself at the beginning, but, over the weeks of reading and writing about introspection, she has developed sufficient expertise to defend her position confidently. She fully acknowledges the limitations of introspection in her paper and can feel comfortable doing that since she is now equipped to offer counterarguments. She is even willing to place introspection within larger research paradigms, as long as their usefulness is not denied:

> To disregard the need for experimental control in our exploration of internal as well as external phenomena would be a step backwards. Yet refusing to investigate internal phenomena that cannot be entirely controlled by an objective experimenter or observer seems to be, if not a step backwards, then at least a refusal to step forward. A more enlightened approach might be to use traditional experimental models to help us limit the possibilities of subjective error while we define the methods of inquiry.

Such a conciliatory stance reflects the voice of a writer who believes her arguments for the value of introspective accounts will stand the test of being subjected to the rigors of other research methodologies. Her substantive knowledge has grown to the point where she does not need charged language to convince her readers of her position; she believes that the logic of her arguments will prevail.

Garnet

Garnet, because she brings more prior knowledge about research methodologies and is also concurrently studying a new research methodology, the naturalistic paradigm, is not so sanguine about accepting introspection within an experimental paradigm. Instead, in her final position paper, she maintains that introspection fits logically, substantively, and virtually exclusively within a naturalistic paradigm. She begins her formal position paper with this introduction:

> A major issue not addressed by [the authors we have read] is the value of introspection in a different paradigm. All have assumed that the experimental paradigm is the one under which introspection must be judged. It seems to me that there is a basic mismatch between using a human instrument like introspection and the experimentalist paradigm which stresses objectivity and sees hu-

man instruments as limitations. In contrast, the naturalistic paradigm views the human instrument not as a detriment but as advantageous to the inquiry.

Garnet notes in her journal on this position paper that she has been influenced throughout the semester by the course she is simultaneously taking on naturalistic inquiry. The juxtaposition of the two courses can be seen to have influenced and shaped her interpretations from the beginning of the semester. She says that the issue of the unwillingness of the authors to place introspection into a naturalistic paradigm has been "bother[ing] me all the way through both class discussions and the articles, but I haven't really addressed it very explicitly." In fact, though, an examination of her papers and journal entries reveals that this topic has been on her mind throughout the semester.

That Garnet would be critical of the stance an author takes vis à vis research methodologies is apparent from her first paper, the reaction statement to Valentine's article. Garnet writes, "Another difficulty I had was that the author would present several sides of an argument and then accept the one that reflected her point of view as a 'fact,' a given, without a sufficiently developed rationale for doing so." The inference is, of course, that Garnet would not do so, that, as a serious researcher, she would provide adequate justification for whatever position she developed substantively or methodologically. She further starts to provide precisely the rationale she will offer later to defend introspection within a naturalistic paradigm rather than an experimental paradigm (and this is the first paper for our course and within two weeks of starting the course in naturalistic research!):

> Any research technique is going to have some limitations but this does not mean that we cannot still gain valuable insights from the technique that otherwise would not be available. What is important is that a researcher use the techniques that have the best fit with the issue or question being investigated in the research.

So, although Garnet may have been initially floundering among the psychological terms and concepts she was introduced to in the articles on introspection, it is clear that as a language education doctoral student well versed in research methodologies, she has a clear philosophy about the selection of research techniques to fit particular issues.

In this first reaction statement (to the Valentine article), Garnet stakes out even the specific issue of the inappropriateness of introspection within an experimental research paradigm that she so cogently later argues in her final position paper:

> The aspect that Valentine stresses the most is establishing the validity and reliability of introspective reports through extensive, empirical investigation. Usu-

ally this means a more tightly controlled laboratory study and this *would seem*
to me to have a negative effect on the introspective report. Putting the re-
spondent in an unfamiliar and tightly controlled setting *would seem* to increase problems of deception and change the process the researcher was trying to take a look at.. . . Many of the characteristics of introspection *would
seem* to make it a good technique to use within the naturalistic paradigm of
research and yet this paradigm is totally ignored in the article [emphasis
added].

Her language is initially cautionary at this point in terms of knowledge both
about introspection and the naturalistic paradigm, but she is clearly already
headed toward the position she will finally and firmly adopt. At this stage in
her thinking, she is still willing to consider the possibility of using introspection within an experimental paradigm, the conclusion ultimately acceptable
to Violet, although, even at this early stage in her thinking, it is not the conclusion Garnet prefers, as she indicates in a later section of this reaction paper:

Many of the problems that introspection has encountered in being accepted as
a legitimate research technique seem to be a result of trying to fit it into a positivist paradigm when many of the basic beliefs of that paradigm conflict with
the technique. While the technique can be used within this paradigm, it seems
to me that its greatest fruitfulness lies within the naturalistic paradigm where its
strengths as a human instrument are considered an asset and not a liability to
the process of inquiry.

This concept of introspection as a strength of the "human instrument" appears virtually unchanged in her final position paper, and it is an issue taken
up by several of the other students as even ethical and religious values are
introduced into the discussion of research paradigms (see the case studies of
Amber and Lionel later in this chapter). But Garnet's complete rejection of
using introspection within an experimental paradigm has not yet been
stated, and it remains to be developed as the semester goes on. Since this
first assignment was to write a "reaction statement" to the Valentine article,
it is clear that Garnet's primary interest lies in the topic of research methodologies, and she continues to examine how introspection fits within various
paradigms as she is simultaneously building knowledge about introspection
and about the naturalistic paradigm.

In her summary of Hebb's critique of introspection within experimental
paradigms, Garnet provides a straight summary of Hebb's ideas with no
evaluative comments or separate evaluative paragraph as Violet had produced. She notes in her accompanying journal entry that she found herself
"defining a summary as very text-based and so [I] worry about putting anything in the summary that I feel is an interpretation of the text." She also

mentions in her journal that she had difficulty understanding some parts of the text so she adopted the strategies of "avoiding putting in something I didn't quite understand or using the author's words because I did not feel able to do much paraphrasing."

Thus, the confident voice of the writer of the reaction statement is reduced to the strategy of omission or direct quotation. Although the relationship of introspection to any research paradigm is not mentioned in either the summary of the Hebb article or the journal comment, she makes it clear in the summary that she believes Hebb has reduced introspection to an inferential tool and denied it the role of direct observation by the mind.

As mentioned earlier, in Chapter 4, when Garnet recognizes her task to write a synthesis *essay* on the Dennett and Hebb articles, she feels the assignment as "more open to reader interpretation and not as much as synthesis of two tasks without much reader interpretation or reaction." The first sentence of her synthesis essay reveals that she has instantly returned to her favorite topic: "The articles by Dennett and Hebb reflect the difficulty *theorists and researchers experience when they try to separate out parts from the whole* in trying to understand any human process" [emphasis added]. She then goes on in her paper to develop the transactional effects mind and body have on each other, drawing on the two readings. But her conclusion returns to the general topic of research methodologies:

> Whether or not one knows her own mind directly or indirectly in the process of introspection is irrelevant in some senses. *It is still one way that cognition can be studied and so is an important technique to use* in inquiry involving the human mind . . . A transactive process means that while there are constraints in the interpretations, no two interpretations of an event or process are going to be exactly alike, nor should they be expected to be. Viewing the mind and body in a transactive relationship with the resulting *multiple interpretations* [a tenet of naturalistic inquiry] seems to be a major step in beginning to get a grasp of the issues raised in these articles [emphasis added].

Apparently, the assignment "synthesis essay" focused her attention again on the issue that seems to have been on her mind throughout the reading and writing tasks of the course and gave her the requisite "permission" to explore it that she had felt had been denied to her in the previous summary assignment. Given the opportunity, she is reading and writing with a growing and strengthened interpretive stance.

For the assignment to write summaries of the positions held by the researchers writing in the *British Journal of Psychology*, Garnet decided that she had a choice on two major issues: either to compare the four researchers' positions on introspection or their views on research. She comments in her journal, "I decided to go with introspection since this is a course in introspection." But she notes in her summarizing paper that the central disagreement is "about the use of introspection in psychological research." Clearly, the topics of introspection and research methodologies remain firmly linked in her mind. In fact, the opening paragraph of her paper concludes with the researchers' positions stated in a methodological context:

> Quinton, Fellows and Morris believe that introspective reports can offer a direct indication of the cognitive processes underlying behavior and that these reports are very helpful in understanding cognitive processes. Evans, on the other hand, argues that introspective reports are not a direct indication of the cognitive processes underlying behavior but that these processes can only be deduced by an experimenter in a carefully controlled laboratory setting.

She goes on to review the major substantive arguments set forward by each researcher, but consistently places these arguments within the context of research paradigms:

> It is obvious that these three researchers [Morris, Quinton and Fellows] feel much more comfortable than Evans in using introspection and not worrying about the tightness of the controls in the experiment. It is interesting that Morris points to these reports of strategies as the best way to begin to understand the cognitive processes people use in real-life situations. This appears to be a direct blow at Evans who emphasizes strictly controlled laboratory research.

So, although Garnet indicates in her journal entry that she has chosen to focus on introspection rather than on views of research, it is clear that she is unable to separate these issues. This, of course, is not surprising, since most of the debates about introspection center on its validity as a research methodology.

Garnet's final position paper can be seen then as a logical outgrowth of her support of introspection as a viable research tool and its appropriate placement within a naturalistic paradigm. Any reservations or cautionary statements she may have uttered during the previous weeks of the semester are swept aside as she now defends, knowledgeably and confidently, the relationships she has tentatively been exploring up to this point. In her final paper, using the five axioms of naturalistic research, she exposes what she believes to be the weaknesses of the experimental paradigm and defends what she believes to be the strengths of the naturalistic paradigm. Now introspection turns out to be an ally as its potential insights buttress the arguments favoring the naturalistic approach. Her conclusion sums up her beliefs:

> It seems to me that many of the problems that these authors [we have read] have discussed in relation to introspection are a result of making a human instrument fit within the experimentalist paradigm where it is always going to be

suspect because it violates so many axioms of that paradigm . . . The human instrument finds its potential within the naturalistic paradigm where it is considered an asset to be exploited rather than a liability to be controlled.

Like Violet, Garnet started with a predilection favoring the use of introspection in psychological studies of cognitive processes. But, for Garnet, a serious issue remained—that introspection be used within a research paradigm where it would be valued, not merely tolerated or downgraded. Only as her knowledge of introspection and the characteristics of the naturalistic paradigm grew simultaneously could she fortify herself sufficiently to take the position of denying the experimental paradigm the "right" to use introspection as a research methodology. Knowledge bred confidence.

In these two case studies, Violet and Garnet are shown to have substantially increased their substantive knowledge about the topic of introspection as a result of their reading and writing activities. Each has prepared herself to defend the position taken in the final paper on introspection, Violet no longer dependent on charged language to critique the views of those she disagrees with, and Garnet able to reject her initial conciliatory position of multiple research paradigms to stand firmly behind the one she finds uniquely suited to utilize introspective accounts. It is true, as these case studies indicate, that both Violet and Garnet were initially predisposed to take the positions they ultimately held, but, without effective knowledge building, neither could have adopted the confident language of their final position papers.

FORMAL STRUCTURES

Genre forms are important in two of the categories of this chapter. In this section, I will be presenting the influence of the argumentative structure, with all its formal requirements, on the writing of one of the students. In the last category section, I will present two case studies of students who selected creative writing as the genre for their final position papers.

Argumentative writing makes special demands on writers and is always the last of the genres taught to composition students because of the rigor required in the formulation of positions defended or attacked. It is not surprising that, by the time an individual becomes a doctoral student, the demands of argumentative writing should be taken very seriously.

Topaz

Unlike Violet and Garnet, from the very beginning of her examination of the topic of introspection, Topaz felt compelled to be able to rigorously justify every statement she made. I don't mean to imply that the others were careless in their statements, but their attention was not drawn to the demands of argumentative writing as Topaz's was. Having been strongly grounded in argumentative writing, studying claims and warrants, implied claims and stated claims, Topaz examined every reading to determine its strength of logic and argument and set about to produce writing that would also stand up to rigorous examination. In her last paper on the topic of introspection, the position paper, she felt released from the bonds of objectivity which had constrained her while she was reviewing other people's work and free to present her own positions and interpretations. But these demanded the same kind of rigorous support she had been conditioned to expect of others writing in this mode. Before this final paper was written, she had been preparing herself all along to identify a position she could defend with her considerable argumentative skills.

She chose a position supporting introspection because she "was not required to choose an objectively valid point to discuss; I was only required to choose what was valid *for me* and to provide logic to extend it." Validity and logic are seen immediately to be crucial factors in her thinking and writing. She noted in her journal that she reread the source texts to find evidence to support her position, thus demonstrating that the point that was valid for her still required evidence for support. She reported that the schema for the structure of the argumentative essay came from the structure of a position paper she had written for a graduate course the previous semester as well as the structure of another position paper she had read on the subject of humanities education. But she was clearly familiar with the structure of argumentative papers, having mentioned in several journal entries her knowledge of warrants and claims in argumentative writing. In fact, the whole issue of structure was central to her approach to the tasks throughout the semester.

In her first reaction paper to the Valentine article, Topaz demonstrated how she approached both reading and writing tasks with structural schemas clearly in mind. In her journal entry, she describes her initial reading strategy:

> To approach the meaning of the article, I first read the title of it and established a mental continuum of movement ("flights") with periodic static points ("perchings") marked on it. This became my tentative global/structural schema to provide an organizational framework for what I read in the article . . . My next step was to read the introduction and conclusion to (1) determine the author's purpose and stance and (2) determine if the author arrived at a logical conclusion based on her original premise . . . Satisfied and tentatively structured, I began reading the article.

In the reaction statement, she focuses on how she perceives "the purpose of the author [to be] to establish the validity and reliability of the use of intro-spection in scientific/empirical studies." She notes also that she has started with a "positive, global reaction to the article as a whole" and moved to a reaction to specific parts of the article, a structural organization she deline-ates no doubt to help her own readers. She then selects "particulars" from Valentine's article, reacting to them from her own beliefs and experiences as well as from prior knowledge related to these points. She returns to her posi-tive global reaction to the article in her concluding paragraph.

In her journal, Topaz reveals that she has mixed feelings about this struc-tural approach to her work which appear to be related to her concern about the grading in the course. She writes in her first journal entry, ". . . and I knew that I was dependent on them [my instructors] for an adequate grade at the end of the semester." She finds that she is structuring her journal just as she had structured the paper, but in the journal she acknowledges that

> this experience is forcing me into a structure that feels artificial. I am more of a free association, "ah-ha" perception person. As I write this, I feel that structure and handwriting are important and both of these constrain me.

Despite this stated ambivalence, the journal structure then resumes its adopted pattern. She goes on to describe her reading strategy through a met-aphoric description, but abruptly relates the metaphor to her need for struc-ture, which seems to go beyond demands she perceives are coming from her instructors:

> In conclusion, reading this article made me realize that reading for me is like submerging into an underwater world where ideas are compressed against one another and against the reader's consciousness like water pressure on the hu-man body. "Ah-ha" perceptions and failure in comprehension (one positive; the other negative) bring the reader up above the water's surface (the text) to think or to emote.
>
> However, I did not "submerge" into the text without a structure: I created one from the title, the introduction and the conclusion. Then I semi-consci-ously compared it to my own knowledge, found it valid in a tentative sense, and then read the article using this structure . . . When I finished the reading, I reaffirmed the initial structure mentally.

At the least, it seems possible to say that structure organizes her schema for reading in ways that predispose her thinking before the actual reading be-gins. In this case, she has predisposed herself to interpret the findings as sound based on her preliminary preview, and it is hard to know whether she would be willing to reject this preliminary view as she read on if this were warranted.

Just as her reading is strongly influenced by her predetermined structure, so is her writing. She notes in her journal that the form of her writing is a well-practiced formula:

> As far as the *form* of what I write goes, it is a "formula" that is so well learned that it is like typing is for someone who has typed for twenty years. It is learned but it is automatic. I know what I need almost intuitively. However, I don't always know if it is *what the reader wants* [emphasis in original].

And then she requests feedback from her readers that we failed to provide to her individually during the semester. In her case, the request for feedback is also related to her concern at being evaluated in the course:

> Is my reaction statement what you wanted? Is this journal written the way you want it? I'm not sure. I need reinforcement, but I wish the Almighty Grade weren't hanging over my head. I wish I could do this for the sheer joy of doing it. I would feel freer—more inclined to experiment, to take a risk in exploring my interpretation, to dare to be wrong. As it is, I feel a constant, self-imposed check on my processes as I read and write. It warns me to be careful: I can be wrong, but not *too* wrong [emphasis in original].

Here, we clearly had an opportunity to reduce Topaz's anxieties which we failed to follow up. I am unable to say then with any degree of certainty whether Topaz's fixation with structure would have been reduced if we had responded to her questions supportively. It seems somewhat doubtful, though, because her strategies for reading and writing fit so strongly into neatly structured patterns. It is difficult to imagine her consciously giving them up.

In the next assignment, Topaz, like others in the class, faced the dilemma of how to summarize the Dennett story. She shaped her response through a combination of her knowledge of structure and her realization that the summary had to report two levels of interpretation. In her journal, she noted:

> My knowledge of summaries told me I had to briefly condense the essence of Dennett's article. My knowledge of his two levels of meaning reminded me I had to briefly mention the wonderfully entertaining literal level but that I had to concentrate in my writing at length on his second/higher level of meaning. Writing the summary was a mental battle for me because I really just wanted to write about the second level and ignore the literal . . .
>
> I felt, as I wrote, to be controlled by the article's title; yet, I felt also that he had understated himself in the title: the purpose was not to determine "where" he was so much as to determine "how" he got there.

She then goes on in the journal to explain that she wanted to rewrite her summary because she "did not have a full sense of structure until I finished writing and realized that what I had written last (not the words but the meaning) should have been used to structure the beginning." She felt that she wanted to change her inductive structure to a deductive structure to make her meaning clearer to her reader. She also noted in her journal that, because of the limitations of the task (to write a summary), she had to deny her reservations about the article.

Topaz had additional reservations about the Hebb article, but, by the time she wrote the summary paper on it, she felt compelled to include some evaluative comments. So, just as Violet had done, she wrote an evaluative paragraph following her summary discussion. The summary itself followed a rough outline she structured before beginning the writing:

> My choices for the outline and the summary were cued by (1) the author's purpose, (2) his conclusions of other writers' theories, (3) his definitions of terms, and (4) his heavy emphasis on objective versus subjective. Using this framework, plus cues from his headings within the article, I began to write.

Thus, although her analysis of the material requires her understanding and interpretation, even these are heavily influenced by the structural requirements she imposes beforehand that emerge at least in part from the structure of the source article.

Disregarding the concerns expressed earlier in her journal entry about the Dennett piece (that she had to deny her reservations), Topaz reveals in this journal entry about the Hebb article that her interpretive remarks can no longer be denied:

> I tried to keep myself from writing any reactions in my summary since my paper was not a critique. However, I had reacted so greatly as I read, that, by the time I reached the end of the summary, I threw caution to the wind and wrote my paragraph of reaction too. It helped relieve the feeling of constraint that hemmed me in as I wrote the summary.

It is only possible to speculate, of course, but perhaps, as Topaz continued to carry out the assignments and introspect herself about her processes, she became more conscious herself about how she was giving up ownership of her papers as she allowed herself to be hemmed in by the structural constraints she practiced in her reading and writing. It may be that this awareness freed her to take the risks she initially seemed reluctant to take.

When it came time to write the synthesis of the Dennett and Hebb pieces, not surprisingly Topaz wrestled with the definition of synthesis. She rejected the definition she believed had arisen out of the class discussion (a bringing together of similarities), and drew on recollections of Bloom and Sanders, who reminded her that "opposites can be synthesized, too, and the emphasis in synthesis is on the creation of a new product rather than on a rendering (rotely) of similarities or differences." As she reread the articles, her summaries and notes, she fell back on her structural security blanket and made a rough outline for herself. She used the four points in her outline to structure her paper, but also gathered quotations and paraphrases from her notes and occasional references back to the articles themselves to support her specific points. She notes in her journal that

> the most important aspects in how I came to select my synthesizing ideas and how I chose materials from the text are (1) definitions presented in the text and (2) claims and grounds set forth in the text. These two aspects are paramount to structuring for me.

No other student in the class put so much emphasis on text-bound structures as the source for writing papers. Topaz does, once again, write two evaluative paragraphs (which she describes as "back burner" material) at the end of her synthesizing paper, but together they consist of about one page of text in a seven-page paper. Her concern with claims and grounds is reiterated in her next assignment, the summarizing of the positions of the authors writing in the *British Journal of Psychology*.

In the formal paper identifying the two positions to be summarized, Topaz distinguishes almost immediately between the *implied* claims and the *stated* claims in the articles. She notes that the positions she will discuss are based on the implied claims, while the stated claims "serve really as subclaims and as grounds (arguments) to support one side or the other of this conflict between innovation and tradition" (as she has labeled the positions she is examining). Her subsequent discussion turns to an evaluation of the claims made by proponents of each view.

She notes in her journal that she has specific "clue words" to look for in the readings that will guide her identification of claims and grounds:

> . . . words such as "therefore," "it follows that," and "I believe/think/assume that" [help me] to find the claims and "since," "because" and "as shown by" to find the grounds. To find both claims and grounds together, I looked for a wording similar to "If . . . , then . . ." Wherever I found a statement worded similar to this, I knew the author had grouped both claims and grounds together.

She also acknowledges in this journal entry that she had previously taken a full semester's course which consisted of

> mapping claims, grounds, warrants and modalities in articles. This course trained me to be more organized, more structured in my approach. It also trained me to be more suspicious and, thus, to not accept stated claims at face value until I had explored implied claims.

Here can be seen, then, the genesis of the structure of her paper with the relationship carefully developed between implied claims and stated claims. It is also possible to see the origin of her structural approach toward the analysis of arguments, the genre she had been reading in the source articles on introspection which had served as the basis for the various writing tasks. It then becomes less surprising to see the strength of a structural focus in Topaz's reading and writing strategies.

Until the final position paper, except for her one "outburst" to evaluate (negatively) Hebb's ideas, Topaz had held to the structured approach she believed suited the assigned tasks. But, when the position paper assignment was made, she was free to adopt the persona she had wistfully called for in her first journal entry when she wrote that she wished she "could do this for the sheer joy of it," feeling freer and more inclined to experiment. The position paper task seems to have given her this freedom:

> . . . I realize that the "how" of my choosing was purely personal because this was a *position* paper: I was not required to choose an objectively valid point to discuss; I was only required to choose what was valid *for me* and to provide logic for it.
>
> My rereading of the text changed. In the past readings, I had been "compiling" objective facts to report or synthesize. This time I was looking for (1) statements that echoed what I was thinking and (2) studies to support my claims [emphasis in original].

Even though Topaz was literated to choose an evaluative stance, her methods of support remained the same and "providing logic" and "supporting claims" remained central to her approach.

Thus, it can be seen that the prior experience with argumentative structure and its logical demands for support dominated Topaz's reading and writing strategies. She grappled with substantive issues and with the appropriateness of using evaluation in assignments that did not appear to call for it, but all of her decisions were dominated by the necessity to present information to readers in rigorous structures that would hold up to careful examination. Proving a position was as important as taking a position.

THE INFLUENCE OF PRIOR KNOWLEDGE

Although all of the students were influenced by their prior knowledge and experiences to some degree in their responses to the reading and writing tasks, in their final position papers two of the students, Lila and Amber, showed how strongly this prior knowledge shaped their responses. But they could not have been more different in terms of how their previous knowledge affected them. Lila, in railing against the authority of researchers and their manipulation of research subjects, reveals a deep seated and long-held hostility toward all psychological research. Amber, influenced by both depth of knowledge about the strengths and weaknesses of empirical research and a strong background in religious studies with serious reflection about moral and ethical values, reasons thoughtfully about the relationship between researchers and research subjects, a topic of concern also for Garnet, but from a different perspective. Although both Lila and Amber reach basically the same conclusion, that subjects need not be dehumanized to make effective contributions to research studies, their assumptions, attitudes, and prior knowledge lead them to very different pathways to the exploration of this topic.

Lila

Lila reveals in her final paper and journal entry that she has a deep mistrust of experimental research, especially that conducted by psychologists, dating back to a strong affective response that she had to reading about an experimental study in her freshman college introductory psychology course. In this experiment, researchers apparently duped subjects to give painful electrical shocks to purported subjects who were actually collaborating with the researchers. The actual subjects were those who had to make the decisions about giving the electrical shocks, thus exposing themselves to feelings of emotional trauma and guilt. Reading about this experiment seems to have so deeply affected Lila that she projects this distrust on all experimental research.

In the formal position paper itself, Lila writes a rather toned-down argument supporting introspection as a research methodology, criticizing experimental methodologies but allowing the counter-arguments to come from the writers of the source articles. She summarizes some of the major points from the source articles, acknowledging in her journal entry that she has included parts of summaries written for previous summary assignments.

It is in the long journal entry accompanying this paper that she reveals her enormous hostility toward experimental research in psychology:

> I consciously chose to tone down the language of the unprofessional and discourteous nature of hacking away someone's argument. I felt comfortable trashing Evans in my summary, but with a "paper" I somehow felt it was a cheap and nasty thing to do.
>
> However, I feel that researchers are backward when trying to use the classic research methodology to answer questions about the mind and human nature. I feel equally repulsed by experimenters who want to control and predict

human behavior. I would fear this knowledge and not be a willing "subject" in such a project. *I am deeply suspicious and hostile toward anyone who wants to control and manipulate me.* For this reason, I am happy that these experiments have yielded little information about human behavior. *I fear this research.* Perhaps other people also fear scientists whose dream is to predict and *manipulate* human behavior [emphasis added].

Thus, the journal outlet permits her the aggressive stance and outlet she feels is "inappropriate" for a "paper" in a graduate seminar. She has apparently been socialized to conventional behavior in formal writing settings (at least in an instructional context) and cannot break away, in the paper, from these constraints. Summary thus becomes a safe outlet for describing views that she wants to criticize.

It is possible to trace back in her earlier papers and journals the hostility Lila feels toward experimental research and its invasion of personal privacy (a central issue for her), whose source she has revealed only in her final journal entry on this sequence of papers on introspection. In her earliest paper, reacting to Valentine's article, Lila notes that introspecting may make "respondents feel an increase in their anxiety level," although the interference from verbalization (in protocol analysis reports) may decrease as may the anxiety levels." It is possible that she is conscious of her own initial anxiety in providing introspective reports on her reading and writing strategies. Continuing her attention on the individual (subject's) response, in her synthesis of the Dennett and Hebb pieces, she notes that "a person's state of mind undoubtedly affects the way a person will respond to certain situations . . ."

By the time Lila writes the paper summarizing the positions of the researchers in the *British Journal of Psychology* articles, she comes up with a metaphor about doctor–patient relationships that begins to convey her attitude about experimental researcher–subject relationships:

Patients cannot heal themselves without doctors; therefore, why should subjects be able to diagnose their thoughts without the expertise of a mental health doctor? At least this seems to be the logic under which Evans is operating. The doctor has the authority, not the patient/subject.

In this last sentence can be seen the underlying objection: the researcher has the authority, controls the subject, and therefore determines the value which should be attributed to the subject's reports. The subject is not deemed capable enough to "diagnose" or interpret his or her own reports.

Her paper goes on to explicitly express her reservations about the experimental paradigm:

Evans obviously believes the only methodology acceptable is that of the experimentalist who is highly trained to produce sound scientific experiments in the laboratory. The closing remark reminds me how conservative and pompous some professors can be: "In any case, it seems very hard to justify the dangerously naive conclusion of Quinton and Fellows which, if taken seriously, might lead us to abandon experimental psychology and regress to the methods of nineteen century introspectionists." Yes, I can understand how threatening Quinton and Fellows might be to someone safely ensconced in their sterile laboratory where their authority is neither questioned nor their methods ever called into question. Numbers are magical and reality is measurable with objective and elaborate tools unavailable to the layman. Evans is special and always RIGHT. By virtue of his authority and his bias towards "subjects" (an appalling substitute for human beings), he is in control which seems to be important to Evans because he lacks the trust that it takes to accept what a human being says about their mental thoughts.

Here again, especially in the last sentence, "authority" and "control" emerge as the central issues in Lila's negative stance toward experimental methodologies. Human beings are seen as reduced to "subjects," and thus incapable of providing insights on their own behavior.

By the time she writes her final position paper, Lila has made two conscious decisions: to tone down the language in the formal paper (no more "pompous professors"), but to reveal her prior experiences with psychological research and its significant impact on the formation of her attitudes. The formal paper, then, is very dry, full of impersonal summaries with only occasional offerings of personal belief ("I do not question that we are influenced by external phenomena, but I have serious doubt that I am *controlled* by external phenomena" [emphasis added]). Personal control remains central to her personality and she must assert it in the paper.

Interestingly enough, in both the journal entry and the paper, she reveals that past experiences may influence present beliefs, but she shies away from how such experiences may have actually influenced her beliefs or behaviors. In the paper, she says: "Furthermore, it is quite plausible that introspection cannot be separated from past experience and personal bias because we constantly interpret our engagings with other external phenomena so that our needs are best served." In this statement, she suggests that her own previous knowledge of the methodologies of experimental research have led her to protect herself from being manipulated and controlled by any such research in which she would be the subject. But only with the revealing comments of the journal entry can we build these bridges to her own experience—she does not reveal anything of her personal or intellectual history in the formal papers themselves.

Lila lets us know clearly in the final statements of her paper that not all is being revealed in the papers and journals:

I feel the accuracy of such interpretations [of introspective reports] is not as important as why people choose to reveal some thoughts and not others. It is that elusive quality that continues to slip through our charts, tests, and measures which intrigues us and ever lures us toward the silent and currently unreachable depths of the human experience.

But it may also be the case that these introspective accounts, accompanied by serious analytic writing, reveal more than even the "subject" may be aware of. Certainly, Lila is conscious of her deep antipathy toward experimental research and the controls she believes it implies, but she may not have realized how deeply this prior experience affected her ability to look objectively at the studies of individual researchers and evaluate these studies on their own merits. Her prior affective responses make this kind of intellectual inquiry virtually impossible for her.

Amber

Amber's final position paper is an exploration of what introspection has to do with knowledge and how it fits into research concerned with validity and reliability. Thus, in some ways, her paper is related to how introspection fits into an experimental paradigm, but she is much more concerned with the ways both researchers and subjects can contribute to studies and how they can share authority. For Amber, the researcher must have a suitable intention and the subject must be both able and honest, both being held to high ethical standards, an essential for any study she could value. Then the "results" can be reported by abstracting about them.

Amber is one who draws deeply on her previous work to draw connections, but who is always simultaneously influenced by what she is doing at the present moment. She is well trained in statistics and so she found it important to connect introspection as a research tool to her earlier training in experimental research. In fact, she says in her journal that she "didn't choose a position—I already had one—so you're just getting the selection of issues." Her statement is reminiscent of Violet's, who also felt that she had had a position all along.

From the very first paper, it is clear that Amber is going to explore how introspection fits into research paradigms that value validity and reliability. In her reaction paper to Valentine's article, she starts to explore this issue in her first paragraph: "Part of the history of introspection, as a term, includes a narrowing of its meaning to get a better fit with the empirical demands for reliability." Amber sees Valentine narrowing introspection to "the process of thinking" rather than "the experience of thinking" and sees that such a narrowing "may be necessary to make it a technical term," but she sees this as circular reasoning when the concepts of validity and reliability have to be handled in the same way in qualitative studies that they are in quantitative studies. She goes on in her paper:

> I think Valentine is forcing introspection into an empirical mold by approaching these two concepts [validity and reliability] from within the empirical model for them. Such a task is certainly possible, but it continues to view subjective experience as a field for objective research. In other words, subjectivity is still held to be within the scope of an objective framework.

So, although Amber is critical of placing introspection within an empirical framework, as Garnet had been, for Amber the background in statistical studies and knowledge of validity and reliability measures are the prime factors influencing her appraisal of placing introspection in a research methodology.

In the journal entry on the Valentine reaction statement, Amber acknowledges some insecurity with the terms she has been presenting in her paper:

> I'm not clear myself—there's some case to be made that the questions of v & r [validity and reliability] should be handled the same for quantitative and qualitative research as parallel—they are models as *Valentine presents it* in that, somehow they are closed systems, self-referencing. I'm not sure about my terms. Reliability depends on agreement of results. Validity depends on the agreement of the content experts. Reliability is measured by numbers. Validity is established by persuasion. I think Valentine is forcing introspection into an empirical mold by trying to deal with these 2 concepts from within the empirical model for them [emphasis in original].

This entire section in her journal is filled with cross-outs (deletions), additions, and re-ordering of phrases as it evidently represents her attempt to clarify her own thinking at this early point in the semester.

Unlike many of the other students in the class, Amber does not address Hebb's views in her summary and synthesis papers in light of research paradigms. She is more interested in the philosophical issues he raises about self and others. But her attention is re-focused on the validity–reliability issue when she reads the four articles in the *British Journal of Psychology* series. Her position summary paper is titled, "The Validity of Introspective Strategy Reports" and deals with how introspective reports "might be used within a quantitative model of explanation."

In her consideration of the positions represented by Evans, Morris, and Quinton and Fellows, Amber is concerned not only with the methodological issues but what she calls the "ethical/moral positions that ought not to be viewed only within the confines of a quantitative model of explanation." For Amber, like Lila, "the issue of power or control appears central." But

Amber's concern is equally with the authority of the researcher and the subject, not with the subject alone as Lila had posited. Amber poses a series of issues that must be confronted:

> Who should—or may—generate hypotheses? The researcher or the subject? Does this question concern scientific rigor? Are the conventions of authority in human experimental situations necessary for validity? Do these conventions circumvent uncontrollable subject and experimenter behavior by refusing to rely on data affected by them—in this case verbal reports of strategies? Or are the behaviors produced by the conventions in such a way that changing the conventions may result in valid reports? Can subject and researcher share responsibility for hypotheses formation? Hypotheses testing?

Because of her greater knowledge about research design, Amber is better able to objectify her questions. Her prior knowledge is not influenced by affective responses, so she can explore the same issues that Lila had raised, but Amber can take that additional step backward to see them in philosophical not personal terms. The difference can be observed in her choice of language as she examines precisely the same issue Lila had, the depersonalization of subjects:

> Evans seems to assume that human subjects ought to be as fully objectified as possible in order to control for social variables inherent in the experimental situation and that such objectification doesn't change the nature of what is being studied—the "human" can be factored out of "human cognitive processes" without changing its designation. Morris et al. seem to assume that subjects will produce genuine reports of strategies if asked by non-directive researchers in a straightforward experimental situation . . . This difference may have to do with whether the model of scientific inquiry is transferrable in whole from the natural sciences to inquiry about human subjectivity, whether human processes can be validly studied by objectifying the human participant. And beyond that, whether they can be studied appropriately. In studies involving human subjects, is experimenter authority inevitable and, thus, the only logical way to control for social variables of the experimental situation or are situational variables manipulable in such ways that the subjectivity of human subjects can contribute to the inquiry.

This carefully worded analysis reflects Amber's background in religious studies and her commitment to consideration of moral issues in every aspect of the intellectual life. For example, in her journal entry, Amber notes her views on Evans' objectivity: "I'm not sure his objectives can be dismissed on anything but ethical grounds—after Auschwitz and Hiroshima, objectifying human beings is unacceptable for *any* purpose even if it makes life more complicated." Amber's views stand in contrast to Lila's more emotional judgments about "pompous professors" who want to "manipulate" her.

Amber understands the need to examine these perspectives within experimental paradigms and then make judgments about the research issue of central concern to her, the validity and reliability of introspective reports in psychological studies. She notes Evans' objections to these reports in her paper: "Introspective reports cannot produce valid statements of strategy or process: the experimental situation is socially constituted and is, thus, never free from desires to please, to save face, to obey authority, all which affect subjects' reports of strategy and process." She considers the alternative position of Quinton, Fellows, and Morris, who "would accept introspective strategy reports as valid under conditions in which the methodology allows their validity and the researcher does not operate insincerely, that is, in which the researcher desires a sincere strategy report and in which the methodology doesn't inhibit or prevent the possibility of such a report." By bringing forward moral values ("the researcher desires a sincere strategy report"), Amber is able to conceive of a research methodology that will value introspective reports and permit the sharing of authority between researcher and subject.

In her final position paper, Amber develops more fully the position that has been emerging from her earlier papers and journals, that validity in research depends upon an able participant and a researcher with a valid intent: "Validity is, thus, the joint responsibility of the researcher and the participant—and it is based on an assumption of honesty or sincerity on the part of both." As she has suggested in her accompanying journal entry, this position was never consciously selected, she already had one. As her earlier observations suggest, she has been gradually bringing together her moral and intellectual positions on research paradigms.

It is clear that Amber is not a naive student of either research methodologies or the human condition. She carefully presents her views in her position paper:

> The participant's responsibility lies both in honesty and in an ability to perform within the intent of the method. Honesty must be taken for granted—but with a grain of salt. Because we all do occasionally, and some of us frequently, operate out of needs to save face or to please others, validity will not be a stable condition, even in different reports of the same participant (saints excepted).

Thus, the participant's "ability" is held to the same high standard as the researcher's "intent."

Because validity and reliability are harder to control in evaluating introspective accounts than other kinds of data might be, Amber proposes that results and conclusions be derived from these reports by "abstracting from them. An appropriate level of abstraction will be such that it helps explain or understand similar types of results." It is precisely through such abstraction, as in the case of the four categories I have proposed for this chapter to analyze textual origins, that I hope to demonstrate the usefulness of the introspective reports collected for this study.

Amber's demand for scientific rigor in assessing the validity and reliability of introspective reports is tempered by her humanistic and ethical demand for "sincerity" as the measure by which the validity of such accounts shall be evaluated. Both researchers and subjects are to be held to high levels of ethical behavior and in the best situation would collaborate to assist each other.

Although prior beliefs, experiences, and knowledge led both Lila and Amber to want to redesign the relationships between researchers and subjects, Lila's strongly affective approach resulted in such harsh suspicions and anxieties that it was impossible for her to imagine sympathetic and supportive collaboration. Although Amber does not suggest that such collaboration would necessarily come easily, her prior knowledge and beliefs encourage her to believe research methodologies should be designed to foster such outcomes.

CREATIVE RESPONSES

Two students, Crystal and Lionel, wrote their final position papers on introspection in fictional form, Crystal's a fable of the Legions of Empire against the hapless Subjects and Lionel's a dialogue between Dr. Jekyl and Mr. Hyde. Although couched in fictional form, Crystal's fable represents a strong position supporting the use and value of introspective reports, while Lionel's dialogue permits him to retain his ambivalence on the use of introspection. Both views, and even their ultimate representation in "nonacademic" prose can be seen to have taken their roots in their earlier papers and journals.

Crystal

In the journal entry for her final paper, Crystal says that she had trouble finding a way to structure her paper although she had no difficulty locating an issue or a position. Then, the night before the paper was due, she "thought about writing a fable and from then on it practically wrote itself."

Although her fable treats the issues more indirectly than Lionel's dialogue between Jekyl and Hyde, Crystal's "empirical" King and her "subjective" Subjects touch directly on many of the controversies addressed in the source articles and class discussions. Her story has a strong narrative line and, interestingly enough, operates on two levels just as did the Dennett science fiction story the class had read earlier. Crystal's "hapless Subjects" are able to outwit the Empire's empirical scientists, whose "information was just too limited" and who were unwilling to ask for the subjective knowledge of those who had created the labyrinth they were trying to explore.

In her earliest paper, the reaction statement to the Valentine article, Crystal indicates difficulty in understanding the concepts and attributes her difficulty to the writer's excessive use of jargon and unclear writing style. At this point in her understanding of the issues on introspection, because of her lack of background in the field, Crystal adopts the stance of the uncritical reader:

> Because I am unfamiliar with the subject matter of Valentine's article, I can only assume that the treatment of the history of introspection is accurate and fair; I have no way of knowing whether or not the "overview" is slanted, but certainly the bibliography seems to be extensive. In addition, the conclusions at the end of the article seem reasonable. Even to one who is a layperson and not an expert, the claim that introspection is the "primary method" for gathering data about thinking processes appears to be justified.

Because of her lack of background in the field, the issue of what kind of research paradigm introspection fits into has not yet been identified as an issue for reflection.

In her formal summary of Hebb's ideas, Crystal gives a straightforward description, in this format not yet suggesting any reservations:

> D.O. Hebb flatly contradicts the notion that one can be directly aware of one's mental processes without the intervention of any sensory process. Hebb does not deny that the workings of the mind are incredibly complex, but says that an individual's access to those workings is limited to inference, that is, to that content which consists of sensations and images.

But, in her journal entry, she presents her first misgivings:

> . . . I found this article very unsettling—the idea of an "unconscious" over which there is literally no control is not a novel one—I accept it and can give numerous examples from my own experience, but it frightens me nevertheless. Body and brain have to exist together, certainly, but what is this "unconscious" or "subconscious" to which we have no rational access? There is, in fact, something in addition to "body" and "brain," something which is in each individual an interaction of the two . . .

Made uneasy about the impossibility of "rational access," Crystal will continue to explore the importance of the individual's self-knowledge until it finally appears as the central controlling element for finding access to the labyrinth in her final fable.

In the synthesizing essay on the Dennett and Hebb pieces, Crystal develops a paragraph using Tarzan as an example of an individual whose "self-concept [is formed] only in reference to those living beings among whom he lived." This example is developed to support her position that "the presence of at least one other person is necessary for the development of self-identity," with Tarzan's initial identity being shaped by the apes with whom he lived. In her journal entry, she makes only a brief passing comment that "even the Tarzan idea could be developed creatively," the first hint that creative responses are options she considers when writing papers. And this observation was made prior to the class meeting when Sharon Pugh raised the option of creative responses as a possible alternative.

When she worked on the essay summarizing the positions of the psychologists writing in the *British Journal of Psychology*, Crystal reported that she went through all the conventional steps for writing such a paper, carefully reading the articles, "mak[ing] notes as to definitions of terms, arguments, and conclusions reached." She quickly identified the two opposing positions, "that introspection works, and that it doesn't." Her third (and final) draft of her paper includes a brief, conventional summary of the issues addressed by the four researchers, and then is followed by a parody which is titled, "They Shoot Psychologists, Don't They?" Two brief excerpts give the flavor:

> A most interesting aspect of this six-year verbal crossfire, however, is that even though the researchers come from a tradition which glorifies the dignified "stiff upper-lip" approach to controversy (and you can tell for sure they're British because they spell funny), their published communications with each other have all the appearance of viciously unrestrained semantic chauvinism.
>
> Predictably enraged by the fellows' [Quinton and Fellows] terminological insouciance, J.St.B.T. Evans (you can tell he's British because who ever heard of an American with three first names?) takes them to task in a response article. [By the time of her final fable, Evans' name has been transformed to James St. Barrymore Tushwell Evans.]

In fact, Crystal deftly deals with all the substantive issues in her parody summary, and it provides her with an approach that feels comfortable to her:

> As to the essay with which I finally ended up, it seemed almost to "start itself." Writing parodies is the writing I most enjoy, and once I begin one I lose track of time while I'm working on it . . . the terminology in these studies easily lent itself to parody, and I was encouraged in the tendency to do it by last week's class discussion, which obviously opened the door to creative essays . . . I

can't remember how it got started . . . suddenly the idea was there . . . [ellipses in original].

I realized when I was writing this essay that I HATE academic writing . . . I have often been criticized for "indirect" prose, for writing criticism that is too "poetic," for using unneeded metaphors or quotations or allusions, for trying to be "cute" . . . in a paper on Faulkner, my syntax was described as being "too Faulknerian" . . . [ellipses in original].

Having creative responses legitimized in our course, Crystal moved quickly to the form in which she could fulfill the assignment confidently and capably. She notes in her journal that she wrote several drafts, "each one expanding on the examples from the articles which lent themselves to parody." She is careful to deal with all the substantive issues in her parody, but allows herself to poke fun at the way researchers debate terminology and endlessly devise subcategories of all categories. Her paper is clearly not an attempt to get out of a difficult task but to transform it into one that can be pleasurable both for the writer and the reader.

Thus, the genesis of the final position paper on introspection in the form of a fable can be clearly seen from the first stirrings of wanting to write a creative paper using the Tarzan story to the parody of the four British researchers' arguments to the fable defending the Subjects against the Legion of Empire. Once again, the fable presents the major substantive arguments regarding the nature and use of introspective reports and takes a strong position supporting their usefulness. After the "empirical legionnaires" fail to negotiate the labyrinth constructed under the fortress by the hapless Subjects, the King summons his subjects:

"Well since you're here, do you mind explaining the labyrinth to me? Did I underestimate its complexity?"

"No, Sweetheart, you didn't underestimate the labyrinth; you underestimated the power of what you so condescendingly refer to as the 'subjective element.' You see—by the way—what *is* your name?"

"James St. Barrymore Tushwell Evans. My friends call me 'Sir'!"

"Figures. You were probably born wearing wingtip shoes. Anyway, each one of us built a different section of the labyrinth according to her own plan, and thus only the builder had direct access to her own section. Your empirical guys did a good job as far as they went, but their information was just too limited. God, my feet hurt. You got any Dr. Scholl's powder, perchance?"

"No. Then what should we have done?"

"Why didn't you ask for directions?"

'BECAUSE YOUR DIRECTIONS WOULD BE SUBJECTIVE AND THEREFORE UNRELIABLE!!"

"Yes, our knowledge of the labyrinth is subjective. Yes, we have to rely on our sensory apparatus to help us find our way around inside. Yes, there's an area in each section that's inaccessible even to us. But look what happened to your guys—one out with a migraine, one in a coma, and one missing in action. The point is that while we may not be perfect, we're the *only* ones who can give you an inside look at the labyrinth. So why don't we put our heads together (figuratively speaking, of course) for a change? We'll give you information that's as objective as possible, and once you have that you can do all your tests and stuff on it . . ." [emphasis in original].

Thus, Crystal's final position is conciliatory—grant introspective accounts credibility and respectability, and they may contribute to knowledge within a range of research paradigms including the empirical. As a literature student not bringing the background in research design that Garnet and Amber had, it is not surprising that Crystal does not have such strong feelings about the sanctity of research paradigms.

Using fictional genres to convey her ideas works for Crystal because it unleashes her sense of humor and allows her to treat serious subjects with just the touch of denigration she feels they apparently deserve. This does not release her of the responsibility of representing researchers' ideas fairly, and this she does while allowing herself—despite her insecurity in a new intellectual field—to retain a touch of her own superiority.

Lionel

For Lionel, the writing of the Jekyl-Hyde dialogue for the final position paper on introspection is a way of resolving a difficult problem. He states in the accompanying journal entry that he feels that he knows very little about introspection "and because of it, I felt unwilling to take a position and staunchly support it." The solution emerged (as he became gradually conscious standing in the shower) that a dialogue could represent his "own voice in its split state as Jekyl-Hyde." The room the two characters are locked in represent the assignment and the house "however, is all this introspection stuff, which requires much exploration on my part." At the end of the dialogue, Hyde escapes from the room (the assignment is completed), " 'But I fear not out of the house,' said Jekyl rising." Thus, the dialogue permits Lionel to complete his assigned task, and he notes in his journal

> that this paper itself will get me out of this particular assignment and its demand for completion of a performance task, juxtaposed with a content with which I feel bewildered, a content which I see "but through a glass, darkly."

In the paper itself, Jekyl, representing the "rational," presents arguments stating that in some cases introspection can reveal limited glimpses "at stages in our mental processes, [but we] can never completely see the process itself." Hyde, the "emotional, instinctive, romantic aspects of my own thoughts," argues that aesthetic experiences go beyond the fragmented data of experience that introspective reports purport to describe. So the paper provides an outlet for Lionel to present both sides of the issue which he feels are entitled to some credible representation. At the same time, the dialogue relieves him of the obligation of taking a specific position.

At the beginning of the semester, in his initial reaction statement to the Valentine article, Lionel is skeptical of Valentine's arguments:

> Valentine has marshalled her information to support the merits of introspection (*although I do not find some of it persuasive*). However, in *her almost desperate attempt* to be balanced and objective about this very subjective method, her writing style is *misleadingly* unsupportive and her tone alternately *aloof and defensive*. Still the study does provide some helpful background information on introspection [emphasis added].

After the sharply critical tone expressed toward Valentine in his short reaction statement, the last conciliatory sentence seems initially surprising, but it turns out to be consistent with the ambivalent stance Lionel takes throughout his examination of introspection as a research methodology.

In his journal entry, Lionel also comments on his interpretation of Valentine's arguments:

> After the first page, I questioned Valentine's premise that introspection was a commonly used scientific method. Though I have no initial objections to information gathered through introspection, I realized it's very subjective and uncontrolled so I doubted its acceptance in the scientific community.

It is somewhat surprising that the language he uses in the reaction statement is so much harsher than the language of the journal entry. Unlike Lila, he appears to have tempered his language for the journal entry while giving it full rein in the reaction statement. That may have had something to do with his interpretation of what a reaction statement entails, but he does not comment on this in the journal entry.

Writing the summary of the Dennett story poses a dilemma for Lionel: "Should I imitate and condense the humor and hypothetical situation, or report the course of ideas at the expense of the humor?" As he grapples with his definition of summary, in his journal entry he reports:

> . . . no purpose is served unless my summary is shorter and simpler than the original which means in my case that the flavor of the original author's style and argument will be lost. Besides, it seems to me that the heart of the article (or *brain* of the article) was the author's speculation about the relationship of mind to body and the location of the essential self. So I decided to organize my summary around the speculations, but mention the farcical situations at least

to suggest by reporting that there was some humor in the original [emphasis in original].

And, of course, in his aside about the "brain of the article," he brings the tone of Dennett's piece to his own journal entry. His decision to develop the philosophical speculations in his summary but to ground them in Dennett's science-fiction tale allows him to present both levels simultaneously, but, of course, the humor of the Dennett tale is essentially eliminated through its philosophical retelling.

In summarizing the Hebb article, Lionel foregoes the highly charged language he had used on the Valentine reaction statement although he acknowledges in the journal entry that he found Hebb's arguments unconvincing. (Perhaps Lionel's definition of summary restricts his use of evaluative language in ways that reaction statement does not.) He provides a straightforward summary of Hebb's views arguing against self-knowledge and self-observation about the mind. But in his journal entry, Lionel notes:

> As I reviewed the article and wrote the summary, I was unconvinced by the arguments and evidence, even though while I was reading I found myself waiting to be convinced. I think that Hebb just did not speak to some of the evidence I have personally experienced as introspection, or else wrote it off too easily as illusion or hallucination.

Lionel's voice here shows new facets of his thinking: He is trying to remain open-minded about introspective accounts, but he is influenced by his personal experience with introspection. Although he does not say so, the suggestion is strong that he ruminated about his own thinking and creative processes long before he came into our classroom. If this is so, then his experience in our class may have been a new opportunity for him to reflect on previous musings that have been meaningful for him. His ambivalence about introspecting may be stemming from his difficulty in connecting his prior experiences with what so-called "experts" have to say about the process.

In writing the synthesis of the Dennett and Hebb pieces, Lionel experiences frustration both with form and content. Just as Crystal had anticipated her first parody, musing on the Tarzan story as a possible creative piece, so does Lionel express his frustration of working within a format he deems unsuitable for synthesis. In his journal, he writes:

> I thought then about format. I considered citing Dennett and Hebb, but decided that would be a report, not a synthesis. *I mused about using the two as characters having a dialogue*, but, that too, might not be true synthesis. So I decided to refer to neither author, so that what I generated was truly a synthesis—a third product as a result of a combination of the first two. This is

> what I did, but I am still uncomfortable because I am not really in the synthesis
> except as writer. The synthesis interests me, but I don't think it expressed my
> opinions and attitudes, except through the subversive use of word choice, se-
> lection, and style [emphasis added].

It is not really until Lionel actually uses the dialogue format in the final position paper that his voices (multiple because of the continued ambiguities he
has difficulty resolving) can emerge.

In the accompanying journal entry, Lionel presents the uncertainties that
the synthesis essay did not seem to allow him to present directly. Unlike
Garnet, the assignment "synthesis essay" provided no liberation for him:

> I explained that my synthesis doesn't accurately say what I think. In fact, I'm
> not sure what I do think about introspection and location of the self. So far, the
> arguments against introspection haven't persuaded me that it doesn't exist, al-
> though I'm not sure it does. I still wonder, for instance, about human beings'
> intuitive sense of divine existence—God or gods. Discrimination of senses
> gives no help, because sensory experience gives no stimulus for constructing
> or conceiving an extrasensory world or force or being, does it? Nor does it
> explain why emotionally I wish to reject the idea as fundamentally untrue that
> what I am is a [sic] the result only of biological-chemical-electrical processes.

So, although from a different perspective than Amber's concern with moral
and ethical values, Lionel's dilemma and ambivalence may also have religious roots, concerned with the existence of the soul and/or higher divini-
ties. At the least, he seems wary of mere physiological existence.

By the time he reaches the series of articles in the *British Journal of Psychology*, Lionel has become a better reader of the research, but he does not
yet have a clearly formulated position of his own. In his journal entry, he
notes that he quickly identified "the value of introspection as a research
method" as the issue being debated. His language again is charged as he
characterizes the positions of the researchers:

> Morris *blatantly* cues the reader to his position in his title, "Why Evans is
> Wrong." Evans opens his response to Morris by *convoluting* Morris' argu-
> ments . . . [emphasis added].

His understanding of the issues has apparently improved to the point where
he has confidence that he is able to recognize when one researcher is apparently misrepresenting the ideas of another. But, in the paper, he attacks all
four researchers for not clearly defining their terms. Like the other students
in the class, he has come to recognize that "[r]etaining introspection for use
in the natural sciences is precisely what is at stake."

In his journal entry, Lionel also introduces the importance of ideas meeting his standards for personal validity:

As I read Evans' first response, I *checked his arguments* against my understanding of research in general for a kind of *personal validity*. By validity I simply mean I compared what I read to what I know to see if the arguments might be affirmed or negated. This affirmation and negation, however, does not appear to me as a consequence of some rational process, but hits me as I am reading—and thinking about what I am reading—much like a little jolt of electricity whose source is internal rather than external. The *comparing for validity*, too, *is not a rational process*, not consciously controlled, and I am not conscious how it works. I just *seems* like I'm comparing as a test for truth [emphasis in original].

Once again, Lionel's quest comes closer to Amber's in that her standards for validity were primarily intellectual with deep moral overtones and his are influenced by his personal truth tests. He never discusses further what this entails except in terms of "what he knows" (and perhaps what he believes).

But, at the end of this journal entry, Lionel indicates his continuing frustration with understanding and "practicing" introspection:

I still don't think I know what introspection is, or if I'm doing it, I imagine I am communicating to you, Sharon, or you, Marilyn.

Of course, what he is communicating to us has to come out of his own experience as he is the only one to have access to his own thoughts (as Crystal pointed out in her fable).

His final position paper on introspection, the Jekyl-Hyde dialogue, allows him to examine the broader issues concerning the validity of introspective accounts while giving voice to the "devil's advocate" counterarguments. Thus Jekyl's argument that at the stage " 'at which we can become aware of our mental processes, I should like to break stage 2 into two divisions, awareness of reasoning and awareness of emotional responses.' Hyde rebuts. 'You can't separate thinking from feeling, man.' " This intellectual/emotional dichotomy that Jekyl represents in the dialogue is unacceptable to Lionel, who has Hyde respond to Jekyl's rational arguments by saying, "I'm not a data bank, Jekyl. I am a man. My very intuition tells me so." His strongest argument against introspection as part of an empirical field comes when Hyde argues:

"I will not consider myself a biochemical computer, Jekyl," Hyde retorted. "It doesn't match up with my intuitive validity, whatever your research reports might say. If what I think is limited only to the fragmented data of my experience, then what accounts for the wave of joy and awe I feel when I see a spectacular sunset, or hear a beautiful piece of music? In my appreciation of art and music and literature, I feel a force much greater than myself, outside myself though I am part of it."

Here Lionel brings together his aesthetic sense and his construct of personal validity to legitimize his rejection of mere physiological existence which he had argued against in an earlier paper. His physiological perspective has been growing slowly until it finds its outlet through Hyde's voice in the final paper on introspection.

He notes his remaining feelings of uncertainty, though, in the journal entry accompanying the dialogue: "I also still have grave doubts about a strict scientific paradigm, as you can see from some of Hyde's remarks, but I haven't found an adequate argument among the doubts and intuition." So, although he may not yet be able to argue a position with the warrants and claims that Topaz would require, Lionel has, nevertheless, achieved an outlet for his understandings of the moment. The creative paper not only allows such expression (it doesn't just "get him out of this particular assignment"), it fosters the exploration of thinking that is still tentative and cautious on a conscious level by allowing risk-taking and speculation through a creative medium.

During the course, both Crystal and Lionel decide to produce creative pieces because this medium furnishes them with opportunities to express their ideas more imaginatively, without obligating them to the strict intellectual evidence that would be required in a more conventional argumentative paper. Both make use of intellectual arguments through the dialogues of their characters, but they know that readers of fables and dialogues do not expect conversations to sound like written treatises. They are thus freed to simplify (in the best sense) the arguments and evidence, keeping in mind that an entertained reader will likely retain more and be more convinced than a bored one.

CONCLUSION

These case studies reveal that, although the students in the class frequently concerned themselves with the same issues (primarily the validity of introspection as a research methodology, the role of introspection in research paradigms, and the relationship between researchers and subjects), they did display sometimes markedly different orientations and approaches toward these topics. Clearly, their previous intellectual and personal histories strongly influenced their interpretations of the readings, their analyses of the writing tasks, and their understanding of their own roles as simultaneously students in a graduate research seminar (where they were "subjects") and serious researchers themselves.

Violet and Garnet, like others who focused on substantive issues, found their major identification as researchers. Both students built knowledge over the semester, although they started from very different levels at the beginning in relation to the topics of introspection and research methodologies.

Even though Violet was a literature major and not very knowledgeable about research paradigms, she was a serious scholar in her own field and felt committed to dealing with the intellectual arguments raised in the course as she felt committed to dealing with intellectual arguments in her own specialty. Garnet came to the course with stronger credentials in educational research, but at a period in her intellectual development when she was being exposed to new ways of looking at this work. Because she was simultaneously taking a course in naturalistic inquiry, she seemed destined to use this opportunity to re-examine old assumptions and evaluate their credibility in light of new information. She could hardly have pursued the topic of our course in any other way. It is certainly not surprising to find mind sets such as these in a group of doctoral students on the threshhold of doing their first major pieces of individual research. What teachers need to understand is how to foster such commitment and responses in students who have not yet found intellectual questioning so exciting.

As noted in the case study of Topaz, the structure of argumentative writing could almost be said to have controlled the approach she took to the tasks on introspection, shaping both her approach to reading and writing. Source authors were evaluated as much on the presentation of their ideas as the quality of their intellect. Topaz held herself to the same high standards that she used to evaluate the work of others: focused argument with logical support. Her experience can alert teachers to the usefulness of showing students how to analyze arguments in the writing of others even as they are preparing to do their own writing. It is clear that, even though so much attention was paid to structure by Topaz, this attention remained focused on the intellectual task of interpreting complex concepts and translating them into concepts that would be meaningful and useful to her. Such an application of structural analysis goes well beyond the analysis itself to its reformulation in the creation of new understandings that will also be accessible to others.

The role of prior knowledge in interpreting tasks and creating new meaning is complex and not always even accessible. Lila's hostility toward all psychological research remained hidden to her instructors until its source was revealed in her journal entry associated with her position paper. What is less clear is whether the basis for this hostility was something she was consciously aware of throughout the semester while she was preparing the earlier papers or whether it was something that suddenly came to her conscious awareness. It is likely the case that she had these negative feelings much earlier than she revealed their source, but it is not so clear whether she herself just felt a general uneasiness or related these feelings immediately to her early experience as a college freshman. In any case, bringing the source to the surface has to be an initial step in examining the basis for one's reactions in order to decide whether these earlier experiences should be re-evaluated in terms of new knowledge and new experience over the intervening period. There doesn't seem to be any indication that Lila was considering any such re-evaluation, but her actions should not be a model for serious intellectual thought. When affective responses are so strong that they may preclude open examination of new material, the individual must try to put them aside, at least temporarily, or they will effectively make it impossible for intellectual reassessment and growth to occur.

Amber's use of prior knowledge, of course, differs markedly from Lila's. Amber's knowledge of experimental research methodology, particularly the concepts of validity and reliability, placed her in a strong position to examine how introspection would fit into the models she was familiar with. Her humanistic background, tempered with strong religious training and experience, also influenced strongly her perception of relationships between researchers and subjects. But, unlike Lila, who could only imagine "manipulation," Amber conceived of high ethical standards for both researchers and subjects as central to the undertaking of meaningful research. Such values need to be transmitted, not only to those who would carry out research studies, but to all involved in the shaping of instructional contexts, including students as well as teachers and administrators. All participants must be "sincere" for their mutual undertaking to be successful.

The desire to shape responses in creative form was especially strong for two of the students in our class, but their experiences demonstrate that just as much intellectual rigor is required for such writing as for more traditional scholarly papers. Without understanding of the issues, even when an ambivalent stand is taken as Lionel did, it is impossible to create parodies, fables, or dialogues. The authors of such writing must know their subject thoroughly, although it must also be acknowledged that somewhat more knowledge may be required of the reader to understand the subtlety that is often expressed in satiric writing. Encouraging students to at least occasionally demonstrate their knowledge in unconventional ways, even in staid graduate seminars, clearly can lead to high levels of engagement and allow those students for whom such writing is a pleasurable opportunity to shine. Who says learning and demonstrating learning can't be fun?

These case studies have shown that, given the same materials and the same tasks, a group of intelligent students cannot help but interpret tasks and carry them out individually as they are influenced by their prior knowledge, their prior experiences and beliefs, their interpretations of the demands being made upon them, their comfort or discomfort in the classroom setting, and their preferred modes of working. No models of the composing process can capture such varied influences, such individual modes of interpretation or behavior. Nor should researchers want to. What we should want is to help students better understand their own preferred ways of mak-

ing and conveying meaning so that we can strengthen their ability to respond meaningfully and make them sensitive to those aspects of their behavior that may be counter-productive for them. There is no question in my
mind that introspective reports of the type that we gathered succeeded in
raising to their consciousness much of what influenced our students' behavior that they had never seriously been aware of before.

CHAPTER 6

Implications for Instruction and Research

IMPLICATIONS FOR INSTRUCTION

Because this book has concerned itself so much with the effects of the class-room context on the reading and writing responses to the tasks, it seems appropriate to begin this chapter with a consideration of what a supportive classroom context should be like. I would like to propose the characteristics of such a classroom and illustrate how these characteristics can be incorporated into curriculum design and implementation.

Characteristics of a Supportive Classroom Context

Just as we encourage our students to learn from their mistakes, so it will be clear in this discussion of what a supportive classroom context should look like that I will be attempting to learn from the experiences of our students just what elements of the context described in this study should be retained and which should be modified.

This discussion will be predicated on the belief that reading and writing must be integrated in classroom settings. The many examples of reading and writing which I have cited demonstrate how these language processes reinforce each other. Even when the most restrictive task designs were imposed (summary writing), students discovered that they learned more from the readings when they had to write something, anything, whether they felt text-bound or freer to impose their own interpretations and evaluations than they would have if no writing activity had followed the reading. For the less-restrictive writing tasks, the writing was often exploratory in nature and gave the students opportunities to try out their reflections on the ideas they dis-

covered in the readings. The requirement to write forced a closer engagement with the reading, and the writing based on reading promoted learning
over time in new areas.

Although some writing classes have used thematically organized readers
in recent years, the emphasis has often been on the transfer of information
through conventional writing tasks such as summaries, analyses, and syntheses. What the experiences of our graduate students have revealed so
strongly is that reading of all types of texts is always constructive and transactional, as the reader response theorists such as Bleich and Rosenblatt have
been telling us is true of literary texts. If students can be moved away from
writing tasks that have "information transfer" as their primary purpose to
tasks that will encourage intellectual and affective responses, then they will
be able to consciously examine how their prior experiences and value systems affect their interpretations. Bringing affective responses to the surface
will enable students to analyze their impact on their responses and modify
their existing knowledge schemas if this seems appropriate. Furthermore, as
the students construct more complex frameworks within which to fit their
perceptions, they will be better able to write critically and evaluatively
about their growing knowledge. But their initial forays should always be
treated as exploratory, and they should be given opportunities to re-read the
earliest materials with which they interacted so they can respond to them
from the more knowledgeable perspective they have gained over time.

A central finding of this study is that there is no monolithic best way for
students to respond to reading and writing tasks. Studies of reading and writing processes have failed to see how such generalized terms as purpose, audience, and genre only come to have meaning when they are interpreted by
individual students. Environments must be created where it becomes, not
only possible, but important, for students to identify meaningful purposes
for themselves. This can only happen in environments where they feel free
to interpret tasks or design tasks for themselves. In such cases, appropriate
purposes and audiences will emerge, as will appropriate genre forms. Content teachers as well as language-process teachers may well select the subject matter for investigation (for at least an initial part of a semester), but they
should make available a multiplicity of writing forms that can be used to
respond to the readings and encourage the students to select forms and audiences that suit their particular learning needs and purposes at particular
points in their investigation of a topic.

What needs to be encouraged is the possibility of having different students doing different things at the same time. For example, all of the students in a particular classroom may be reading the same set of materials
over a month's time, but they should be given the opportunity to respond to
these readings in ways that seem fitting to them as they determine their purposes at different points in time. We short-circuited our students' first con-

sideration of their initial materials in their self-designed projects when we asked them to write summaries of these articles. Instead of such an activity, students should be encouraged to decide whether their initial encounters with materials require immediate analysis, or whether they should just try to read for a "gist," take exploratory notes, go on to other materials to soak up further background, or even take a step back and search for more basic materials to help them orient themselves to the topic at hand. Students' backgrounds do differ, and their readiness to handle complex materials in different topical areas will also vary. If larger units of time could be built in for the comprehension of a set of materials rather than discrete and immediate mastery of each item in a sequential set of materials, individual students could adjust their strategies to their needs, needs which might differ markedly for the same students in different areas. Within monthly units, for example, students could still consider themselves responsible for the same basic set of materials, but they might wish to approach the reading of these materials and design the accompanying set of writing tasks in individual ways to meet the intermediate goals they have set for themselves within this larger time period. Such an approach would doubtlessly complicate the logistics of running a classroom, but it would facilitate learning because it would accommodate the different learning styles and backgrounds of individual students. Students who wish could form small writing communities and share their explorations with each other and design goals they feel are appropriate at intermediate stages. The pacing of different groups could be determined by the group members who would voluntarily join together. Individuals who wished to remain independent could choose to do so.

This is, of course, only one possible configuration of a curriculum design, but it could work equally well in content-area classes or language-instruction classes where a common topical area is being used for investigation for at least part of the semester. A teacher, in such a classroom, would become a facilitator. The teacher would meet with individuals or groups and help them evaluate their understanding of the materials they are working with, the usefulness of the goals they have designed, the appropriateness of the strategies they are using to achieve these goals, and their success in articulating the meanings they wish to convey to the audiences they feel are appropriate. Such a classroom context would return responsibility to the students and give them ownership over the tasks they are undertaking and the papers they eventually produce.

The Safety of Risk-Taking

An essential quality that a supportive classroom context must provide is an environment within which risk-taking is encouraged and valued. Students all have instructional histories within which many have learned over long, often hard years, just what is expected of them in their classrooms, i.e., to give the teacher just what the teacher wants. Unfortunately, that has too often been a regurgitation of the teacher's own views or evidence of rote information transfer. At the same time, teachers have said that they valued individual thinking and creative responses, but such responses all too often resulted in negative evaluations. It is essential that over time trust be built up between students and instructors, so that risk-taking becomes such a commonplace that it loses the connotation of risk and becomes fruitful exploration.

One way of achieving this is to encourage exploratory writing where it is assumed that students are not giving final opinions or judgments or assessments of their reading and thinking, and where there is no evaluation attached. Rather, students are encouraged to actively seek associations with prior knowledge, beliefs, and value systems that are supported or threatened by the new materials they are encountering. They should be given opportunities to respond both affectively and intellectually, so that they are aware of the reasons they interpret materials in the ways that they do and how past experience has affected their responses. They must become aware that every act of reading is an interpretive act. Their meaning grows alongside the meaning they see placed in the text by the author, and creates the interpretation which must arise from every such encounter. Journal accounts of the type that our students produced would be of value here, serving as safety-valves for the students, who can probe into their backgrounds in trying to make sense of the meanings they are making from their new experiences and who can share their uncertainties with the instructor who serves as a supportive reader.

Our students' responses to the tasks frequently showed that the genre of a particular form of writing was intrinsically limiting, as in the example of summary writing, but even in such cases those students who believed in a transactional model of reading and writing realized that every experience involved some degree of interpretation and meaning-making. Students can readily be shown that they are bringing legitimate prior experiences and associations to their readings, and that they are therefore creating original and individual meanings already. What needs to be demonstrated to them is that such activities and responses are not only legitimate, but that they are also valued.

Challenging but not Frustrating

In our class at Indiana University, Sharon Pugh and I had wanted to allow the students to experience the difficulty of working through materials in an area that we felt would be essentially new to them, i.e., the articles on the topic of introspection. Although the students' papers and journals did reflect their working through the articles that were initially quite difficult for them, I feel now that we would have had more realistic and meaningful activities for them if we had provided some introduction to the major concepts and some framework around which they could have focused their readings. I am not suggesting that such frameworks establish the only legitimate perspective from which to view the topic (although that is clearly a danger, even if scrupulously unintended). Rather, the introduction to the materials could provide some brief historical perspective suggesting the ways that terms may have been defined or altered as the field developed or changed. Such an introduction, I believe, would mitigate the high level of frustration that was encountered by our students who were far more sophisticated and motivated than we might expect underclassmen to be. (Two of the reading students, Daisy and Opal, told me, as I was writing this last chapter, that they debated vigorously during the first few weeks of the semester whether they should drop the course, so great was their frustration with the reading materials.) In addition, we should have indicated what the sequence of activities would be so that the students could see the overall plan and how each task supported the larger structure. So it should be possible to identify and structure reading materials that will challenge students but will also take into account what a reasonable level of challenge should involve. If we can anticipate that the field will be entirely new to our students, we must provide a level of introduction that will make it possible for the students at least to believe that they can establish some relationship to the materials even if only at an introductory level initially. We must validate exploratory thinking but also stimulate challenge rather than frustration.

Writing tasks must also be challenging, but this is a somewhat more complex topic to deal with than reading tasks. Writing tasks become challenging to the writer when the writer has internalized a need to understand something at a fairly sophisticated level (for that individual) and has also acquired a need to communicate that understanding to someone else. (It is true that a writer might choose to write for himself or herself at some earlier time, but that would usually be an intermediate point before the writer feels prepared or motivated to share that understanding with others.)

An important part of that component of challenge is the need to communicate with an audience that is expected to be simultaneously critical and supportive. Our students made clear to us that they would produce their best work when they had developed meaningful, intrinsic goals, but the response of an audience who shared their interests and wanted them to develop their meanings was a significant stimulus. An essential ingredient of that relationship would be appropriate feedback, feedback of a substantive sort, not at all necessarily linked to evaluation of the work. When I attempted such feedback through a dialogic journal with the graduate students at City College, they noted in their course evaluations at the end of the semester that that had been an important motivating stimulus for them. Until they trusted me enough to disabuse themselves of the idea that my journal responses to them were not intended to be evaluative, some told me that they put off reading my journal entries for several days after the class had met. But as they saw that my comments were directed mainly to their attempts to introspect about their reading and writing strategies, and supportively toward the substance of their papers based on the readings, they relaxed somewhat and began to feel more confident about their grasp of the difficult articles. This happened also in the class at Indiana for most of the students after several weeks, but some remained intimidated and frustrated during the entire first half of the semester. I believe now that we could have mitigated this frustration considerably by providing an introductory conceptual framework and feedback to the journals and papers in some individualized form, not just through the classroom discussions.

Setting Goals and Purposes

As I have already started to suggest, the setting of goals and the establishing of purposes for writing are complex issues. Previous research in writing, based primarily on the carrying-out of a single task, has suggested that the writer establishes goals, both intermediate and long-range, that will facilitate the performance on the particular task. But the vast majority of writing that individuals do involves a series of writings that eventually culminates in a longer paper or project. Thus, the intermediate goals may not necessarily reflect the same objective that the final product will have. For example, several of our students, even when researching and writing the final papers for our course, noted that these papers were only part of a longer-range plan they had that would provide them with expertise in a large area of which the topic explored in our course was only one component. Thus, for that purpose, the objective of attaining greater understanding of that specific sub-area *for themselves* was a perfectly legitimate goal, even though the paper appeared to be a final product in and of itself. If, in undergraduate teaching, we could foster such goals for students in the full realization that they are only beginning to acquire familiarity with new areas, even the areas of their gradually developing majors, we could encourage them to see their own gradual learning as the central focus of their explorations.

Such an approach would also encourage exploratory writing and risk-taking as the students could genuinely try out their analyses and interpretations on a supportive audience that could then respond to neophytes in the field and encourage them to follow up some of their explorations, or guide them to new readings that would help them become aware of understandings in the field that they might not have known at this particular stage in their experience. If such an apprentice philosophy could be taken within courses and between courses, students could be made to feel less inadequate and more like explorers simultaneously learning from the past and anticipating new directions.

Within introductory reading or writing, or preferably reading and writing, courses, students could spend the first half of the semester, as our students did, in reading on a particular topical area and engaging in a variety of writing tasks. In the second half of the semester, they could be encouraged to identify a question of their own in that same topical area and explore it in individual research. This relationship between the first set of readings and their own projects would demonstrate the benefit of bringing prior knowledge to bear on individual research and give them opportunities to integrate known with new information. It would also make them more sophisticated readers and evaluators of the material related to the question they were researching.

An alternative to this approach, one that might be more applicable to advanced writing courses, would be to encourage each student to develop a topic for investigation and spend the entire semester researching that subject, setting intermediate goals, and writing frequent short papers during the semester that would intentionally be exploratory in nature. This idea has been suggested by others, and I mention it here because it seems so clearly validated by the experiences of our students. Students could establish goals for themselves for each stage of their research, observe how these goals change as their knowledge grows, and alter their writing as they deem appropriate.

To be meaningful, it is clear that goal-setting must energize the individual. Without commitment to the writing, writers will continue to produce the perfunctory, passionless papers we have seen for so long. It should be possible in all courses where writing is valued to provide an environment where students are encouraged to identify topics and purposes and audiences that really matter to them. We have, unfortunately, seen the debilitating effect that the absence of any of these components can have.

Balancing Directed Tasks and Self-Designed Tasks

It is the case, though, that in some instructional contexts it may be desirable for teachers to give students experience with a range of writing tasks so that they gain familiarity with genre types that they might not otherwise know about. I believe that this can be implemented within the kinds of contexts I have been describing. That is, teachers can still select or have the students select areas of knowledge for exploration through readings. Then, the students can be asked to respond to the readings in a range of genre types, as our students were, for some part of the semester. What would be of value would be for the instructors not to define each genre type, but rather ask the students to come up with their definitions of these genre types *after* they have written their responses. The reason they should write the definitions afterward is that they cannot know what decisions they will have to confront until after they have attempted to respond to the task. If the students can come up with the kinds of questions our students came up with about what legitimately is permitted in a summary or a reaction statement, they will have come a long way toward understanding the roles that each genre type can play. They can also come to see the necessity for flexibility in the definitions of these genre types as the forms must be flexible enough to meet a variety of needs. It would be hoped that questions would arise such as for whom the summary or reaction statement is needed, and the variability in the definition seen to be desirable as the answers differ.

The students in our class showed great competence with genre types and, except for their frustrations with what they perceived the limitations of some of these genre types to be, they could write such papers fluently and auto- matically (thus often not "heeding" the role that genre type played in their writing). But such automaticity comes only with practice, and so students must not only be asked to practice such ranges of writing, but they must be conscious of the flexibility and usefulness of these genre types to help them meet specific purposes in their own writing.

After students have had exposure to a range of genre types, they might be asked to write something about a series of readings, consciously select the genre types they are going to use for their responses, and then write journal entries in which they explain why particular genre types were appropriate for the goals and audiences they had identified. This period of self-consci- ousness may be necessary for less practiced writers with the expectation that, over time, these choices can be made automatically, because the strat- egies will have become internalized. Thus, instructors will be varying teacher-designed tasks with a modified form of self-designed tasks. The in- tention, of course, is to follow this sequence with opportunities that are truly open-ended, allowing students to design fully their own tasks, and, ideally, even selecting the reading materials on which their writings will be based.

Time for Incubation and Reflection

One of the clearest outcomes of this study is that students need time for in- cubation and reflection. Whether it be a week, a series of tasks over a month at a time, or a semester's work, students need to have opportunities to read, reflect, think, talk with others if they feel comfortable doing this, write, and re-write, especially in exploratory fashions. Studies of the composing pro- cess that demand that students compose in one or two sittings, in front of a tape recorder or a video camera, can only dimly record the preparation that has preceded the actual writing event (if, in fact, any preparation time has even been built into the experience). As teachers and researchers ourselves, we know how essential the factor of time is in our planning, carrying out and re-doing the many activities we participate in. We must build into our courses such opportunities for reflection for our students so that they can come to see in practice the value of such a period of time. It will likely not be adequate to just allow a week's time, for example, from the giving of an assignment to its being due as we did for our advanced graduate students. It is more likely that, for undergraduates, we may have to specify that they design intermediate goals with deadlines and work toward each over the designated period of time. The important point to stress is that the extended time period is intended to give them opportunities to alter their goals as their knowledge and competence increase. That is, students should be heeding the availability of the time, but given freedom about how they will modify what they are doing during the time period.

In basic writing or freshman writing courses, for example, students might be encouraged to explore a community where they live. They might be asked to identify a few preliminary questions about the community, then begin to read about it, interview people of different generations, occupations, and ethnic groups, and try to find out how the community has changed in relation to the issue they are examining. In a sense, the students become beginning ethnographers. They are looking at the larger issue all the time, but they can set intermediate goals for themselves as they do their reading and interviewing, realizing that these goals can be changed as they become more knowledgeable. Such tasks also have the advantage that, while the students may be studying different communities and/or different questions, they are doing the same kinds of things so they can feel comfortable talking with each other and often learning about the process from the shared experiences of their classmates.

The Social Dimension of Learning

Our students made very clear to us that, during the first half of the semester, we short-circuited their usual experience of building a community of learners. They were accustomed to "talking over" the content of their course materials, to trying out new ideas on each other, and to giving and receiving help from each other when they had difficulty with complex concepts. Cut off from these familiar, comfortable, and important channels, particularly under stressful conditions when they were confronted with new and difficult readings, they reacted with frustration and even rage. Although, of course, we had imposed such restrictions in the belief that they would help the individual students examine their own strategies in confronting such tasks, we inadvertently imposed an unnatural context in which they would be examining these strategies.

Often, such restrictions are imposed for reasons entirely different from the ones we had, that students who "collaborate" in any way are "cheating" because they may "steal" ideas from each other. Instructors may be concerned that they will be unable to discern from a body of work which students have been successful in understanding materials and which have not. However, in most of the classroom settings where instruction focuses on literacy skills, it is frequently the case that instructors really want to evaluate the language skills of their students. In such settings, each individual student still has the ultimate responsibility for demonstrating his or her level of understanding through the presentation of that understanding in some forms of writing. Thus, the ability of the student to explain ideas in clear, coherent, and appropriate language to meet a particular purpose for a particular audience still remains that student's responsibility.

There seems, then, no reason to discourage active collaboration in the language-centered classroom. A setting must be created within which such collaboration is possible *for those who desire it*, but the forms of the collaboration are often best left to the designs of the students. As I have suggested earlier in this chapter, students could be encouraged to form groups with shared interests or shared strategies, try their ideas and exploratory writings out on each other, and receive feedback and recommendations from their peers.

Audience

The issue of self or other as audience in student writing needs to be considered more carefully than it has in the past. In instructional settings it has always been assumed that the instructor is the final and appropriate audience. Of course, peer audiences have been widely used in recent years, particularly as the readers of emerging drafts of papers. But rarely have students been encouraged or even permitted to view themselves as the appropriate and even final audiences for their writing. The reason for this is that it has almost never been the case that writers have been encouraged to see their own thinking on a topic as *part* of a larger whole that they are gaining expertise in. Such practices could easily be adopted in sequences of courses that students take in their majors, each course and each final paper seen as part of a growing understanding that a student might be encouraged to synthesize in a final seminar course in his or her senior year.

But even in courses specifically designed to facilitate the use of language to demonstrate literacy skills, emerging expertise can be viewed as tentative by the students' readers, even by the teacher who may have to assign a grade, but should do so on the basis of how well the paper demonstrates the ability of the student to express his or her current understanding.

Response and Evaluation

Clearly, the intention in our course was to have it operate in a non-evaluative mode. Unfortunately, we failed to realize that eliminating evaluation from the course experiences did not relieve us of the responsibility of responding. A great deal has already been said about the effects of failing to provide individual, meaningful feedback to the students while they were undertaking the various tasks.

We recognized only later how essential it was to distinguish between the roles of response and evaluation. It became clear that the absence of individual responses led some of the students to feel that they could produce perfunctory responses to the tasks and no one would notice, care, or take them to task for this. From a research perspective, we found such an attitude interesting in that it told us a great deal about the role that response plays in affecting student's motivation, but from an instructional perspective we began to see that this approach was destructive because it led to a decrease of the challenge and stimulation that all instructors wish to foster.

Feedback must be supportive and critical at the same time. Writers need to know that a thoughtful reader is taking their work seriously, valuing their exploratory efforts, but also being prepared to guide them to alternative perspectives or additional sources of information as might be appropriate. Instructors might choose to respond to students in journal form, commenting as any interested reader might, but keeping such comments clearly non-evaluative.

In most instructional settings, of course, a time for evaluation will come, and both instructors and students must be prepared for this. We told our students that we would evaluate them on the basis of their commitment to the activities they undertook, both the specific reading and writing tasks, and the keeping of the journal. Only one student, Lila, failed to complete all the tasks satisfactorily and turned in a perfunctory final paper which we refused to accept. She decided that she herself was not interested in revising it, and she finally turned in a mediocre substitute paper.

It is essential that the criteria for evaluation be clearly stated and understood from the very beginning of a course. If some part of the work is going to be clearly exploratory, it should be responded to but never evaluated. When the work is prepared for evaluation, the evaluation should be constructive and take into account the appropriate level of expertise to be demanded, whether it be in terms of the content or the expression of the ideas.

Instructional Strategies

Although it might be expected that a study of composing processes such as this one would try to come up with a model of composing, the intention of this study has been exactly the opposite, to demonstrate the range of strategies that competent readers and writers use to approach a range of teacher-designed and self-designed tasks. What is apparent is that competent students have a wide range of strategies available to them, and they pull out of this bundle the one or combination of several that seems appropriate because it will facilitate the carrying-out of the task at hand.

When a task is particularly difficult, students will fall back on what they characterize as "basic skills" strategies, quoting, paraphrasing, summarizing, taking detailed notes, annotating, making outlines. Naturally, the level of sophistication with which they handle these skills exceeds the level used by actual basic skills students. But it is important to note that they have these strategies available to them and do not hesitate to use them when appropriate settings call them forth. So although they may not heed such strategies when they are in settings in which they feel more confident, they have had to go through learning activities which made these strategies accessible when they were needed.

We must therefore expose our students to a wide range of reading and writing processes in the expectation that many of these processes may become automatic for the students as they become more fluent in their work with language, but secure in the knowledge that they will be retrievable on occasions when they are needed. Only by giving students wide exposure to genre types and the flexibility offered within them, to the freedom to explore their own thinking in settings in which response rather than evaluation will be the primary source of feedback, to the integration of reading and writing so that each enhances the other, and to contexts in which risk-taking is not only permitted but encouraged, can we begin to establish the contexts for learning in which students who examine their own reading and writing processes can say, "I understand what I am saying, why I am saying it, how I am saying it, and for whom I am saying it."

IMPLICATIONS FOR RESEARCH

The rich accounts provided by our students' introspective journal entries of their reading and writing composing strategies demonstrate the range and complexity of such activities in a way not available through any other research methodology. The previous accounts of composing, through protocol analysis in sterile laboratory-like settings, arise from a research perspective that is still trying to control variables and hold independent the process being examined. But reading and writing are activities so intrinsically bound up with the entire life experience of individuals that it becomes clear that such controlled descriptions can account for only a small part of the composing process, and even that part is being distorted by the unnatural conditions under which the protocols are taken. Similarly, stimulated recall descriptions may try to allow for time to elapse, as the individual may be video-taped in several sequences, but the restrictions of the media itself inhibit the natural movements, interruptions, delays, or procrastinations writers are prone to. Even more important, neither of these research methodologies permit any description of how prior experiences or values of the writer may have influenced the decisions the writer made or the shape that the writing eventually took.

By being a-contextual, such descriptions also fail to take into account how the circumstances of a particular reading and writing episode affect its shape or how this specific episode fits into the larger experiences and goals of the writer. It is clear from the descriptions of the reading and writing activities or our students that complex individual interpretation is involved in the decisions made in relation to each aspect of each task. In classroom settings, there is always the context of the specific classroom, the instructional history and knowledge base that each student brings to the setting, the relationships between the students and the instructor(s), the relationships the students have established or will establish among themselves, and the individual's own personal set of objectives and goals in relation to the tasks placed before him or her.

Introspection in the form of retrospective journals offers many advantages into gaining insights into the composing strategies of readers and writers. The journals can provide an outlet for students to express their concerns and questions about the tasks they are being asked to undertake. Such accounts provide a picture of what is likely to be troubling the students, the information being "heeded" at the time. The journals can also be the basis for seeing how contextual factors are affecting the responses.

Although they are retrospective and this necessarily means that some information will be lost, the journals are the least intrusive method of collecting descriptions from students of what factors influence their composing behaviors over time, in the real context in which they are occurring, with the real interruptions and interferences of their lives, with the real interpersonal relationships among students and instructors.

A natural follow-up study of the type carried out here should examine the processes of less proficient language users to see what aspects of composing they "heed" as they attempt to respond to the cues in their classrooms and their lives. Here again, we should not seek schematic models of composing, but rather rich ranges of strategies which will reflect the complexities of these students' experiences. After at least one extensive study of novice writers is carried out, it will become possible to examine more fully the contrasting strategies used by novice and expert writers. Existing studies have looked at revision processes or goal setting, but these studies have always been limited to examining single episodes of writing and have not attempted to note what strategies readers and writers consistently call upon, or how these strategies may differ according to interpretations of multiple tasks and differing contexts. North has noted:

> Knowledge-making is essentially a two-stage process. Over time, the community develops a collection, a canon, of first-level knowledge in the form of what I have been calling stories, accounts of individual cases or communities. When the collection is deemed large enough to warrant the effort—and that can happen as soon as there are two studies—it is possible to make a second-level kind of knowledge by trying to connect one study with another, to see what individual studies do or do not share (278–79).

In order to generalize, then, about reading and writing strategies, it will be necessary to have studies of a variety of writing communities over real time with accompanying detailed ethnographic descriptions. Studies by Emig, Perl, Pianko, and others began by studying individual writers of different communities through protocol analysis reports of several writing episodes; now the research community must move beyond the studies of individuals in laboratory-like settings to studies of communities in meaningful settings over substantial periods of time. Berkenkotter's study of Donald Murray points the way for further studies of individuals; I hope this study of a community of graduate students will provide another model.

Generalizations that will reveal the complexity of reading and writing strategies can only come from naturalistic studies carried out over extended periods of time that give the participants opportunities to reveal as much as they can of the factors that influenced their interpretations of tasks and the shape of the outcomes.

REFERENCES

Bartlett, F.C. *Remembering*. Cambridge: Cambridge University Press, 1932.

Beach, Richard and JoAnne Liebman-Kleine. "The Writing/Reading Relationship: Becoming One's Own Best Reader." *Convergences: Transactions in Reading and Writing*. Ed. Bruce Petersen. Urbana, IL: National Council of Teachers of English, 1986, 64–81.

Berkenkotter, C. and Donald Murray. "Decisions and Revisions: The Planning Strategies of a Published Writer" and "Response of a Laboratory Rat—or, Being Protocoled." *College Composition and Communication* (1983) 156–172.

Blanchard, Jay S. "What to Tell Students About Underlining . . . and Why." *Journal of Reading* 29.3 (1985) 199–203.

Bleich, David. *Subjective Criticism*. Baltimore: Johns Hopkins University Press, 1978.

Bleich, David. "Cognitive Stereoscopy and the Study of Language and Literature." *Convergences: Transactions in Reading and Writing*. Ed. Bruce Petersen. Urbana, IL: National Council of Teachers of English, 1986, 99–114.

Bloom, B. et al. *Taxonomy of Educational Objectives, Handbook I: Cognitive Domain*. New York: David McKay, 1956.

Bracewell, Robert J. "Investigating the Control of Writing Skills." *Research on Writing: Principles and Methods*. Eds. Peter Mosenthal, Lynne Tamor and Sean A. Walmsley. New York: Longman, 1983.

Brandt, Deborah. "Writer, Context, and Text." Paper presented at the Conference on College Composition and Communication, Detroit, MI., 1983.

Britton, J., T. Burgess, N. Martin, A. McLeod, and H. Rosen. *The Development of Writing Abilities (11–18)*. London: Macmillan, 1975.

Brooks, Peter. "Fictions of the Wolfman," *Diacritics*, 9 (1979), 74 cited in Eakin, 165.

Brown, Ann L. "Theories of Memory and the Problem of Development: Activity, Growth and Knowledge." *Levels in Processing in Memory*. Eds. L. Cermak and F.I.M. Craik. Hillsdale, NJ: Erlbaum, 1979.

Brown, Ann L. "Metacognitive Development and Reading." *Theoretical Issues in Reading Comprehension*. Eds. Rand J. Spiro, Bertram C. Bruce and William F. Brewer. Hillsdale, NJ: Erlbaum, 1980.

Brown, Ann L. and J.C. Campione. *Inducing Flexible Thinking: A Problem of Ac-*

cess. (Technical report no. 189). Urbana-Champaign: Center for the Study of Reading, University of Illinois, January 1980.

Bruner, Jerome. "The Act of Discovery," *Harvard Educational Review* 31.1 (1961) reprinted in Jerome S. Bruner. *Beyond the Information Given*. Ed. Jeremy M. Anglin. New York: W.W. Norton and Co., 1973, 401–412.

Collins, J.I. and E. Seidman. "The Struggle for Meaning." *English Education* 12 (1980) 5–9.

Cooper, Marilyn M. "The Ecology of Writing." *College English* 48.4 (1986) 364–375.

Culler, Jonathan. "Jacques Derrida." in Sturrock. *Structuralism and Since*, 169–170, cited in Eakin, 224.

Dennett, Daniel C. "Where Am I?" *Brainstorms*. Reseda. CA: Bradford Book Publishers, 1978.

DiVesta, Francis J. and G. Susan Gray. "Listening and Note Taking." *Journal of Educational Psychology* 63 (1972) 8–14.

Dobrin, David N. "Protocols Once More." *College English* 48.7 (1986) 713–725.

Durkin, H.E. "Trial and Error, Gradual Analysis and Sudden Reorganization: An Experimental Study of Problem Solving." *Archives of Psychology*, 1937, 210.

Eakin, John Paul. *Fictions in Autobiography: Studies in the Art of Self-Invention*. Princeton: Princeton University Press, 1985.

Emig, Janet. *The Composing Processes of Twelfth Graders*. Urbana, IL: National Council of Teachers of English, 1971.

Emig, Janet. "Writing as Learning." *College Composition and Communication* 28.2 (1977) 122–128.

Ericsson, K. Anders and Herbert A. Simon. "Verbal Reports as Data," *Psychological Review* 87 (1980) 215–251.

Ericsson, K. Anders and Herbert A. Simon. *Protocol Analysis: Verbal Reports as Data*. Cambridge, MA: The MIT Press, 1984.

Evans, J.St.B.T. "A Critical Note on Quinton and Fellows' Observation of Reasoning Strategies." *British Journal of Psychology* 67 (1976) 517–518.

Evans, J.St.B.T. "A Reply to Morris." *British Journal of Psychology* 72 (1981) 469–470.

Flower, Linda. "Writer-Based Prose: A Cognitive Basis for Problems in Writing." *College English* 41 (1979) 19–37.

Flower, Linda and John R. Hayes. "A Cognitive Process Theory of Writing." *College Composition and Communication* 32.4 (1981) 365–387.

Flower, Linda and John R. Hayes. "The Pregnant Pause: An Inquiry Into the Nature of Planning." *Research in the Teaching of English* 15 (1981) 229–243.

Flower, Linda and John R. Hayes. "Plans That Guide the Composing Process." *Writing: The Nature, Development, and Teaching of Written Communication*. Vol. 2. Eds. C.H. Frederiksen and J.F. Dominic. Hillsdale, NJ: Erlbaum, 1981, 39–58.

Flower, Linda, John R. Hayes, Linda Carey, Karen Schriver and James Stratman. "Detection, Diagnosis, and the Strategies of Revision." *College Composition and Communication* 37.1 (1986) 16–55.

Fodor, J.A. *The Language of Thought*. New York: Thomas Y. Crowell, 1975.

Gardner, Howard. *The Mind's New Science: A History of the Cognitive Revolution*. New York: Basic Books, Inc., 1985.

Harré, Rom, David Clarke and Nicola DeCarlo. *Motives and Mechanisms: An Introduction to the Psychology of Action.* New York: Methuen, 1985.

Harste, Jerome C., Virginia A. Woodward and Carolyn L. Burke. *Language Stories and Literacy Lessons.* Portsmouth, NH: Heinemann Educational Books, 1984.

Heath, Shirley Brice. "Protean Shapes in Literacy Events: Ever Shifting Oral and Literate Traditions." *Spoken and Written Language: Exploring Orality and Literacy.* Ed. Deborah Tannen. Norwood, NJ: Ablex, 1982. 91–117.

Hebb, D.O. "Self-Knowledge and the Self." *Essay on Mind.* Hillsdale, NJ: Erlbaum, 1980.

Hillocks, George. *Research on Written Composition.* Urbana, IL: National Council of Teachers of English, 1986.

Hirsch, E.D. "Reading, Writing and Cultural Literacy." *Composition and Literature.* Ed. W. Horner. Chicago: University of Chicago Press, 1983.

Jones, E. "Rationalisation in Everyday Life." *Journal of Abnormal Psychology,* 3 (1908) 161–169, cited in Sherwood, 175.

Kant, I. *Critique of Pure Reason.* trans. by N. Kemp Smith. New York: Random House, 1958. (Orig. work published in 1781).

Kantor, Kenneth J., Dan R. Kirby and Judith P. Goetz. "Research in Context: Ethnographic Studies in English Education." *Research in the Teaching of English* 15 (1981) 293–309.

Kucer, Stephen L. "The Making of Meaning: Reading and Writing as Parallel Processes." *Written Communication* 2.3 (1985) 317–336.

Lakoff, Robin Tolmach. "Why You Can't Say What You Mean: Review of Edwin Newman's Strictly Speaking." *Centrum* 4.2 (1976) 151–170, cited in Tannen, 156.

Lakoff, Robin Tolmach. "Persuasive Discourse and Ordinary Conversation, with Examples from Advertising." *Analyzing Discourse: Text and Talk.* Ed. Deborah Tannen. Washington, DC: Georgetown University Press, 1982, 25–42.

Langer, Judith A. *Children Reading and Writing.* Norwood, NJ: Ablex, 1986.

Langer, Judith A. "Learning Through Writing: Study Skills in the Content Area." *Journal of Reading* 29.5 (1986) 400–406.

Mishler, E.G. "Meaning in Context: Is There Any Other Kind?" *Harvard Educational Review* 49 (1979) 1–19.

Morris, Peter E. "Why Evans is Wrong in Criticizing Introspective Reports of Subject Strategies." *British Journal of Psychology* 72 (1981), 465–468.

Myers, Miles. *The Teacher-Researcher: How to Study Writing in the Classroom.* Urbana, IL: ERIC/NCTE, 1985.

Norris, Christopher. *Deconstruction: Theory and Practice.* London: Methuen, 1982.

North, Stephen M. *The Making of Knowledge in Composition.* Upper Montclair, NJ: Boynton-Cook, 1987.

Perkins, D.N. *The Mind's Best Work.* Cambridge, MA: Harvard University Press, 1981.

Perl, Sondra. "The Composing Processes of Unskilled College Writers." *Research in the Teaching of English* 13 (1978) 317–336.

Pianko, Sharon. "A Description of the Composing Processes of College Freshman Writers." *Research in the Teaching of English* 13 (1979) 5–22.

Quinton, Graham and Brian J. Fellows. "Perceptual Strategies in the Solving of Three-Term Series Problems. *British Journal of Psychology* 66 (1975) 69–78.

Reid, Wallis. "Linguistics and ESL: The Constructivist Relation Toward Language and Thought." Unpublished paper, 1984.

Rosen, Harold. *Stories and Meanings*. London: National Association for the Teaching of English, 1984.

Rosenblatt, Louise M. *The Reader, The Text, The Poem*. Carbondale, IL: Southern Illinois University Press, 1978.

Rubin, Donald L. and Bennett A. Rafoth. "Social Cognitive Ability as a Predictor of the Quality of Expository and Persuasive Writing Among College Freshmen." *Research in the Teaching of English* 20.1 (1986) 9–21.

Ryle, Gilbert. *The Concept of Mind*. London: Hutchinson, 1949.

Scribner, Sylvia and Michael Cole. *The Psychology of Literacy*. Cambridge, MA: Harvard University Press, 1981.

Sherwood, Michael. *The Logic of Explanation in Psychoanalysis*. New York: Academic Press, 1969.

Short, Kathy G. *Literacy as a Collaborative Experience*. Bloomington, IN: Indiana University. Unpublished Dissertation, 1986.

Smith, Sharon L. "Learning Strategies of Mature College Learners." *Journal of Reading* 26.1 (1982) 5–12.

Spence, Donald P. *Narrative Truth and Historical Truth: Meaning and Interpretation in Psychoanalysis*. New York: W.W. Norton and Co., 1982.

Steinberg, Erwin R. "Protocols, Retrospective Reports, and the Stream of Consciousness." *College English* 48.7 (1986) 697–712.

Sternglass, Marilyn S. "Commitment to Writing and Complexity of Thinking." *Journal of Basic Writing* 5.1 (1986) 77–86.

Sternglass, Marilyn S. and Sharon Lynn Pugh. "Retrospective Accounts of Language and Learning Process." *Written Communication* 3.3 (1986) 297–323.

Tannen, Deborah. *Conversational Style: Analyzing Talk Among Friends*. Norwood, NJ: Ablex, 1984.

Tierney, Robert J. and Margie Leys. "What Is the Value of Connecting Reading and Writing?" *Convergences: Transactions in Reading and Writing*. Ed. Bruce Petersen. Urbana, IL: NCTE, 1986, 15–29.

Tierney, Robert J. and P. David Pearson. "Toward a Composing Model of Reading." *Composing and Comprehending*. Ed. Julie M. Jensen. Urbana, IL: ERIC Clearinghouse on Reading and Communication Skills, 1984, 33–45.

Tomlinson, Barbara. "Talking About the Composing Process: The Limitations of Retrospective Accounts." *Written Communication* 1 (1984) 429–445.

Valentine, Elizabeth. "Perchings and Flights: Introspection." *Thinking in Perspective: Critical Essays in the Study of Thought Processes*. Eds. Andrew Burton and John Radford. London: Methuen, 1978.

Wallas, G. *The Art of Thought*. London: Jonathan Cape, 1926.

White, Hayden. *Tropics of Discourse: Essays in Cultural Criticism*. Baltimore: The Johns Hopkins University Press, 1978.

Williams, Melvin G. "Making Sense: What Happens When You Read?" *English Journal* 75.4 (1986) 33–35.

Author Index

Subject Index